1973

INTRODUCTION TO
BIOPSYCHOLOGY

INTRODUCTION TO
BIOPSYCHOLOGY

RICHARD F. THOMPSON
UNIVERSITY OF CALIFORNIA, IRVINE

ALBION PUBLISHING COMPANY

SAN FRANCISCO

ALBION PUBLISHING COMPANY
1736 STOCKTON STREET
SAN FRANCISCO, CALIFORNIA 94133

Library of Congress Catalog Card Number 72-86236
ISBN 0 87843 610 3

Printed in the United States of America

TO JUDITH

PREFACE

Man is an animal, but a very special and unique "psychological" animal. To understand ourselves and our fellow-humans properly we must know something about both our psychology and our biology. This volume serves as an elementary introduction to the biological basis of behavior and experience. Biopsychology goes by many names: physiological psychology, psychobiology, neuropsychology. The basic goal is to understand human behavior and experience in terms of underlying physical and biological mechanisms, particularly the brain and its functions.

This Introduction to *Biospychology* has been adopted from portions of a more general text (*Psychology*, Harlow, McGaugh, and Thompson, Albion, 1971) and is designed to be used as an elementary text in biopsychology or as supplementary reading for introductory courses in psychology and biology.

Many individuals have contributed to this book. I am indebted to Norman Weinberger for contributing to Chapter 3 (Sleep, Dreaming, and Attention), to Gary Lynch for contributing to Chapter 4 (Motivation), to Gerald McClearn and James McGaugh for their contributions to Chapter 5 (Heredity), and to Nancy Kyle and Cheryl Real for preparing the manuscript, and most particularly to my wife, Judith, for her help and patience.

RICHARD F. THOMPSON

CONTENTS

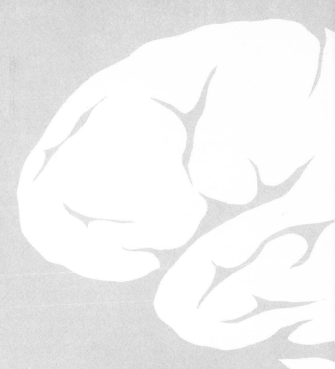

CHAPTER ONE

THE NEUROLOGICAL BASIS OF BEHAVIOR

Neurobiology is the study of the neural basis of behavior, which comes down to the study of the brain and how it functions to control behavior. The human brain is the most complex structure in the known universe. An average human brain has on the order of 12 billion nerve cells, and the possible number of interconnections and pathways among them in a single brain is greater than the total number of atomic particles making up the universe. The physical basis of everything that we are and do, both as members of the species Homo sapiens and as individuals, is to be found in the brain. All our response and behavioral patterns, everything that we have learned and experienced throughout our entire lifetimes, are in some way coded in the brain. Indeed, our actions and subjective experiences are but outward reflections of the patterns of physical activity in the brain. If we could understand the brain we would understand the reasons for all aspects of human behavior.

Although the human brain is an enormously complex mechanism, there are certain principles of organization, in terms of both its structure

2

NEUROBIOLOGY

and its functions, that permit us to gain a relatively simple overview of what the brain is and how it actually works. The entire field of neurobiology has undergone a major revolution—a knowledge "explosion"—in the past few years, and in the process a great many fundamental and extremely important discoveries have been made about the brain. We shall touch only on some of the highlights of this exciting and many-faceted story.

We are rapidly approaching a level of knowledge and understanding of the brain that will permit us for the first time to determine more about what a person is experiencing by recording the activity from his brain than he is able to describe to us himself, at least in some situations. For example, a wire may be glued to the surface of a person's scalp to pick up the electrical activity, or voltage, that is generated by the underlying brain. Of course these electrical signals are very weak; they are in the microvolt (millionths of a volt) range. The signals are led through an amplifier and are displayed on a polygraph, usually an ink record made on moving paper. This record is termed an *electro-encephalogram* (EEG). A simplified version of such a recording device is shown in schematic form in Fig. 1-1.

3

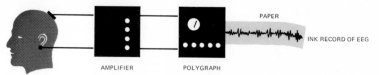

PAPER

INK RECORD OF EEG

AMPLIFIER   POLYGRAPH

FIGURE 1-1   *General method of recording brain activity in man.*
Activity is picked up by a wire on the scalp, amplified, and written out
on moving paper by a polygraph. The paper record is thus a graph
of the changing voltage generated by the brain (on the ordinate) over
time (abscissa). The wire on the ear serves as a neutral reference
point.

Examples of EEG tracings are shown in Fig. 1-2. These are simply tracings of the voltages generated by the brain over time. The upper tracing is typical for a person who is alert and attentive; there are few obvious waves, but in general the activity (voltage change) is small, irregular, and fast. The next tracing is typical of a subject who is resting quietly but is awake. A regular rhythmic wave pattern, the *alpha rhythm*, becomes quite clear. The alpha wave occurs at a frequency of about 8 to 12 per second and waxes and wanes. When the subject is asleep and not dreaming the waves tend to be slower than alpha and of large amplitude (this condition is called *slow-wave sleep*). In the last tracing the subject has started to dream. The pattern has become much more like that characteristic of the alert awake state, but the subject is still asleep. If we were to awaken him at this point, he would report that he was dreaming. If we were to wait until he awakened naturally, he would probably be unable to tell us whether he had been dreaming or not, but we could tell with a good degree of accuracy simply by looking at the EEG.

The EEG is a record of the ongoing or spontaneous electrical activity of the brain, measured, of course, at some distance from the brain on the surface of the scalp. It is a kind of overall average of what many thousands or millions of nerve cells in the brain are doing. With the same simple arrangement of a wire glued to the scalp we can also record electrical activity evoked by a stimulus. In the recording setup shown in Fig. 1-1 the recording wire is at the back of the head overlying the visual area of the brain, where visual information is processed. If we suddenly flash a light or a visual pattern in the eye, a relatively clear electrical response will be picked up by the wire on the scalp. The activity is generated by many thousands of neurons in the visual area of the brain. These responses are actually averaged by a computer; individual responses are hard to see because there is so much brain "noise."

A striking example of the information conveyed by the averaged brain response is shown in Fig. 1-3. Simply by noting the characteristics of the responses, we can determine whether the subject is viewing a square or a diamond, regardless of what he chooses to tell us, and regardless of the size of the object. However, if the subject for some reason mistakes the two objects, the brain response seems to correspond to what the subject *thinks* he sees, not what is presented to him. Even more remarkably, if the subject is asked to imagine one of the stimuli,

4

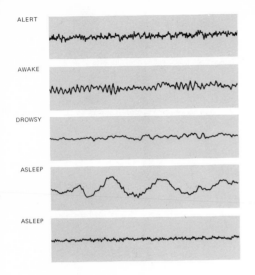

ALERT

AWAKE

DROWSY

ASLEEP

ASLEEP

FIGURE 1-2   *Typical human EEGs taken from subjects in different states, ranging from alert wakefulness to deep sleep [Brazier, 1968].*

FIGURE 1-3   *Human averaged evoked potentials. Stimulus forms are shown on the left, and the brain response evoked by each stimulus is shown on the right. Both the square and the diamond evoke the same first wave, but the diamond also evokes a later wave, independent of the size of the diamond. [John et al., 1967]*

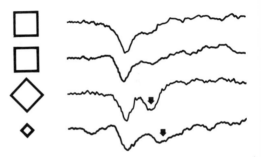

the brain response may correspond to the stimulus he is thinking about even when no stimulus is present. This type of averaged brain response may provide us, for the first time, with a way inside the mind—an objective method of measuring mental events.

THE BRAIN AND NERVOUS SYSTEM

We shall discuss here only a brief overview of the structural organization of the brain. Each of the regions described will be considered in detail later in connection with the important psychological processes to which they relate, particularly sleep and waking, motivation, sensation and perception. It is perhaps useful at this point to review a few simple definitions. The *brain* refers to the enlarged collection of cells and fibers inside the skull at the head end of an animal; it becomes the *spinal cord* as it leaves the skull (see Fig. 1-4). The *central nervous system* (CNS) includes both the brain and the spinal cord and is composed of nerve-cell bodies and their characteristic fiber processes, glial cells, and a variety of other types of cells making up blood vessels, membranes, etc. A complete nerve cell with its cell body and fibers is called a *neuron*. The functional connection from one neuron

5

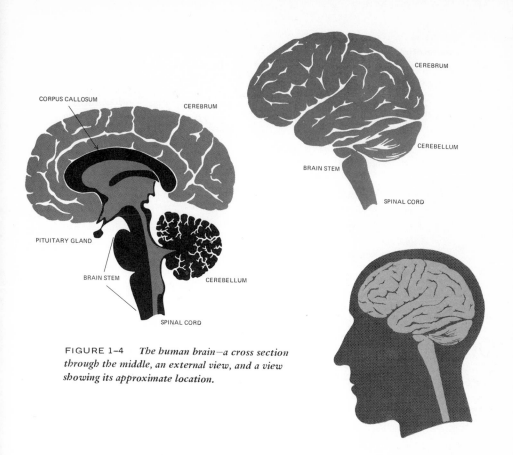

FIGURE 1-4   *The human brain—a cross section through the middle, an external view, and a view showing its approximate location.*

to another is called a *synapse*. The word *nerve* refers to a collection of nerve fibers (not including the cell bodies) outside the CNS; inside the CNS it is called a *tract*. Collections of nerve cell bodies are called *nuclei* if they are inside the CNS and *ganglia* outside.

COMPARATIVE AND DEVELOPMENTAL ASPECTS OF THE BRAIN

Most of what you see when you look at the brain in Fig. 1-4 is actually a surface structure of the forebrain, the *cerebral cortex*. In man and other higher vertebrates the cerebral cortex has enlarged enormously. In fact it has pushed out over all the rest of the brain, so that the basic tubular arrangement of the nervous system cannot be seen at all in the human brain, even at birth. However, we can get a clearer view of how the brain is formed by comparing the brains of simpler animals with man, and by comparing the adult human brain with the developing brain of the human embryo from early stages after conception to birth.

The basic organization of the vertebrate brain and spinal cord is perhaps most easily seen in certain invertebrates, particularly worms. A series of brains ranging from the flatworm (planaria) and earthworm to man are shown in simplified form in **Fig. 1-5.** The fundamental plan is that of a segmented tube. This is evident in the earthworm, where each body segment has nerves going into and out from the corresponding segment of the tubular nervous system. Even in the worm there is an enlargement of the "head" end in relation to specialized receptors. The human brain maintains the basic tubular organization from spinal cord up to about the middle of the brain (midbrain). However, the front end of the tube is enormously expanded and laid back over the core tube to form most of what we usually refer to as the brain.

The hindbrain and midbrain of the human are a continuation of the tubular organization of the spinal cord and resemble the worm nervous system. In mammals the tubular portion of the nervous system is, of course, only relatively tubular. There is a very small central canal filled with *cerebrospinal fluid*. The tube is thus mostly wall, composed of nerve cell bodies and fibers, glial cells, blood vessels, and so on. However, the forebrain of the higher mammals is, as we noted earlier, so enlarged that it becomes most of the brain. It is worth emphasizing that the forebrain differs embryologically from the hindbrain in that they come from different types of primitive tissues. It is this relative enlargement of the forebrain, particularly the cerebral cortex, that distinguishes men from monkeys and monkeys from lower mammals. This is "where the action is" in the control of complex behavior.

FIGURE 1-5   *The general appearance of a series of brains ranging from worm to man. The drawings are not shown in scale. In actual relative size the flatworm (planaria) brain would be a dot too small to see on the human brain, and the frog brain would be about the size of the "O" in the label "frog". [Truex and Carpenter, 1964]*

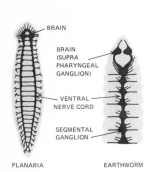

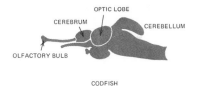

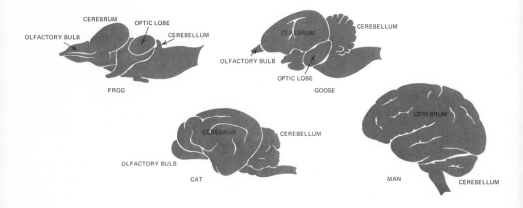

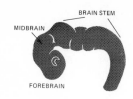
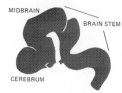
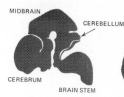
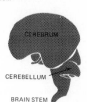

FIGURE 1-6   *Embryological development of the human brain (not to scale) at 4 weeks, 6 weeks, 7 weeks, and 12 weeks after conception. The brain at 12 weeks is actually 10 times larger than it is at 4 weeks.* [Peele, 1954]

It is a fundamental biological principle that "ontogeny recapitulates phylogeny"—that is, in embryological development the individual organism passes through many of the forms that comprise its evolutionary history. As the novelist Aldous Huxley [1928] put it:

... something that has been a single cell, a cluster of cells, a little sac of tissue, a kind of worm, a potential fish with gills ... [will] one day become a man.

This principle is clearly illustrated by the developing human nervous system. Some of the embryological stages of the human brain are shown in Fig. 1-6. The brain of the 5-millimeter embryo is basically similar to the primitive vertebrate adult brain. However, there is already a sharp bend in the midbrain. By the time the embryo is 11 millimeters long the brain shows several subdivisions and is beginning to fold back on itself. At 15 millimeters the cerebrum is beginning to grow out, as is the cerebellum. Finally, the brain of the 53-millimeter embryo shows a marked similarity to the adult brain, although the cerebrum has not yet grown out to cover the midbrain.

ANATOMY OF THE NERVOUS SYSTEM

THE PERIPHERAL NERVOUS SYSTEM   The *peripheral nerves* are the nerves lying outside the central nervous system which connect to skin, muscles, and glands. There are in fact *two* peripheral nervous systems, the somatic system and the autonomic system. Each contains both sensory and motor nerves, but their functions are quite different. The *somatic nervous system* controls all the striated muscles—the muscles that we contract when we walk, write, talk, make all types of voluntary motions, and make involuntary adjustments in posture and other reflex functions. The somatic motor nerves thus control most of what we normally call behavior. The *autonomic nervous system*, in contrast, controls glands, smooth muscles and the heart, and what might be called the emotional aspects of behavior. Crying, laughing, fear, anger, and love involve the autonomic nervous system. Sensory input to the somatic nervous system is from skin, joint, and muscle receptors and includes touch, pressure, temperature, and pain. Sensory input to the auto-

8

nomic nervous system is from glands and smooth muscle and is generally much more diffuse, conveying a vague sense of feeling, pain, and organic sensations.

To add to the confusion there are two subdivisions of the autonomic nervous system, the *sympathetic* and *parasympathetic*, which have their ganglia in different locations. Often the functions of the two systems are opposite. Activation of the sympathetic system causes contraction of arteries, acceleration of the heart, inhibition of stomach contractions and secretion, and dilation of pupils, whereas activation of the parasympathetic system causes dilation of arteries, inhibition of the heart, stomach contractions and secretions, and constriction of pupils. It appears that the sympathetic system functions to mobilize the resources of the body for emergencies, whereas the parasympathetic system tends to conserve and store bodily resources. Thus in a sudden emergency a person will experience increased heart beat, inhibition of stomach activity, widening of pupils, and energy mobilization as a result of the sympathetic system. Such conservative functions as digestion, basal heart rate, and bladder control are carried on in periods between stresses by means of the parasympathetic system.

THE SPINAL CORD   Two general categories of activity are handled by the spinal cord. *Spinal reflexes* are muscular and autonomic responses to bodily stimuli which occur even after the spinal cord is severed from the brain, as in a paraplegic accident victim. In addition, a wide variety of *supraspinal* activity is channeled through the spinal cord. The cerebral cortex and other brain structures controlling movement of the body convey activity down the spinal cord to motoneurons, which in turn control the muscles, and all bodily sensations are conveyed up the spinal cord to the brain. Analogous sensory and motor relations for the head are handled directly by the cranial nerves, which are like peripheral nerves but go directly to the brain rather than to the spinal cord.

THE BRAIN STEM   The *brain stem* refers to the structures of the midbrain and hindbrain, which are overlain by the cerebral hemispheres as indicated in Fig. 1-4. The hindbrain represents the continuation and expansion of the spinal cord in the brain and contains all the ascending and descending fiber tracts interconnecting brain and spinal cord, together with a number of important nerve-cell nuclei. The vital autonomic control nuclei concerned with respiration, heart action, and gastrointestinal function are located in the lower brain stem.

The brain stem *reticular formation* has extremely important functions which have only recently been appreciated. Anatomically it is a complex mixture of cell bodies, fibers, and nuclei extending from the spinal cord to the cerebrum, generally located in a somewhat ventral (lower) position in the brain stem (see Fig. 1-7). The two major aspects of reticular function concern descending influences on spinal and cranial motoneurons and ascending influences on the cerebral cortex and other brain structures. Stimulation of descending portions of the reticular system

9

FIGURE 1-7   *The ascending reticular system, shown as a large central arrow that acts upward and outward on the brain [Magoun, 1954].*

may cause either decreases (inhibition) or increases (facilitation) in the activity of the motoneurons controlling the skeletal musculature. In a classic paper Moruzzi and Magoun [1949] demonstrated that stimulation of the ascending reticular formation, or the ascending reticular activating system, resulted in an arousal response on the EEG, a pattern of low-voltage fast cortical activity characteristic of the waking state (see Fig. 1-2). Destruction of the midbrain reticular formation tends to yield a sleeping or stuporous animal [Lindsley et al., 1949].

The ascending reticular formation thus appears to be critically involved in the control of sleeping and waking. It also seems to play a fundamental role in behavioral alerting and possibly in attention as well [Lindsley, 1958]. The reticular formation receives input from all sensory systems and is in fact the major ascending system for the pathways mediating pain. Still another very old brain stem system that has acquired a new significance is the *raphé nuclei*. These are groups of cells lying in the midline and extending throughout the brain stem. There are relatively few neurons in the raphé system, but they seem to play a significant role in regulation of sleeping and waking and form a very important chemical circuit in the brain.

The brain stem developed early in the course of evolution and is surprisingly uniform in structure and organization from fish to man. There are, of course, some variations among species. A general principle of neural organization is that the size and complexity of a structure is related to the behavioral importance of that structure. In fish, which have no cerebral cortices, the midbrain region contains the important centers of seeing and hearing and is relatively large. Among mammals, the bat, for example, has a much enlarged midbrain auditory nucleus, corresponding to its extensive use of auditory information. As you probably know, the bat employs a system much like sonar. It emits very-high-frequency sound pulses and determines the location of objects in space by the echo sounds of the reflected pulses. The relationship of size of structure to behavioral importance provides a number of clues about possible functions of the various brain structures.

In summary, the brain stem contains all the fiber systems interconnecting the higher brain structures and the spinal cord; it also contains the cranial nerves and their nuclei (except for the olfactory and optic nerves), nuclei subserving vital functions, emotional expression, and many higher-order nuclei concerned with various sensory modalities. When all brain tissue above the midbrain is removed in a cat, for example, the animal is still capable of an amazing variety of behaviors. It will live for long periods, can walk, vocalize, eat, sleep, exhibit some components of emotional expression, and may even be capable of very limited learning [Bard and Macht, 1958]. Humans, on the other hand, rarely survive if all tissue above the midbrain is absent or destroyed, and if they do, they exhibit only primitive reflex responses.

THE CEREBELLUM AND BASAL GANGLIA   The cerebellum is in evolutionary terms a very old structure and was probably the first to be specialized for sensory-motor coordination. It overlies the brain stem (see Fig. 1-4) and is typically very much convoluted in appearance, with a large number of lobules separated by fissures. The cerebellum is basically similar from snake and fish to man. Although it may be involved in a number of other functions as well, the cerebellum is primarily concerned with the regulation of motor coordination. Damage to the cerebellum produces characteristically jerky, uncoordinated movement.

The *basal ganglia* are a group of large nuclei (ganglia is really a misnomer) lying in the central regions of the cerebral hemispheres. These nuclei appear to play an important but as yet poorly understood role in the control of movement. Although their specific functions remain a mystery, we are beginning to learn something about a most interesting and important chemical circuit involving the basal ganglia.

THE HYPOTHALAMUS AND LIMBIC SYSTEM   The hypothalamus encompasses a group of small nuclei that lie generally at the base of the cerebrum close to the pituitary gland, or *hypophysis*. The pituitary gland, the "master gland" of the endocrine glands, is actually controlled by neurons from the hypothalamus. In recent years it has been found that the interrelationships between these two structures are critical in the neural regulation of endocrine gland function. The very small nuclei that comprise the hypothalamus are of fundamental importance to the entire organism. They are critically involved in eating, sexual behavior, drinking, sleeping, temperature regulation, and emotional behavior in general. The hypothalamus is the major central brain structure concerned with the functions of the autonomic nervous system, particularly with its sympathetic division.

The hypothalamus interconnects with many regions of the brain. A number of these structures, including old regions of the cerebral cortex (the cingulate gyrus), the hippocampus, the septal area, the amygdala, portions of the reticular formation, and the hypothalamus itself, are viewed by many anatomists as an integrated network of structures called the *limbic system* (see Fig. 1-8). Many of these structures seem to be involved in aspects of behavior such as emotion, motivation, and reinforcement.

11

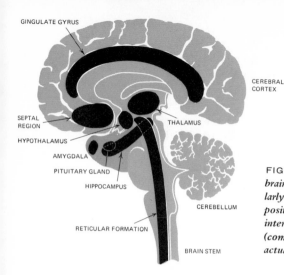

GINGULATE GYRUS

CEREBRAL CORTEX

SEPTAL REGION

THALAMUS

HYPOTHALAMUS

AMYGDALA

PITUITARY GLAND

HIPPOCAMPUS

CEREBELLUM

RETICULAR FORMATION

BRAIN STEM

FIGURE 1-8 *The limbic system of the human brain. These older structures are involved particularly in activation, motivation, and emotion. The position of the thalamus, a newer structure with interrelations to the limbic system, is also shown (compare with Fig. 1-4). The limbic structure are actually within the hemisphere, not on the midline.*

THE THALAMUS   The thalamus is a large grouping of nuclei located just above the midbrain. Its general shape is somewhat like that of small footballs, one in each cerebral hemisphere (see **Fig. 1-8**). One region of the thalamus, the lateral or sensory thalamus, is concerned with relaying sensory information to the cerebral cortex from specific sensory pathways for vision, hearing, touch, taste, and perhaps pain. Another region of the thalamus, the diffuse thalamic system, does not seem to be involved in relaying specific sensory information, but it plays an important role in the control of such processes as sleep and wakefulness and is considered a part of the limbic system.

THE CEREBRAL CORTEX   Biopsychologists have long been particularly fascinated by the structure and functions of the cerebral cortex. A number of considerations justify viewing this structure as the major system for the more complex and modifiable aspects of behavior. The cerebral cortex represents the most recent evolutionary development of the vertebrate nervous system. Fish and amphibians have no cerebral cortices, and reptiles and birds have only a rudimentary indication of one. More primitive mammals such as the rat have a relatively small, smooth cortex. As the phylogenetic scale is ascended, the amount of cortex relative to the total amount of brain tissue increases accordingly. In more advanced primates such as the rhesus monkey, the chimpanzee, and man the amount of cerebral cortex is enormous and disproportionately large. Of the approximately 12 billion neurons in the human brain, 9 billion are found in the cerebral cortex. There is a general correlation between the cortical development in a species, its phylogenetic position, and the degree of complexity and modifiability characteristic of its behavior.

All incoming sensory systems project to the cortex, each to a specific region. Motor systems controlling the activity of muscles and glands arise in other regions of the cortex. Interestingly enough, the basic organization of the cortical sensory and motor areas does not appear to differ markedly from rat to man. However, with ascending position

12

on the evolutionary scale there is a striking increase in the relative amount of *association* cortex—areas that are neither sensory nor motor and have often been assumed to be involved in higher or more complex behavioral functions. Studies done on monkeys indicate that the different association areas of the cortex may play rather different roles in the mediation of complex intellectual processes. In particular, the frontal areas (frontal lobes) may be concerned more with short-term memory and the temporal areas with processing of complex sensory information [Harlow, 1952]. Rough-scale drawings of the cerebral cortex in rat, cat, monkey, and man are shown in Fig. 1-9. Note the remarkable increase in absolute brain size, the increase in the number of indentations or fissures, and the increase in relative amount of association cortex. The depths of the fissures are also covered by cerebral cortex. In fact the development of fissures permits a vast expansion of the amount and total area of the cerebral cortex; the human brain has more cortex in the fissures than on the outer surface.

Man, incidentally, does not have the largest brain. The porpoise, the whale, and the elephant all have larger brain masses, although the packing density of cells may be less. The cortex is a multiple layer of nerve cells about 2-millimeters thick which overlies the cerebrum. An actual photomicrograph of a cross section of the visual area of the cerebral cortex in a human brain is shown in Fig. 1-10.

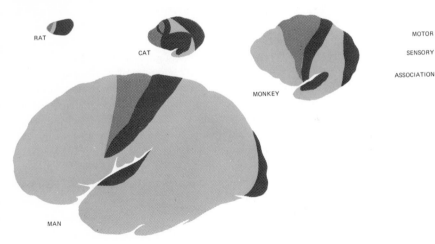

RAT

CAT

MONKEY

MAN

MOTOR

SENSORY

ASSOCIATION

FIGURE 1–9   *Rough scale drawings of the cerebral hemispheres of four mammals. Note the increase both in size and in the relative amount of association cortex. [Thompson, 1967]*

FIGURE 1–10   *Photomicrograph of a cross section through the visual area of the human cerebral cortex. The surface of the cortex is at the top. Each small dot is a neuron. [Sholl, 1956]*

The cerebral cortex is the last or highest region in the brain where sensory information from the eye, the ear, the skin, and other senses is represented. If the visual region of a man's cerebral cortex is destroyed, he will be blind. If the auditory region is removed, he will be deaf. Similarly, if the motor region is destroyed, he will be very awkward and clumsy in his movements. However, the cortex is much more complex than this. A relatively small lesion in one region of the dominant hemisphere makes it impossible to speak (aphasia). Complete destruction of the cerebral cortex transforms a complex human being into a primitive reflex machine. The cerebral cortex is the neural substrate of all higher and more complex behavior in man and is essential to such phenomena as learning, language, and thinking. Not only does it distinguish man from other animals, but it marks the difference between one man and another.

THE BIOLOGY OF THE NEURON

The basic processes of the brain occur at the level of the individual neuron, the fundamental functional element of the nervous system. Various ways of studying the neuron have become artificially separated into different fields. Neuroanatomy is concerned with the fine structure of the neuron, neurochemistry deals with the chemistry of the neuron, and neurophysiology is concerned with the function of the neuron, particularly in terms of electrical or electrophysiological activity. Actually, it makes a good deal more sense to view the neuron and its synapses from all these points of view together.

The individual nerve cell, the *neuron*, resembles most other types of living cells. It has a cell membrane, a nucleus, various structural elements within the cell body, and is a single isolated or individual entity—that is, it is not structurally continuous with other cells. The neuron is specialized, of course, to conduct and transmit information. This is reflected in the fact that neurons have long fibers to conduct information to other neurons or to muscles and glands and the fact that they form *synapses*, the functional connections between neurons.

A typical nerve cell has several characteristic features. The cell shown in Fig. 1-11 is a common type called a *pyramidal cell*, which has a relatively long axon fiber. There are, of course, many specialized forms and shapes of neurons. However, the general features shown here are common to many types of neurons. The main cell body contains the cell nucleus and is referred to as the *soma*. It has many short fibers extending out from it, called *dendrites*, which serve to receive activity from adjacent cells. Synapses form on these dendrites and conduct this activity to the cell body. The long fiber which transmits activity to other neurons is called the *axon*. Actually, the axon will conduct in both directions, but impulses can cross the synapses between nerve cells in only one direction, from the axon of one cell to the cell body or fibers of another. The

14

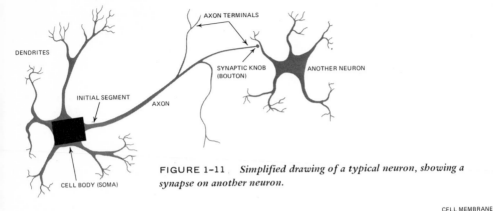

FIGURE 1-11 *Simplified drawing of a typical neuron, showing a synapse on another neuron.*

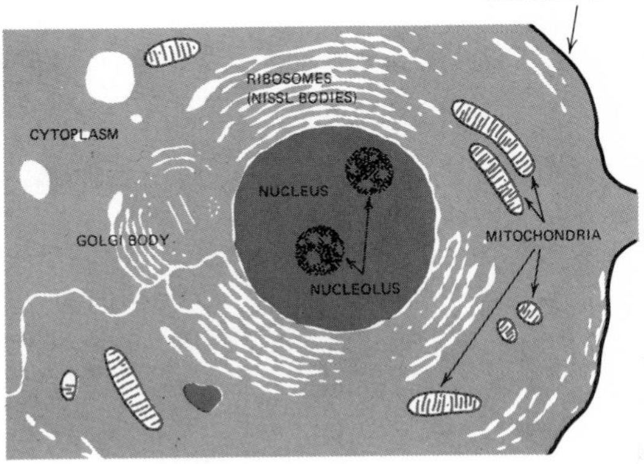

FIGURE 1-12 *Enlargement of the area marked off by a square in Fig. 1-11, showing the characteristic small organelles within the cell body.*

initial portion of the axon is called the *initial segment*. The presynaptic axon terminals are typically very fine as they branch out to end in knobs or *boutons*, in close apposition to other neurons to form the synapses.

The cell body or soma region marked off by the square in **Fig. 1-11** is enlarged in **Fig. 1-12**. Several quite specialized structures called *organelles* ("little organs") are found within the cell body. Recent basic work in cellular biology on the organization and functions of these organelles, which are found in most living cells, has led to something of a revolution in our thinking about how cells function. In particular, we now know that such fundamental processes as the use of food energy (metabolism), use of oxygen (respiration), the synthesis of new chemicals and tissues, and of course reproduction of new cells do not occur uniformly throughout tissue or protoplasm, but occur instead in the specialized organelles within the cell.

Some of these organelles are indicated in **Fig. 1-12**. The *cell membrane*, which covers the entire nerve cell and all its fibers, is specialized to perform a very remarkable task—to conduct information. This process takes place only along the nerve-cell membrane, and not in tissue inside the neuron. The *nucleus* of the neuron contains the genetic material, the deoxyribonucleic acid (DNA), which is present as many

15

thousands of genes which make up the chromosomes. There is another structure within the cell nucleus, the *nucleolus*, that is made up of ribonucleic acid (RNA). This is the system involved in the synthesis of protein and is therefore of fundamental importance. In fact there are several theories that attempt to link RNA to learning and memory. After it is formed in the nucleus, RNA moves out into the cytoplasm of the cell, where it exists as particles called *ribosomes*. In nerve cells the ribosomes are very numerous and are called *Nissl bodies*. The *Golgi bodies* are found in neurons and other cells that are specialized to secrete substances (for example, cells in the pancreas that secrete insulin). It is believed that the Golgi bodies are involved in the manufacture and/or storage of the substances secreted. This is of particular significance for neurons, since it now appears that synaptic transmission, the transfer of information from one neuron to another, is accomplished through the manufacture and secretion of chemical transmitter substances. The last major type of organelle in the neuron is the fairly large football-shaped *mitochondrion*. The interior of the mitochondrion is literally a metabolic factory. It is here that the cell converts foodstuffs and oxygen into biological energy to run the machinery of the body.

Metabolism is a general term which refers to all the chemical processes in the body related to the production and utilization of energy. Considerable amounts of energy are used continuously by all living organisms, even under conditions of minimal activity. This energy is available to the organism only in the form of chemical energy, obtained from foods. When foods are ingested, they are broken down into component substances by the processes of digestion and transported to all cells via the bloodstream. The most common food substance carried by the blood is glucose, a sugar derived from natural carbohydrates. The processes of metabolism whereby glucose and other compounds are broken down to form energy occur separately in all individual cells of the body. Each cell contains a number of mitochondria. The major form of this biological energy is the substance adenosine triphosphate (ATP), produced in the mitochondria. Thus when muscles contract or nerves are active, they use ATP as a direct source of energy.

The brain uses only glucose as the food supply from which to make the energy substance ATP. This process requires oxygen, which means, of course, that the brain must be well supplied with blood. Although the human brain constitutes only about 2.5 percent of the total weight of the body, it receives 15 percent of the total blood supply and uses 25 percent of all the oxygen used by the body. The brain literally lives off the body. Interestingly enough, the energy requirements of the human brain are remarkably steady and constant. The amount of energy used in sitting quietly and not thinking about anything in particular for an hour and the amount of energy used in sitting and solving a problem or studying for an exam for an hour would differ by the equivalent of about half a peanut—and most of the half peanut would be used not for the intense mental effort, but for the increased muscle tension that usually accompanies intense mental effort.

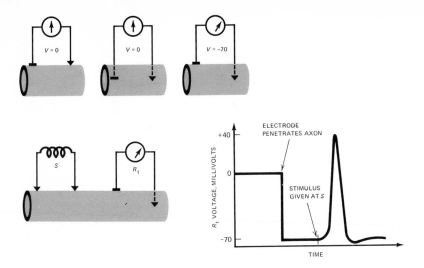

FIGURE 1-13   *Recording the membrane potential from a single nerve fiber axon. Above, the resting membrane voltage (−70 millivolts) is generated only across the axon membrane and does not occur if both electrodes are outside or inside the axon. Below, the conducted nerve action (spike) potential. When the electrode from R_1 penetrates the axon, the resting membrane potential of −70 millivolts is recorded. An electrical stimulus is then given at S, which induces a spike action potential that travels down the axon and is recorded at R_1.*

All the stimuli impinging on us, all our sensations, thoughts, feelings, and actions, must be coded into the "language" of the neuron. Every neuron uses two quite different sorts of language to transmit information. Activity is initiated in a given neuron by the process of synaptic transmission. Once the nerve cell has been activated, the nerve action potential, or spike, develops in the initial segment of the axon and is conducted down the axon to the axon terminal boutons to induce activity at synapses on other neurons. Thus information has to be translated into two codes—synaptic *transmission* when it passes from one neuron to another and action potential *conduction* when it is conducted out along the nerve cell axon from the neuron cell body to the next neuron in the system. Our understanding of the two basic neural processes of transmission and conduction has been due in large part to the work of Hodgkin [1964] and Huxley [1964] in England (nerve action potential) and Eccles [1964] in Australia (synaptic transmission). These studies, for which all three shared the Nobel prize in medicine in 1963, rank among the great intellectual achievements of the twentieth century.

The basic kind of experiment used by Hodgkin and Huxley to study the nerve action potential is shown in Fig. 1-13. They used the giant axon from the squid, which is a single nerve fiber many times larger than axons in mammals and will live for some time after it is removed. In their early

THE AXON AND THE NERVE ACTION POTENTIAL

17

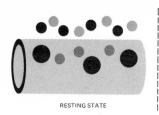
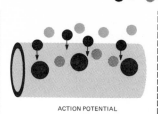
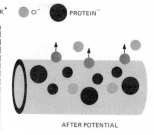

● Na⁺ ● K⁺ ● Cl⁻ ● PROTEIN⁻

RESTING STATE ACTION POTENTIAL AFTER POTENTIAL

FIGURE 1-14   *The distribution of ions inside and outside the axon. In the normal resting state, when the axon is not conducting an action potential, protein and potassium ions are more concentrated inside and sodium and chloride ions*

experiments they tried recording from this axon without removing it from the squid. However, when the fiber was stimulated, the squid gave a powerful flip that smashed their recording electrode. It is easy to see from the figure that the electrical activity of the axon occurs entirely at the nerve membrane. If both electrodes to R_1 are outside the axon there is no voltage; if both are inside the axon there is no voltage. However, if one is outside and one is inside the axon, as shown, a steady voltage will be recorded regardless of where the internal electrode is, as long as it is inside. The graph portion of the figure shows what happens when the internal electrode is inserted through the membrane. The voltage, or potential, shifts from 0 to −70 millivolt (nearly 1/10 volt). This is called the *nerve resting membrane potential*. It is present at about the same value in all neurons, even the very tiny neurons in the human brain. Although the amount of voltage may seem small (it is about one-fifteenth the voltage in an ordinary flashlight battery), it is actually quite substantial in view of the tiny size of most neurons. Cells in the electric eel, using the same basic mechanisms, can develop several hundred volts, enough to stun a man.

The actual mechanisms that produce the resting membrane potential (which, incidentally, occurs in most types of cells, not just in neurons) are beyond the scope of our present discussion [see Thompson, 1967]. However, the essence of the situation is indicated in **Fig. 1-14**. The nerve membrane is semipermeable; in effect, it has small holes that allow some ions to cross, but not others. In the resting state the nerve membrane allows chloride ions (Cl^-) and potassium ions (K^+) to cross rather freely in both directions. However, it will not allow the protein ions, which are mostly inside neurons, to pass out, and it also has a specific barrier that keeps sodium ions (Na^+) from passing in. The actual level of the nerve resting potential, −70 millivolts, is determined entirely by the relative concentrations of potassium ions inside and outside the cell.

As we saw in **Fig. 1-13**, when the axon is stimulated at S, some distance away from the recording electrodes, an action potential develops and travels down the axon. The actual speed of the action potential

18

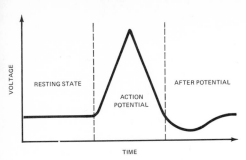

VOLTAGE

RESTING STATE | ACTION POTENTIAL | AFTER POTENTIAL

TIME

are more concentrated outside. As the initial large spike of the action potential develops, sodium ions rush into the axon. During the later afterpotential phase of the action potential, potassium ions move out. The drawings indicate the movements of ions at the same location on the axon during different periods of the action potential.

is relatively slow—from a few feet to several hundred feet per second, depending on the size and other characteristics of the axon. The action potential is constant in amplitude; it does not decay as it travels down the axon, but always stays at the same height, which is about 100 millivolts. It is best viewed as a localized and temporary disturbance of the membrane which moves along the axon much as a wave moves across the surface of water.

The actual mechanisms that yield the action potential, although complex [see Thompson, 1967], are not difficult to describe. When the action potential begins to develop, the membrane barrier to sodium ions breaks down very briefly, and sodium ions rush in (see Fig. 1-14). This creates the 100-millivolt shift in the positive direction (depolarization) that is the major component of the action potential. After this there is a somewhat longer period when the membrane becomes more negative than usual (hyperpolarization, or afterpotential). This is due to a later outward movement of potassium ions. The membrane then returns to its resting level of –70 millivolts and is ready to respond again. The spike action potential is *all-or-none*; it either does not fire at all, or it discharges to its full height and travels down the axon.

When the activity induced in a neuron by synaptic transmission causes the membrane potential of the cell body and initial segment of the axion to depolarize about 10 millivolts, to the spike discharge threshold of about –60 millivolts, the spike develops in the initial segment (see Fig. 1-11) and travels down the axon. It had generally been assumed, incidentally, that when a spike travels down the axon it activates all the small axon terminal branches, but recent evidence suggests that this may not always be the case. Under some conditions not all axon terminals may be activated. When the action potential reaches a branching point, where the axon branches into two smaller axons, the spike may or may not continue in both branches. It is as though there might be some basic element of uncertainty, chance, or "free will" in the system. In any event, the action potential travels down the axon to many of the axon terminals, where it initiates the process of synaptic transmission to activate the next neuron in the system.

19

SYNAPTIC TRANSMISSION

The most important process in the human brain is synaptic transmission. As far as we know, the only way that a neuron can communicate with other neurons is through the synapses. The synapse is not an actual connection, but a close approximation to one. The distance between the axon terminal bouton of one neuron and the cell body of the other neuron is about 200 angstroms (approximately 1/50,000 millimeter). The presynaptic terminal contains a number of circular structures called *synaptic vesicles*, each of which is believed to contain the chemical synaptic transmitter substance which is released across the synapse to act on the postsynaptic membrane of the other cell. The presence of synaptic vesicles is characteristic, indeed even diagnostic, of the appearance of a synapse. The presumed transmitter chemical may be manufactured in the cell body, perhaps by the Golgi bodies, and then transported down the axon by some means and stored in the synaptic vesicles. Alternatively, the chemical may be formed in the terminal itself, where the vesicles are found.

Synapses are localized primarily on dendrites and cell bodies. The dendrites are the region of the cell where incoming information is summed and, in a very real sense, evaluated. Recent work indicates that there are important specialized structures on the dendrites called *dendritic spines*

FIGURE 1-15   *Synapses. In a typical neuron of the cerebral cortex, the dendrites are covered by many thousands of dendritic spines. Each spine is a synapse. The type 1 dendritic knob synapse (drawn from electron-microscope pictures) is characteristically excitatory. The presynaptic axon terminal knob is filled with small vesicles, presumably containing the chemical synaptic transmitter substance, and the postsynaptic membrane has a dark thickened region, presumably containing chemical receptors for the transmitter substance. On the type 2 synapse, which occurs on the cell body of the neuron, there is no spine or thickening of the postsynaptic membrane. This type of synapse is characteristically inhibitory.*

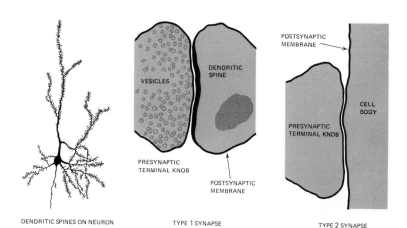

DENDRITIC SPINES ON NEURON   TYPE 1 SYNAPSE   TYPE 2 SYNAPSE (see Fig. 1-15). These very small knobs or spines cover all parts of the dendrites but are not found on cell bodies or axons. They are particularly numerous on the pyramidal type of neuron found throughout the cerebral cortex and certain other regions of the brain. The enlargements in the figure show the nature of the spine synapse in greater detail. Each spine is a place where an axon terminal from another neuron forms a synapse with the neuron dendrite. The many thousands of spines that appear on the dendrite are all terminations of other neuron processes. Thus each dendritic spine provides the means by which a fiber from another neuron can increase this neuron's excitability or tendency to be active. A different type of synapse, however, is found on the *cell body* of a neuron (see also Fig. 1-11). These synapses have no spines. Recent evidence indicates that there is also a fundamental difference in their function—the dendritic spine synapses (type 1) excite the neuron and cell body synapses (type 2) inhibit it.

There are several aspects of the dendritic spines that are of great significance. First, in higher mammals they seem for the most part to develop after birth. In the cat, for example, spines first become apparent about seven days after birth, a time when the infant kitten is just beginning to explore and learn about his world. They are not fully elaborated until the kitten is several months old. Equally important is the fact that if activity on the spines is decreased by damaging the input fibers to the spines, they do not develop normally. Even such a simple procedure as keeping an animal in the dark for a month leads to changes in the spines of cortical cells in the visual region. From this it is a relatively small step to the enormously important hypothesis that the dendritic spines are the fundamental structural locus of memory in the adult brain. Very recent evidence provides some support for this idea. It appears that if rats are raised in an "enriched" environment, with many more types of objects and stimuli than are usual in a rat cage, they develop more than the normal number of dendritic spines in cortical cells [Schapiro and Vukovich, 1970]. This finding opens up a most exciting possibility in the search for the memory *engram*—the physical basis of memory. It is also possible that the dendritic spines, if they reflect the structural development of synapses, may have a more general function than simply the coding of memory. They may reflect all the patterns of interconnections established among neurons in the brain during the growth and development of the organism.

In terms of structure, neurons, with their many thousands of dendritic spines, are far and away the most highly specialized cells in the body. All behavioral patterns—indeed, all the countless billions of elements of information and experience that we acquire in a lifetime—appear to be coded in the structural-functional relations among the neurons. Neurons are the only cells in the body that do not reproduce after birth. We are born with all the neurons we will ever have. As we grow up and grow older, we simply lose neurons. It has been estimated that on the order of several hundred neurons die each day in the adult human brain. If all memory is in fact coded in part by structural features of neurons such as the spines, then it would not be feasible for neurons to reproduce. If they did, the structural relationships would change, and the very fabric of memory would shift and dissipate. Although it is difficult to imagine an information-storage system in a higher organism in which the elements reproduce themselves, speculation on the kinds of psychological processes that might occur has resulted in some classic science fiction [van Vogt, 1940].

EXCITATION OF NEURONS

The operation of synaptic transmission is shown in Fig. 1-16. The presynaptic axon terminal contains vesicles of the transmitter chemical. The particular chemical transmitter shown here, acetylcholine (ACh), is in fact the chemical transmitter at the neuromuscular junction (where the motoneuron axon ends on the muscle fiber and induces muscle contraction), in certain synapses in the peripheral autonomic system, and in

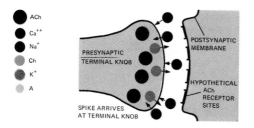

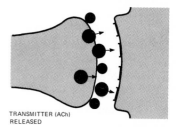

TRANSMITTER (ACh)
RELEASED

FIGURE 1–16   *Chemical actions that occur during synaptic transmission. The action potential arrives at the presynaptic terminal, causing sodium ions (Na⁺) to move in (and potassium ions out), which in turn causes calcium ions (Ca⁺⁺) to move onto the membrane. This produces release of the transmitter, in this case acetylcholine (ACh). When acetylcholine arrives at the "receptor" sites on the postsynaptic membrane, the postsynaptic electrical response is generated. The transmitter, acetylcholine, is broken down at the receptor sites into acetyl (A) and choline (Ch), which can then be reabsorbed by the presynaptic terminal and reformed into acetylcholine.*

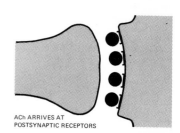

ACh ARRIVES AT
POSTSYNAPTIC RECEPTORS

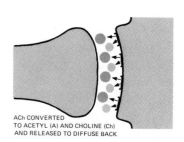

ACh CONVERTED
TO ACETYL (A) AND CHOLINE (Ch)
AND RELEASED TO DIFFUSE BACK

some brain synapses as well. When the action potential reaches the terminal, as shown, a reaction is started which leads to release of the transmitter. Recent work indicates that the important process here is an action of calcium ions (Ca^{++}) on the membrane. The influx of calcium is apparently started by the arrival of the action potential and the associated inward flow of sodium ions and outward flow of potassium ions. When the calcium ions move onto the membrane, the transmitter substance ACh is released into the synaptic space. The ACh molecules diffuse across the synapse, attach to receptor sites on the postsynaptic membrane, and induce an electrical response in the postsynaptic membrane. Since the excitatory synapse is on a dendritic spine, the electrical response occurs in the dendrite and cell body of the neuron.

The receptor sites on the postsynaptic membrane are not fully understood. They may actually be an enzyme that breaks down ACh into its components, acetyl and choline. This enzyme, acetylcholine esterase, is in fact present in all acetylcholine synapses. Such a receptor mechanism would indeed be a great convenience. The same process that inactivates the transmitter by breaking it down also induces activity in the postsynaptic membrane. The chemical receptor functions as both a receptor and an inactivator for ACh. If the ACh were not inactivated, the cell would respond for a long time instead of briefly. The components of the acetylcholine are then taken up, perhaps into the presynaptic terminal, to be reformed into ACh and used again.

If a recording electrode were placed inside the postsynaptic neuron, it would indicate a change in the membrane potential when the ACh arrived at the postsynaptic membrane. As shown in Fig. 1-17, the resting potential of the neuron is –70 millivolts, and the spike discharge threshold is –60 millivolts, the same as in the axon. The electrical change in the postsynaptic cell membrane during synaptic excitation is a very brief decrease in the membrane potential—a depolarization. If only a single synapse on a cell is activated, there will be only a small depolarization. If we activate a few synapses on the cell together, the depolarization will be larger. When enough synapses are activated to cause the membrane potential to reach the spike threshold level of the cell, then a spike develops at the initial segment of the axon and travels down the axon to act on other neurons. This kind of synaptic depolarization, which seems to occur particularly on the dendritic spine synapses (type 1), is called an *excitatory postsynaptic potential* (EPSP).

The actual mechanism that yields the EPSP is very similar to that producing the spike. When the cell membrane potential reaches the spike threshold point, the irreversible chemical reaction that generates the spike—the breakdown of the sodium barrier and the inward rush of sodium ions—occurs. The EPSP itself results from a brief, limited breakdown of the barriers to sodium and other ions on the postsynaptic membrane at the synapse. Since this occurs only at the synapse, the effect for one synapse will be small. The size of the EPSP, however, depends on the number of synapses activated. Hence it is a graded response; that is,

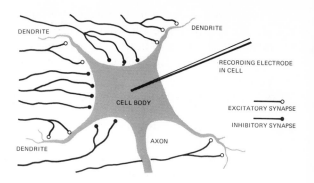

FIGURE 1-17   *Synaptic transmission. Schematic
of a neuron with excitatory synaptic terminals (light)
on the dendrites and inhibitory synaptic terminals
(dark) on the cell body. A recording electrode has
been inserted into the cell to measure the changes in
the cell membrane potential during synaptic excitation and inhibition. During synaptic excitation the
electrical response of the membrane to a weak excitation from only 1 or 2 synapses is a brief deplorization*

it can vary continuously in amplitude. This is in sharp contrast to the
all-or-none action potential. The fact that the EPSP is graded is of
fundamental importance. The neuron is continuously being bombarded
by the actions from many synapses. It averages or integrates all this input activity into an overall graded level of membrane potential. When
this level reaches the spike threshold, the neuron fires the action potential, thus converting the continuous graded synaptic activity or information into a discrete, fixed-amplitude, all-or-none spike discharge. For
readers familiar with computers, every neuron is like a complex hybrid
computer, the graded synaptic activity is comparable to an analog
computer, and the all-or-none spike is comparable to a digital computer.
People say that the brain is like a computer; it is in fact like 12 billion
complex computers, each interacting with many others.

INHIBITION OF NEURONS

If the brain were composed entirely of excitatory synapses of the type
we have been discussing, any stimulus that induced neural activity
would immediately cause a runaway buildup of excitation to the point
where the brain would be in a permanent state of massive continuous
discharging, as in an epileptic seizure. Indeed, certain drugs that block
inhibition, such as strychnine, produce just this effect—massive epileptic-
like discharges of neurons. It is therefore necessary to consider processes
of inhibition in order to account for the neural functioning of the brain.

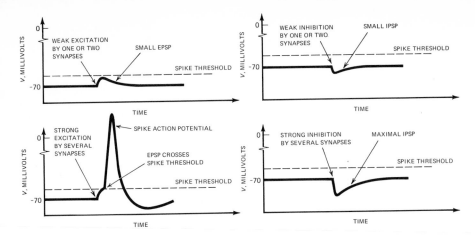

(EPSP) *that does not reach spike threshold (upper response). Strong excitation from several synapses produces an EPSP large enough to cross the spike threshold level of the cell, which results in a spike developing at the initial segment of the axon and traveling down the axon (lower response). During synaptic inhibition the postsynaptic cell-membrane potential becomes greater in the negative direction (hyperpolarized) during inhibition. This response is called the inhibitory postsynaptic potential (IPSP). Weak inhibition from only 1 or 2 synapses (upper response) produces a small increase in negativity of the membrane and strong inhibition (lower response) produces a maximal negativity. The IPSP inhibits synaptic excitation by preventing the cell from developing an EPSP to excitatory input.*

Perhaps the simplest possible way that an inhibitory synapse could act would be to do just the opposite of what an excitatory synapse does and *increase* the negativity of the membrane potential beyond that of its resting level. As noted above, the resting membrane is normally about −70 millivolts and an excitatory change of about 10 millivolts to the threshold level of −60 millivolts initiates spike discharge. If the membrane potential could be shifted in the opposite direction to a value of, say, −75 millivolts, then an EPSP of 10 millivolts that had previously caused discharge of the cell would just shift the membrane potential back to −65 millivolts, still 5 millivolts below the spike discharge threshold. This is essentially what does take place during inhibition; there is a brief *increase* in the negativity of the membrane potential.

Examples of inhibitory synapses are also shown in **Fig. 1-17**. These are the type 2 synapses on the cell bodies, which have no spines. Stimulation of an input fiber that exerts an inhibitory effect on the postsynaptic neuron causes release of a chemical inhibitory substance that diffuses across the synaptic space to act on the postsynaptic membrane of the cell body. However, the cell membrane potential is shifted toward a greater degree of polarization—that is, the cell membrane becomes hyperpolarized. The actual membrane potential may shift from −70 to −75 millivolts. This is termed the *inhibitory postsynaptic potential* (IPSP). When an IPSP occurs an excitatory action that previously depolarized the cell to firing threshold will no longer produce a depolarization sufficient to reach spike threshold. The ionic mechanism of the IPSP is different from that of the EPSP. The sodium barrier does not break down,

25

but is instead made stronger by small increases in the movement of potassium and chloride ions across the membrane. Examples of IPSPs produced in a neuron by weak and strong actions from inhibitory nerve fibers are shown in Fig. 1-17. The IPSP appears to be roughly a mirror image of the EPSP. Note that it grows in a *graded* fashion with increasing stimulus strength, just as does the EPSP. However, it moves the membrane potential level of the cell farther away from the spike threshold, and so, of course, no action potential is developed.

Postsynaptic excitation (EPSP) and postsynaptic inhibition (IPSP) are the major types of synaptic processes that occur in the brain. Remember that the spike action potential begins at the initial segment, where the axon leaves the cell body. Excitation occurs on the dendrites, some distance from the initial segment. However, the development of the spike at the initial segment is entirely due to synaptic excitation. Inhibition, in contrast, occurs on the cell body adjacent to the initial segment. Thus inhibition has a much more immediate and potent controlling effect than excitation on the tendency of the cell to fire spikes and hence influence other cells.

In the mammalian nervous system, where the basic mechanism of synaptic transmission is chemical, essentially all interactions among neurons take place through the processes of excitation (EPSP) and inhibition (IPSP). Virtually every nerve cell body and dendrite has an essentially continuous covering of synaptic terminal knobs (see Fig. 1-18), and in the normal state the cell is continuously being bombarded with thousands of excitatory and inhibitory synaptic influences. The extent to which the cell is or is not firing all-or-none spike potentials down the axon is determined by the dynamic balance among these classes of synaptic events. This complexity of organization makes it very clear that the usual simple diagrams and neural models, which show each neuron synapsing on only one or two other neurons and all synapses as excitatory, must inevitably fail to predict the complexity of behavior of the real nervous system.

The EEGs we discussed at the beginning of the chapter are averaged records of the electrical activity generated by literally millions of neurons. A basic question in the study of brain activity has been the nature of the processes in the neurons that produce the EEG. If all the neurons were acting differently, we would see nothing but noise in the record.

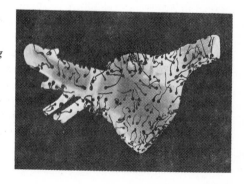

FIGURE 1-18   *A realistic drawing showing only the largest synapses in the cell body of a neuron [Haggar and Barr, 1950].*

Instead, under many conditions we can record clear wave patterns (see Fig. 1-2). The processes that act together to produce synchronous wave patterns are primarily the graded synaptic potentials we have been discussing. The brain activity that is shown in an EEG is the summed graded synaptic potential, both excitatory and inhibitory, generated on the dendrites and cell bodies of millions of neurons in the brain.

SYNAPTIC TRANSMITTER SUBSTANCES

The fact that synaptic transmission in the human nervous system is a chemical process means that chemical substances must play a fundamental role in learning, thinking, and other complex aspects of behavior. We can make very good guesses about the nature of some chemical substances that may serve as transmitters in the brain. However, there is a great deal more to be learned about this fundamental and important field than we know today.

ACETYLCHOLINE   As we noted earlier, acetylcholine is the transmitter at the neuromuscular junction, certain peripheral autonomic synapses, and in certain regions of the brain. It appears that ACh is substantially present in a large ascending system of neurons tentatively identified with the ascending reticular activating system. This system, which originates in the brain stem and projects anteriorly to the hypothalamus, the thalamus, the limbic system, and other regions, plays a fundamental role in the regulation of sleep, waking, and arousal. Thus ACh might have a very specific and important function in the control of sleep and waking, of behavioral arousal, and possibly attention as well.

NOREPINEPHRINE, DOPAMINE, AND SEROTONIN   There is considerable evidence that norepinephrine and two closely related compounds, dopamine and serotonin, may be synaptic transmitter substances in the brain. These three *biogenic amines*—amines which have biological activity or effects—are derived from naturally occurring amino acids, the major components of meat and other proteins. Norepinephrine is in fact formed from dopamine, which in turn is formed from the amino acid tyrosine. Serotonin (5-hydroxytryptamine, also referred to as 5-HT) is simply derived from the naturally occurring amino acid tryptophan.

Norepinephrine is a transmitter in portions of the peripheral autonomic system. Recently a group of scientists in Sweden developed a technique for identifying the presence of biogenic amines in the brain by converting them to highly fluorescent substances [Hillarp et al., 1960]. Norepinephrine and dopamine fluoresce with a greenish color and serotonin fluoresces with a yellow color. They have been able to show that there appear to be biogenic amine systems in the brain. Thus there is a norepinephrine system with cell bodies in the brain stem that send axons via the medial forebrain bundle (a fiber pathway) to the hypothalamus, the hippocampus, the limbic system, and the cerebral

27

cortex. This system appears to be similar to the acetylcholine system described above and may also be related to the organization and functions of the ascending reticular activating system. There is a particularly high concentration of norepinephrine in the hypothalamus, the small region in the depths of the brain that is most directly concerned with the motivational and emotional aspects of behavior.

Although norepinephrine is formed from dopamine, dopamine appears to exist and function independently in the brain. Hillarp et al. have demonstrated that there is a dopamine system in the brain that is quite distinct from the norepinephrine system. The cell bodies of this system lie in the *substantia nigra*, a dark-staining group of neurons in the region of the midbrain. The axons from these cells go to the basal ganglia, large masses of cells in the cerebrum that appear to have functions related to the control of movement. It is of considerable significance that parkinsonism, which produces forced involuntary repetitive movements of the hand and arm, is generally associated with degeneration of cells in the *substantia nigra*. Furthermore, in this disease there is a pronounced decrease in the dopamine content of the basal ganglia. Parkinsonism has been treated by making lesions in the basal ganglia, the region of termination of the dopamine system whose cell bodies originate in the *substantia nigra*. Very recently dopamine has been used with apparent success in treating this disease. Interestingly, it also seems to be of great benefit in the treatment of depression.

Serotonin is found in many portions of the central nervous system. Essentially all the serotonin neurons in the brain have their cell bodies in the raphé nuclei of the brain stem. These cells project to wide areas of the forebrain, including the hypothalamus, the septal area, and other regions of the limbic system. It appears that the projections of these cells can account for all of the brain serotonin. In other words, it seems likely that all serotonin is manufactured in these cell groups of the raphé nuclei and is then distributed to various other brain regions by the axons of the cells. The raphé nuclei appear to be involved in regulation of sleep and wakefulness, and the regions to which they project, the hypothalamus and the limbic system, are involved in the motivational and emotional aspects of behavior. It is as though the raphé cells were a very ancient system with its own neural transmitter, serotonin, concerned with such primitive aspects of behavior as sleep and basic emotion.

Schildkraut and Kety [1967] have developed an interesting theory relating the biogenic amines to emotion. In surveying the effects on mood and emotions of a number of drugs that influence brain levels of the biogenic amines they found that drugs which tend to cause *decreases* in brain levels or activity of biogenic amines tend to produce depression or sedation, while drugs which *increase* or potentiate the brain levels or activity of biogenic amines are associated with behavioral *stimulation*, excitement, or even mania, and in general have a clear antidepressant effect in man. This leads to the very simple and intriguing theory that depression is due to a deficiency of brain biogenic amines and elation is associated with an excess of such substances in the brain; in short, happiness is having lots of brain biogenic amines. This theory is, of course, only in the stage of speculation, but it could have enormously important implications for the understanding of mental illness.

OTHER TRANSMITTER SUBSTANCES   Although a good many other chemicals have been suggested as synaptic transmitters, current evidence is strong for only three substances—glutamic acid, glycine, and gamma-amino butyric acid (GABA). Interestingly enough, they are all simple amino acids. Glutamic acid appears to be a transmitter chemical at certain excitatory synapses, and glycine and GABA seem to be transmitters for certain inhibitory synapses. Glycine is the simplest amino acid and one of the simplest of all biologically active chemicals. The fact that the nervous system appears to have utilized the simplest and most commonly occurring natural biological chemicals as transmitters is strong testimony to the elegant simplicity of evolution. If we wanted to design a system with roughly a trillion functional connections, each requiring chemicals to work, the ideal solution would be to use chemicals that are simple and widely present in the system. The brain has done just this. The chemistry of synaptic transmission, literally the chemistry of the mind, is an exciting and fundamental area of research.

THE EFFECT OF DRUGS ON BEHAVIOR

Drugs can exert extremely potent and sometimes lethal influences on behavior. Indeed, among the major influences on behavior, drugs can be of overriding importance because of their capability to *control* it. *Drugs* are usually defined as chemicals that have effects on animals. In this sense almost every substance might serve as a drug. The study of drugs that influence experience and behavior is termed *psychopharmacology*.

Since the interactions among neurons occur at synapses, and synaptic transmission is chemical, we might expect that many different drugs would have an effect on brain function and behavior. Such is indeed the case; many drugs do alter brain activity by acting on the chemical mechanisms involved in synaptic transmission. In some invertebrate animals certain synapses are electrical (the presynaptic spike directly induces an electrical response in the postsynaptic neuron). Because electrical synapses are not subject to chemical influences, it is very difficult to modify their actions in any way. However, there are no electrical synapses in the human brain; in fact in higher mammals all brain synapses are chemical. This is a great advantage in terms of flexibility. Chemical synapses can be modified very easily, not just by drugs, but by normal chemical and structural factors. It is probable that the great plasticity, or modifiability, inherent in the human brain—our capacity

29

to learn so much so well—is due to the fact that our brain synapses work by chemical rather than electrical processes.

Although psychopharmacology has existed as a field for only about 20 years, references to drugs that affect experience are as old as history. According to Homer, Helen of Troy was an opium addict; alcohol is at least as old as Western society; Herodotus described how the ancient Scythians heated hemp seeds on hot stones, inhaled the vapors (marijuana), and "shouted for joy." It is probably a safe generalization that every primitive culture in the world has discovered and developed its own brand of "trip" from naturally occurring substances. The major categories of drugs that influence behavior, with examples and typical effects, are given in **Table 1-1.**

NARCOTIC ANALGESICS

Morphine, heroin, and the other opium alkaloids are among the most severely addictive of all drugs. They have been used for centuries to ease pain; in fact morphine is still one of the most widely used drugs in medicine. The modes of action of the narcotics are unknown. In moderate doses they produce a sense of euphoria (a feeling of well being), drowsiness, and most important, a marked analgesia (relief of pain). Even the most severe chronic pains, from toothache to terminal cancer,

TABLE 1-1   *Psychopharmacological drugs.*

DRUG CLASS	EXAMPLES	EFFECTS
Narcotic analgesics	Morphine, heroin	Relieves pain; produces sense of well-being; highly addictive
Stimulants	Amphetamines, caffeine	Increases alertness; can produce anxiety; moderately addictive
Psychotherapeutics		
Antipsychotics	Reserpine, chlorpromazine	Aids some forms of mental illness
Antianxiety drugs	Meprobamate, chlordiazepoxide	Reduces some forms of anxiety
Antidepressants	MAO inhibitors, imipramine	Reduces some forms of depression
Psychogenics	Lysergic acid diethylamide Mescaline Marijuana	Produces psychoticlike symptoms

are markedly and often completely relieved by morphine. It is important to note that although chronic pain is eliminated, awareness is not.
The pain threshold and the feeling of unpleasantness from a pinprick
seem relatively unchanged after analgesic doses of morphine. It is often
said that morphine does not alter the immediate sensation of pain, but
only the patient's reactions to that sensation. Although this may convey the essential character of the morphine syndrome, it is probably not
a scientifically tenable distinction. Furthermore, under many conditions,
narcotics may reduce the response to imposed pain in man and animals.

STIMULANTS

A wide variety of substances can be categorized as stimulants in terms of
their general effects on behavior. *Strychnine*, *picrotoxin*, and *metrazol*
(pentylenetetrazol) are potent stimulants of the central nervous system
which lead in overdoses to convulsions and death. Strychnine and picrotoxin, incidentally, are among the very few drugs whose actions on nerve
cells are to some degree understood; they block particular forms of
neural inhibition, thus leading to "runaway" excitation and convulsions.
These three drugs and related substances are of particular interest to
physiological psychologists because of their effects in facilitating certain
kinds of behaviors, particularly learning [McGaugh, 1969].

Widely used mild stimulants include *caffeine* (in coffee, tea, and
cocoa) and *nicotine* (in tobacco). One cup of coffee, for example, contains about 200 milligrams (0.2 gram) of caffeine, a dose sufficiently
high to produce stimulation of the central nervous system. The effects of
these drugs as stimulants are relatively mild. Caffeine in particular appears
to be an almost ideal stimulant. It seems to allay drowsiness and fatigue,
increase the "flow of thought," and increase motor activity, and for most
people it has few or no side effects. There has never been a death attributed to an overdose of caffeine.

Amphetamines and related drugs—dexedrine, benzedrine, "speed,"
methedrine—are perhaps the most widely used and abused of the
potent stimulants. They lessen depression and fatigue, increase motor
and verbal activity, and can lead to increased alertness, lessened need
for sleep, and lessened appetite. Elevation of mood, however, is followed by a corresponding letdown which can increase severely with
successively higher doses.

Amphetamines are most commonly prescribed to overcome le-
thargia during pregnancy and to decrease the appetite in overweight
patients. The effect on appetite, however, is quite variable in humans.
Although dogs given amphetamine an hour before feeding will refuse
food, and will even starve to death under such conditions, amphetamines often have little or no effect on appetite in humans.

Amphetamines are strongly addictive; in fact amphetamine addiction has become a serious social problem in both Europe and the United

31

States. It is significant from both a practical and a theoretical standpoint that amphetamines are the only drugs known to produce a psychotic state that is clinically indistinguishable from a naturally occurring psychosis, paranoid schizophrenia. A fact of great interest in this context is that the chemical action of amphetamines leads to an increased activity of biogenic amines in the brain.

PSYCHOTHERAPEUTICS

Psychotherapeutic agents, drugs used in the treatment of psychological disorders, have led to a genuine revolution in the care and treatment of the mentally ill. Their advent has enabled many thousands of persons who just a few years ago would have spent their lives in the back wards of mental institutions to live and function in society.

Psychotherapeutics do not, of course, cure mental illness. They are effective in varying degrees with different patients in treating and controlling the symptoms, particularly in cases of depression. However, this does not mean that we understand the causes of mental illness or that we understand why these drugs have the effects they do. Much of the work has been on an entirely empirical and even accidental basis. The psychotherapeutic effects of reserpine, for example, came to light as a more or less unexpected side effect when it was being used to control hypertension, a form of high blood pressure.

ANTIPSYCHOTICS   There are two major categories of antipsychotic drugs—the phenothiazine derivatives such as chlorpromazene, and the rauwolfia alkaloids, such as reserpine. The phenothiazene derivatives grew out of biochemical work on antihistamines and related substances. Although there are a great many similar substances now available, chlorpromazene, synthesized in 1950, is still most widely used. The rauwolfia alkaloids are derived from a naturally occurring plant that grows in India. Ancient Hindu writings recommend the use of rauwolfia for both hypertension and insanity—its two modern applications. Reserpine is the purified synthetic form of rauwolfia in present use. Although the drugs are chemically unrelated, many of the general behavioral effects of chlorpromazene and reserpine are similar. One major difference is that reserpine produces marked depression of mood, whereas chlorpromazine does not. As is true for most drugs, the mechanisms and modes of actions of the antipsychotic drugs are essentially unknown. It is noteworthy, however, that reserpine also causes a significant decrease in biogenic amines in the brain.

TRANQUILIZERS   Antianxiety drugs, usually referred to as tranquilizers, produce a generally relaxed and anxiety-free state somewhat similar to that produced by alcohol and barbiturates, but without their marked sedative effects. Two common but chemically unrelated anti-

32

anxiety drugs are meprobamate (Miltown) and chlordiazepoxide (Librium). Meprobamate was initially developed as a muscle relaxant, and its tranquilizing properties were discovered later. The usual clinical dose has no effect on tested performance but alters the EEG slightly in the direction of that seen during sleep. According to subjective reports, it reduces anxiety and induces a mild euphoria. The mechanisms by which antianxiety drugs produce these effects are as yet unknown.

ANTIDEPRESSANTS   The antidepressant agents are a particularly interesting group of drugs which provide rather dramatic relief from certain forms of severe depression. Although amphetamines might also be classified as antidepressants, their effect is of much shorter duration, and they are generally classed as a stimulant. However, the mode of action is in some ways similar. There are two general types of antidepressant drugs, *MAO inhibitors* and *imipramine*. They are chemically unrelated, but they both seem to act in such a way as to increase the brain level of norepinephrine, one of the biogenic amines.

It was observations such as this that led Schildkraut and Kety to the theory that biogenic amines are related to emotions. Tranquilizers such as reserpine decrease brain amines, and stimulants and antidepressants such as MAO inhibitors, imipramine, and amphetamines increase brain amines. Hence the general level of emotional state may be determined by the levels of biogenic amines, particularly norepinephrine, in regions of the brain such as the hypothalamus and limbic system, which are involved in emotional and motivational aspects of behavior.

PSYCHOGENICS

The most widely known psychogenic agents are lysergic acid diethylamide (LSD or "acid"), mescaline (from the peyote cactus), psilosibin (from mushrooms), and marijuana. These drugs have been variously described in terms of their effects as psychotomimetics (imitating psychosis), hallucinogenics (inducing hallucinations), and psychedelics. Psychogenic, perhaps the best term, simply refers to the fact that these drugs produce psychoticlike symptoms.

LYSERGIC ACID DIETHYLAMIDE   LSD is one of the most potent and dangerous drugs known; the effective dose is as low as 100 micrograms (1/10,000 gram). It produces a variety of bizarre subjective experiences and behaviors that in many ways resemble insanity, and for a while there was hope that it would provide a good model of psychosis for experimental study. However, there appear to be some fundamental differences. Hallucinations, subjective experiences of stimuli that are not physically present, are common to both situations, but the type of hallucination induced by LSD is primarily visual, whereas in naturally occurring psychosis they tend to be predominantly auditory (hearing voices that are

33

not there). Furthermore, a normal person who has taken LSD is aware that he is under the influence of LSD; a psychotic person does not believe that he is psychotic. Following is a description by a normal subject of his experience with LSD [Farrell, 1966, pp. 8-9]:

I'm a hard-headed, conservative, Midwestern, Republican businessman. Under no circumstances would I consider myself a person who goes around taking strange drugs.

But my wife took LSD at a friend's house, and in order to get her to agree to come home, I took the stuff myself.

We got in the car, and I had only driven about three blocks, when suddenly the pavement in front of me opened up. It was as though the pavement was flowing over Niagara Falls. The street lights expanded into fantastic globes of light that filled my entire vision. I didn't dare stop.

It was a nightmare. I came to traffic lights, but I couldn't tell what color they were. There were all sorts of colors around me anyway. I could detect other cars around me, so I stopped when they stopped, and went when they went.

At home I flopped in a chair. I wasn't afraid. My conscious mind was sort of sitting on my shoulder—watching everything I was doing. I found I could make the room expand—oh, maybe a thousand miles—or I could make it contract right in front of me. All over the ceiling there were geometric patterns of light. To say they were beautiful is too shallow a word.

My wife put on a violin concerto. I could make the music come out of the speaker like taffy, or a tube of toothpaste, surrounded by dancing lights of colors beyond description.

A friend showed up. He was talking to me, and I was answering, all in a perfectly normal way. Then, I saw his face change. He became an Arab, a Chinese, a Negro. I found I could take my finger and wipe away his face and then paint it back again.

I made a chocolate sundae and gave it to him for a head. A great truth appeared to me. The reason he had all those faces was this: he was a reflection of all mankind. So was I.

I asked myself, "What is God?" Then I knew that I was God. That really sounds ridiculous as I say it. But I knew that all life is one, and since God is Life, and I am Life, we are the same being.

Then I decided to examine my own fears, because I wasn't really afraid of anything. I went down into my stomach and it was like Dante's inferno—all steaming and bubbling and ghastly. I saw some hideous shapes in the distance. My mind floated to each one, and they were horrible, hideous.

They all got together in a mob and started to come up after me— a flood of bogeymen. But I knew I was stronger than all of them, and I took my hand and wiped them out.

Now, I think there lies the real danger with LSD. Anyone who motioned with his hand and couldn't wipe out those creatures. He has to stay down there with them, forever.

The danger of LSD lies not only in its immediate effects on subjective experience, but also in the extreme and bizarre behavior that may arise from this experience. People on "bad trips" have fatally injured themselves and others. Moreover, there have been reports that the symptoms recur at a later date in the absence of LSD.

LSD is known to be a potent inhibitor of brain serotonin. Although the exact mechanisms are not known, it seems to inhibit or decrease activity of cells in the raphé nuclei, which apparently influence such basic functions as sleep and emotion. Of course, it is a long step from this information to a clear understanding of what LSD actually does.

MARIJUANA   The most widely used psychogenic agent is marijuana, the dried flowers and leaves of the hemp plant. In its naturally occurring form the dosage of its effective ingredient, tetrahydrocannabinol, is relatively low. However, the highly concentrated form hashish has long been known to induce pronounced psychoticlike behavior. The word "assassin" derives from the Arabic "hashshāshīn," a Mohammedan sect addicted to hashish, whose terrorist activities were notorious during the time of the crusades. The most frequently reported effect of marijuana is a mild euphoria. There are also occasional reports of increased appetite, a heightened sense of taste and smell, and some alteration of time perception. The drug itself is not known to have any long-range biological effects. The fact that it tends to lower productive activity levels may, of course, have social, if not biological, consequences.

DRUG ADDICTION

Addiction is a complex phenomenon, but a very real and prevalent social problem. Psychogenic agents such as marijuana and LSD do not appear to be addictive, at least in the sense that they do not appear to produce a strong biological need for their continued use. Addiction to heroin, barbiturates, amphetamines, and alcohol produces an extreme biological need. Sudden withdrawal from such drugs causes severe and violent withdrawal symptoms which in some cases may even be fatal. In contrast, a regular user of marijuana experiences no particular biological effects from sudden withdrawal. He may continue use simply because he likes it. However, since we know that "likes" are fundamentally biological phenomena—indeed, they are the result of brain processes—the distinction between addiction and nonaddiction may in part be only a matter of degree.

Sharpless, Jaffe, and others have developed a most interesting *hypersensitivity* theory which explains many withdrawal effects in drug addiction [Jaffe, 1965]. It appears that whatever effects the drug produces will occur in opposite form during withdrawal. If stomach contractions are decreased by the drug, for example, they become abnormally strong and produce stomach cramps during withdrawal. Since amphetamines produce a sense of well-being, the patient becomes severely depressed during withdrawal. The explanation of these effects is that during drug use

35

the biological systems that are inhibited or depressed by the drug compensate by stepping up activity, so that their base levels of activity are much higher than normal. As a result, when the drug is withdrawn the biological systems which had been artifically depressed are left in a hyperactive state and produce the symptoms of withdrawal. The duration of withdrawal symptoms corresponds to the duration of action of the drugs themselves. Heroin is relatively short acting; the withdrawal symptoms are relatively brief and extremely severe. A new synthetic drug, methadone, has effects similar to those of heroin, but it is much longer acting. The patient can be shifted from heroin to methadone addiction without difficulty. If he is then taken off methadone, his withdrawal symptoms are of much longer duration but much less severe. This fact provides a basis for what appears to be a most promising approach to the treatment of heroin addiction.

This chapter is only a very brief review of how the human brain is organized, how information is coded into the language of the neuron, and how synaptic transmission, the communication between neurons, works. The human brain is the most complex structure in the universe. Neurobiology, the study of how the brain controls behavior, is the most fundamental aspect of biopsychology. We are at the forefronts of knowledge in this exciting and challenging field. What remains to be learned is much more than that which we already know.

SUMMARY

The vertebrate nervous system has developed from the segmented tube of the lowly flatworm to the enormously complex nervous system of man. The peripheral nervous system includes all sensory and motor nerves of both the somatic system, which controls bodily movement, and the autonomic system, which controls emotional and other involuntary reactions. The central nervous system includes all structures contained within the spinal column and skull. The autonomic part of the peripheral nervous system is further subdivided into the sympathetic system, responsible for energy mobilization, and the parasympathetic system, which controls the processes of the internal organs. The lower portion of the central nervous system, the spinal cord, is responsible for spinal reflexes and for channeling all sensory and motor information going to and from the brain.

The brain itself is divided broadly into three sections. The *hindbrain* includes the reticular formation, ascending and descending fiber tracts, and many important nuclei. The *midbrain*, which is important in motivation and emotion, includes the hypothalamus and pituitary gland and the sensory relay centers for the brain, the thalamus. Overlying the midbrain is the cerebellum, important in sensory-motor coordination. The *forebrain*, the most recent evolutionary development, appears to distinguish man from other animals; it is predominantly cerebral cortex, which is important in such higher mental processes as language, speech, and thought, as well as the higher-order control of movement and sensation.

The individual unit of the nervous system, the neuron, has all the general properties of other living cells, including the nucleus and other organelles that allow for the processes of metabolism, synthesis, and respiration. It is more specialized, however, in that its axon, dendrites, and synaptic connections with other neurons allow it to conduct and transmit information.

Synaptic transmission within the mammalian nervous system is a chemical process. The resting potential across the cell membrane is temporarily altered by a change in the permeability of the membrane to various species of ions, especially sodium. This alteration, an all-or-none spike discharge which results from stimulation of the cell above a critical threshold, propagates unchanged down the axon of the neuron until it reaches the axon terminals, where a transmitter substance is released to cross the synaptic cleft and excite or inhibit the neuron next in line. Synaptic connections may be on the dendritic spines or the cell body of another cell. Excitation takes place by depolarization of the cell body, causing an excitatory postsynaptic potential (IPSP). Excitatory transmitter substances include acetylcholine, which functions at the neuromuscular junction; the biogenic amines; and various other naturally occurring substances in the brain. The drug effects on behavior take place primarily by interaction with these important chemical determinants of neural activity and behavior.

A drug is any substance that affects behavior, and psychopharmacology is the study of these effects. The narcotic analgesics include heroin, morphine, and the opium alkaloids, which are highly addictive. Stimulants include the amphetamines, strychnine, and picrotoxin. Various psychotherapeutic drugs, such as antipsychotic agents, tranquilizers, and antidepressants, have been useful in the treatment of mental illness. The psychogenics, which produce psychoticlike symptoms, include peyote, LSD, and marijuana. Drug addiction has become a serious social problem, and its treatment is an area of active interest.

CHAPTER TWO

SENSATION AND
PERCEPTION

Look up from your book for a minute. As you look around you experience a number of stimuli. You see a whole range of different colors; you see many different objects and forms. You also see depth; some objects are closer than others, and they all appear three-dimensional, How is it that we have these experiences? Why does blue look blue and not red? Why do some objects look round and others rectangular? More generally, why does the world look the way it does to us?

A superficial answer is that things look the way they do because that is the way they are. However, a little thought should disabuse us of this notion. Optical illusions do not look the way they "are." The figures in a moving picture do not really move. The objects we see in dreams are not "real." Furthermore, the physicist tells us that real objects, such as watches and tables, are actually empty space occupied by a few electrons and protons, no matter what they look like to us.

This whole question of why the world looks the way it does is actually fundamental to any knowledge we have of the world around us. Philosophers and scientists have argued the matter for centuries. We can

SENSORY-MOTOR
INTEGRATION

take comfort in the fact that the question seems ultimately to come down to our own common experiences. A theoretical physicist who conceptualizes the real world as clouds of elementary particles distributed unevenly in an n-dimensional space must ultimately rely on his own and other people's simple subjective experiences of what color a chemical solution is, what a dial reads, and what numbers appear on a counter. The basic measurements in science are all this kind of simple observation. The entire edifice of modern scientific knowledge is in fact built on the rather shaky and uncertain foundation of subjective observations. Fortunately, so far as we can tell, there is a high degree of similarity in such simple experiences for different people. Moreover, we are beginning to understand the physiological bases of these experiences. We now have some clear idea why colors look the way they do, why we see objects as having shape and form, and why one tone sounds high and another low.

However, understanding why things look the way they do is not enough. People are not inanimate objects; they respond to stimuli. In order to understand the appearance of things, our perceptions of the world, we must also know something about how we respond to things. Indeed, the way we act on the world has some effect on the way the

39

world looks to us. All you need do to convince yourself of this is to watch a baby exploring his world—a world full of strange, interesting, and sometimes frightening things which seem continually to change, particularly when he makes them move. In this chapter we will discuss what is known about the way things appear and how we respond to them, in other words the sensory and motor systems and how they function together to yield the smooth, integrated behavior of the perceiving and responding organism.

Look at the painting in Fig. 2-1. What is your reaction to it? Perhaps you consider it trivial, odd, interesting, or even ridiculous. You react to it in an overall, integrated manner; in fact you evaluate it. This is an example of a very complex perceptual process. Psychologists are fond of distinguishing between sensation and perception, the idea being that *sensation* is an immediate experience of stimuli—in this case the various forms of the painting—and that *perception* is a more complex response to it in terms of past experience. In other words, perception is an interpretation of sensation in the light of learning.

The distinction between sensation and perception is traditional, but it is probably more correct to refer instead to a greater or lesser *degree* of interpretation of stimuli. The sky at the top of the painting could be viewed simply as a horizontal stripe. However, even this statement would require a knowledge, based on past experience, of "horizontal stripe." In fact we cannot really translate pure sensation into words at all, since all words involve learning. The object in the left foreground could be described as an irregular shape with a border and symmetrical markings, but we immediately identify it as a watch—even though it may be unlike any watch we have seen before. We know from experience that watches are usually round and have dial markings and hands. We also know that watches are hard to the touch and rigid—not limp like soft-boiled eggs. This, of course, is what makes the painting unusual—the depiction of familiar objects as having properties that are different from those we normally experience.

An even more extreme example of interpretative perception of the stimuli in this painting is evidenced in the following description by an art critic [Canaday, 1961] :

. . . the symbolism is clear enough. At a glance the theme is concerned with time and decay. The most obvious symbols are the watches and the dead tree, and the jellyfish-like monster melting on the beach. Scavenger ants attack one of the watches, with no success. We deduce from this that the symbolism is also concerned with immortality, the triumph of something or other over the forces of decay. The watches are a symbol not only of time but of infinite time, eternity, impervious to the frustrated insects who would devour them. They are also limp; somebody has bent time to his will. Who? The artist, of course, since he painted them that way. Thus seen, the picture is a restatement in fantastic terms of an old idea, popular in antiquity and in the Renaissance: the idea that through creative works during his mortal life, the artist defeats time and achieves immortality.

FIGURE 2-1   *The persistence of memory, Salvador Dali,*
1931 [collection, The Museum of Modern Art, New York].

This is admittedly a complex "perception," since it is based on individual past experiences that have little connection with the immediate stimuli of the painting.

Some of the more spectacular advances in psychology to date have been in the study of sensory processes. This was one of the earliest branches of psychology to develop, undoubtedly because of the ease of specifying the physical characteristics of stimuli. Learning, motivation, and other inferred processes have no such obvious physical starting points. We have found out a great deal about sensory processes simply by presenting physical stimuli such as lights and tones and asking a subject to describe what he experiences.

The fundamental problem in sensory function concerns the manner in which stimuli are coded by the brain. Physical stimuli come in a variety of forms—light, sound, heat, pressure, soluble molecules, women—which can change continually, often in several ways. A light can change in intensity, in wavelength, in area, in complexity, and in duration. Since we can perceive literally millions of different physical stimuli, it is obvious that stimulus characteristics must somehow be coded by the sensory receptors and sensory nerves. In what manner do we identify and respond to a physical stimulus as red, cold, high or low in pitch, female, or fragrant?

In 1826 Johannes Muller published his formal theory of "specific nerve energies" concerning the way in which nerve fibers code sensory stimuli. From the time of the Greeks people had assumed that a given stimulus somehow impressed its characteristic directly on the "mind," or brain. Muller noted the now obvious fact that gross sensory quality depends on *which* nerve is stimulated, not on how it is stimulated. Visual receptors of the retina and the optic nerve can be stimulated by

41

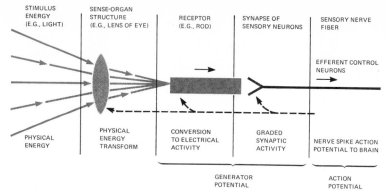

FIGURE 2-2   *The sensory coding process. Stimulus energy is focused or transformed be accessory sense-organ structures and then activates the receptors. Receptors develop graded electrical activity, the generator potential, which influences the sensory nerve fibers. This graded activity induces an all-or-none spike action in the sensory nerve fibers. Efferent pathways from the brain (dashed line) influence the coding process.*

anything—light to the eye, pressure on the eyeball, electric shock, mechanical irritation—and in all cases the subject reports *visual* sensations. It is not the stimulus that determines gross sensory quality, but the receptors and nerves that are activated by stimuli.

The sensory modality that is experienced, of course, depends on the portion of the brain to which the sensory nerve leads. Activation of the optic nerve produces visual sensations because this nerve projects to the visual system of the brain; similarly, activation of the auditory nerve produces auditory sensations because this nerve goes to the auditory pathways. The mechanisms underlying finer distinctions within a given sensory modality—distinctions between colors, frequencies of tone (pitch), or touch and pressure—are less obvious. Recent studies indicate that different stimulus characteristics activate different cells in the general brain area in question. For example, stimulation of the fingertip by either a very light touch or a strong pressure will activate the sensory cortex of the brain, but within this small region different nerve cells are stimulated by the light touch and the strong pressure.

The most direct and obvious type of coding process concerns the transformation of physical stimuli into nerve impulses by the various sensory receptors, a process referred to as *transduction*. Most receptors share a number of common features, schematized in Fig. 2-2. External energy in the form of light, sound, pressure, heat, or soluble molecules impinges on receptors, which in turn initiate spike discharges in sensory nerve cells. Some receptors have accessory structures, such as the lens of the eye or certain membranes in the ear, which serve to focus, alter, amplify, or localize the particular stimulus. The stimulus then activates receptor cells, such as the rods and cones in the retina of the eye or the hair cells in the cochlea of the ear. Activation of receptor cells produces a graded electrical activity, the *generator potential* (analogous to synaptic potentials in neurons). If this graded response is sufficiently large

42

to cross the firing threshold, it initiates an all-or-none spike discharge in the sensory neuron, which is then conducted along the sensory nerve fiber into the central nervous system. Finally efferent neural pathways terminating on receptor systems permit the CNS to influence, or "gate," the activity of accessory structures, receptors, and sensory neurons.

THE BIOLOGICAL BASIS OF VISION

Light is a form of electromagnetic radiation, or radiant energy. Visible light is a very small region of the total electromagnetic spectrum, or range of wavelengths, which extends from radio waves (particularly AM waves, which have wavelengths of many miles) to visible light, which has wavelengths in the range of 380 (violet) to about 760 (red) millimicrons (1 millimicron is one-billionth of a meter). Cosmic rays are still shorter, with wavelengths of only 0.00005 millimicron.

As shown in Fig. 2-3, the wavelengths of visible light to which the human eye is most sensitive are green and yellow; we can see dimmer shades of these colors than of violet or red. Of course, light itself has no color; light simply has different wavelengths. Color is merely our *subjective experience* of these differences in wavelengths. Psychologists often use the term *hue* to refer to our experience of color.

Light also varies in intensity, the strength of the electromagnetic waves. The physicists tell us light itself consists of elementary particles called photons; the intensity of light could be expressed in terms of the

FIGURE 2-3 *The visible colors of light and their wavelengths. The graph shows the relative sensitivity of the human eye to color (we are most sensitive to greenish-yellow). The dots on the curve indicate relative absorption of light energy by chemicals in the cones of the eye. Our sensitivity to color is thus determined entirely by the chemical properties of the cones.*

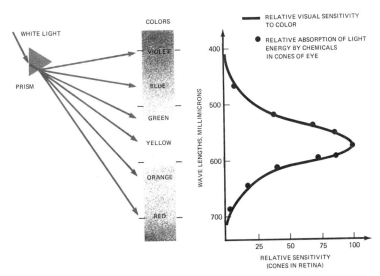

density of photons. The physical intensity of light, its *luminance*, is not the same as the degree of intensity we see or experience, its *brightness*. As shown in Fig. 2-3, violet and green lights that have the same luminance—that is, the same amount of physical energy—will not look equally bright; the green light will look brighter. The human eye, incidentally, is amazingly sensitive; we can see as few as seven photons. No physical measuring instrument developed is this sensitive to light.

A third aspect of light that we perceive is its "purity," the extent to which only one wavelength or a narrow band of wavelengths is present. Psychologists refer to our experience of this as *saturation*. Red, for example, may look very red (saturated), or it may look weak and faded (unsaturated). A weak red looks weak not because it has fewer red wavelengths, but because it contains many other wavelengths in addition to the red ones. In contrast, the light from a laser looks very saturated because it has almost no other conflicting wavelengths.

THE STRUCTURE OF THE EYE

Most organisms, even single-celled animals, can respond to light energy. However, the vertebrate eye is designed to do much more than simply signal the presence or absence of light. A detailed image of the external world is projected on the *retina*, the layers of receptors and nerve cells at the back of the eye. This structure transforms and codes the image into nerve impulses which carry a representation of the external visual world to the brain. The precision of detail vision is surprising. The image of the full moon on the retina has a radius of only about 0.1 millimeter, and considerable detail can be seen within this image. Lines that are much narrower than the single receptor cells of the retina can easily be seen. The vertebrate visual system is also particularly sensitive to movement of objects in the visual world. Most predators, animals that hunt to live, have eyes that point forward and focus together to give a clear, three-dimensional image of the object or prey being perceived and pursued. Most prey animals, such as rabbits and deer, have eyes far apart on the sides of the head, so that they can see better to the sides and behind to detect the predator. The faster a predator normally moves, and the faster its prey moves, the more acute the movement vision of each must be to ensure survival. Man has the eyes of a predator.

In general the retina functions more like a television camera than like a photographic camera. According to Rushton [1962, p. 13]:

Its purpose is not to fix a picture upon the retina, but rather to transmit in a code of nerve impulses the more dramatic features of the ever changing retinal scene. Our rods and cones are 100 million reporters seeking "copy." That which continues unchanging is not "news" and nothing will induce them to report it.

It has been demonstrated that if an image is stabilized on the retina it fades away. Normally the images are continually shifting back and forth

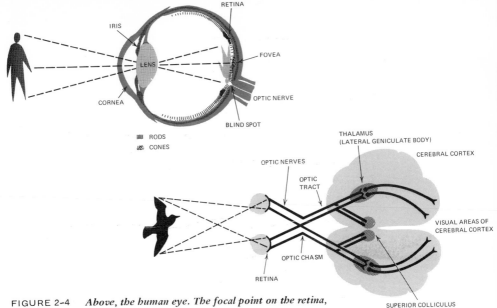

FIGURE 2-4   *Above, the human eye. The focal point on the retina,
the fovea, is the region of best detail vision. The fovea has no rods and
has the greatest density of cones. The rods are most dense about
20 degrees away from the fovea. At right, the visual pathway in
primates (top view). The right half of the visual field projects to the
left side of each eye. These two left sides project to the left hemisphere
of the brain, to the relay in the thalamus, and thence to the visual
area of the left cerebral cortex. Similarly, the right half of each eye
projects to the right cerebral cortex. The optic tracts also give off
pathways to the visual midbrain (superior colliculus).*

on the retina because the eye is always making small, rapid movements
or oscillations. Riggs et al. [1953] devised an optical system in which
the visual object was reflected to a viewing screen from a small mirror
attached to the side of a contact lens on the cornea of the eye. The
image moved with the eyeball and thus was always projected on the
same retinal elements. Under these conditions most objects tend to fade
out in a few seconds. This rather striking adaptation does not generally
occur because the image is always being shifted to different receptor
cells by rapid eye movements.

As indicated in Fig. 2-4, the rods and cones, the two basic types
of light-sensitive receptor cells in the eye, are in close approximation to
neurons. There are several types of neurons in the retina. The retina is
actually a very complex neural system and is perhaps best thought of as
a "little brain" lying between the photoreceptors and the brain. Embryologically, the retina is an outgrowth of the brain rather than a
peripheral formation.

Rods and cones serve different functions. The rods are sensitive
to very dim illumination (*scotopic* vision), whereas the cones require
greater intensities of light and are more involved in acuity and color
aspects of visual function (*photopic* vision). Rods and cones are easily
differentiable in terms of structure in mammals. This differentiation of

45

structure and function in rods and cones is of fundamental importance. The center of the visual field, the region we see most clearly when we look at an object, projects on the *fovea*, which is composed entirely of cones. The foveal cones have an almost one-to-one relation to outgoing nerve fibers. The rods have their greatest density at about 20 degrees of visual angle; this is the angle between the direct line of sight projecting to the fovea and the projection of any other position in the visual field away from the fovea (see Fig. 2-4). Thus you can see a dim star best if you look about 20 degrees away from it. There are about 125 million rods and 6 million cones in the human retina, but only about 1 million optic nerve fibers. Hence many receptors will activate each nerve fiber, particularly in the peripheral regions of the retina, where rods are predominant.

There are at least two visual pigments (chemicals responsive to light) in receptor cells of the mammalian retina, *rhodopsin* in the rods and *iodopsin* in cones. When light falls on a rod, the rhodopsin immediately breaks down into two chemicals, *retinene* and *opsin*. Retinene has a relatively simple chemical structure closely related to vitamin A (thus the necessity of vitamin A for adequate night vision), and opsin is a complex protein. The visual pigment of the cones, iodopsin, breaks down on exposure to light into two substances—retinene, in the same form as that from rhodopsin, and a different protein, *photopsin*. In other words, the visual pigments of the rods and cones are both made up of retinene and a protein, with only the protein differing; the chemical reactions of both are comparable. Actually human cones appear to have three iodopsins, made up of retinene and three different opsins.

A number of aspects of visual sensation, particularly those relating to brightness and color, can be deduced very accurately from the biochemical properties of rhodopsin and the iodopsins. Foremost among these is the virtually perfect correspondence between spectral sensitivities (sensitivity to different wavelengths of light) and the chemical-absorption spectra of the rod and cone pigments (see Fig. 2-3). Another striking correspondence concerns the time required for rod and cone *dark adaptation*. After exposure to a bright light it takes up to 30 minutes in the dark for the rods to dark adapt—that is, reestablish maximum sensitivity to dim light. The spontaneous rate of synthesis of rhodopsin in solution follows virtually the same curve as does the rate of rod dark adaptation. Cone dark adaptation is much more rapid; it requires only about 6 minutes. The rate of synthesis of iodopsin in solution is also about 6 minutes.

THE CODING OF VISUAL STIMULI

Our eyes receive a continual and everchanging barrage of light energy. The characteristics of visual stimuli are many and complex; however, in discussing the ways in which the visual system responds to light it is convenient to distinguish three different categories—response to the

46

presence of light; response to the form, pattern, or spatial distribution of light energy, and response to wavelength (color). To understand how the visual system operates we must, at the very least, understand something about these basic coding processes.

In lower vertebrates such as the frog the eyes function as two independent visual systems; the nerve fibers from the right eye all go to the left side of the brain, and the nerves from the left eye go to the right side of the brain. However, in higher mammals there is *bilateral projection*; a part of each eye goes to each side of the brain. This tendency is most developed in primates, particularly man. As shown in Fig. 2-4, the left half of each retina goes to the left side of the brain, and the right side of each retina goes to the right side of the brain. This makes possible binocular vision with depth perception. The optic nerves carry the nerve fibers from cells in the retina to a visual relay nucleus in the thalamus called the *lateral geniculate body*. Here the fibers from the two eyes come together on each side of the brain and synapse on neurons that go to the visual areas of the cerebral cortex.

There are thus three major stations along the way from eye to cortex—the retina sending out the optic nerve, the lateral geniculate body of the thalamus, and the visual area of the cerebral cortex. Some fibers from the optic nerves also go other places, particularly to serve as the visual input for certain reflex functions such as control of pupil diameter. In lower vertebrates that have no cerebral cortex, a midbrain visual region called the superior colliculus serves as the visual brain and receives the optic nerve fibers. This system is also present in higher vertebrates, but its functions are not well known. In birds there is also a pathway from optic nerve fibers to the hypothalamus that plays a major role in reproduction and migrating behavior. Thus the critical stimulus that starts them on their migratory flight seems to be the relative length of day and night. In man the major visual path is from retina to lateral geniculate body to visual cortex.

THE PERCEPTION OF FORM

When we look at an object, it is projected onto the retina by the lens of the eye, as in a camera. This visual image on the retina activates the receptors, the rods and cones, and hence the appropriate neurons of the retina, to produce an accurate spatial layout of the visual world. Neurons in the visual cortex are then activated in such a way that a representation or spatial layout of the image is formed over the visual area of the cerebral cortex. This is termed *retinotopic projection*. A similar fundamental spatial coding mechanism exists in all sensory systems. The sensory receptor surface is laid out spatially over the sensory area of the cerebral cortex.

Some highly significant distortions take place in the visual image when it is projected to the visual cortex. If you look at someone's nose from a few feet away, the image of the entire person and his surroundings will be projected accurately on the retina of your eye. However, the neural projection onto the visual cortex will be quite different; half the projected neural image will be nose, and the remainder will include the rest of the person and his surroundings. When we focus our eyes on an object, the line of sight projects to the fovea at the center of the retina. As we noted above, this region of densely packed cones is where our detail vision is best. We see small objects in good light best when we look directly at them. The fovea, which takes up only about 1 percent of the retinal area, projects to nearly 50 percent of the visual cortex. Half the visual area of the cerebral cortex is thus devoted to this very small central line-of-sight region of the retina. Our detail vision is so much better when we look directly at an object because a much greater relative area of the visual cortex is involved in the analysis of information that is focused on the central fovea of the retina. This fact is another illustration of the general principle, mentioned in Chapter 1, that the relative amount of brain tissue devoted to a particular region or function is proportional to the behavioral importance of that region. The center of vision is the region involved in detail vision; hence a great deal of the visual cortex is used to analyze the spatial pattern projected on the small foveal area of the retina. We see best in the line-of-sight gaze not because it is the center of the retina but because a relatively larger area of visual cortex is concerned with it.

Our experiential or perceptual visual world does not of course *look* distorted. It corresponds very closely to the real world. However the details are clearer at the point where we look. To convince yourself, close one eye and focus the other eye on one word in the center of this page. If you are very careful not to move your eye you will only be able to recognize three or four words in any direction around the word at which you are looking. The entire page is projected onto your retina, and hence to the visual cortex, but insufficient brain tissue is available for analysis of the rest of the page.

The retinotopic projection of the retina to the visual cortex can explain detail vision and our general perception of the spatial layout of the visual world. For some time scientists have attempted to explain *form* perception—the fact that we see lines, angles, rectangles, circles—solely in terms of the retinotopic projection. However recent and very fundamental work suggests that quite different mechanisms may be involved. Hubel and Wiesel [1965] have found that form is coded by single cells in the visual cortex. The experiment involves using a microelectrode to record spike discharges from single neurons in the visual cortex. The spike discharges show up as spikes—vertical lines of fixed amplitude on the baseline. This record is essentially the same as the recordings of spike discharges we saw in Fig. 1-13, except that they are recorded from outside the cell. Whenever the neuron is activated by the appropriate visual stimulus presented to the eye, it will discharge spikes. Examples of form-coding cells are shown in Fig. 2-5. One neuron responds only to a horizontal bar. It fires only when the horizontal bar is present at the correct place on the retina but does not respond if the bar is tilted away from the horizontal. An even more complex example is

48

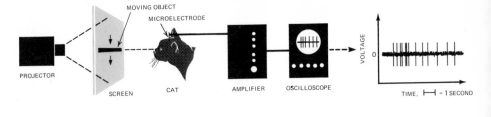

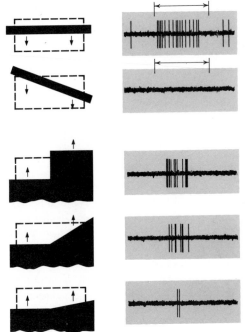

FIGURE 2-5   *Coding of visual form by single neurons in the visual area of the cerebral cortex. A small electrode is inserted in the visual cortex of the anesthetized animal and records the spike discharges of single neurons activated by stimuli presented to the eye. Center, a horizontal-bar-detector cell in the visual cortex. The bar stimulus induces spike discharges on the neuron as shown by the graph alongside. As the line above the spike discharges indicates, the cell does not respond when the bar is tilted away from the horizontal. At the bottom, a right-angle-detector cell in the visual cortex. The cell fires best (the most spikes) in the presence of a right angle. [Hubel and Wiesel, 1962; 1965]*

the right-angle-detector cell, which will respond only to an angle moving across the visual field and responds best to a right angle. This cell is an angle detector in the cerebral cortex; however, the story is a little more complicated in that there are several visual areas. In the primary visual area (area 17 on the striate cortex), cells respond best to simpler stimuli such as lines and edges, and in the higher-order visual areas 18 and 19, cells respond to angles, rectangles, and more complex forms. However, the overall picture is clear—forms are coded by single cells in the visual cortex. We see lines, angles, shapes, and forms as clearly as we do because the cells in the visual cortex are so wired that they respond selectively to these types of stimuli. We see the forms of the visual world the way we do because the neurons in our visual cortex are wired that way. We do not see forms simply because they are there; we see them because our visual cortex is put together in particular complex sets of networks connected together in very specific ways to code forms. Such a view provides a partial answer to the question of why we see the world the way we do. We see visual forms because that is the way our visual brain is wired.

49

Color is probably our most profound visual sensation. Young children can match colors to samples correctly long before they can learn the names for colors. Indeed, although we can denote a color by name, color is such an immediate given experience that we simply cannot describe it in words. Try to imagine how you would describe a color to someone who had never seen it. As we noted above, the physical basis of colors is the different wavelengths of light. The light itself, however, is not colored; color exists only in the eye of the beholder. It is in this way that color differs fundamentally from form. Form exists in the external world; color does not. Many of the greatest minds have attempted to solve this fundamental problem. Da Vinci, Newton, Helmholtz, and many others all developed theories of color vision. It is only in the past few years, however, that we have come to understand how it is that we see color.

Two differing theories have been held for some time in psychology about color vision, the Young-Helmholtz *three-receptor theory* and the *opponent theory*. It now appears that both theories are correct, at least up to a point. The Young-Helmholtz theory, first proposed by Thomas Young in 1802, assumed simply that there are three primary color receptors in the retina most sensitive to red, green, and blue. Any color attained its appearance from the relative degree it activated these three primary color receptors. Hering's opponent theory assumed, in contrast, that the receptor and neural processing of color in the retina was in the form of opponent functions. One process coded black-white and all shades of gray. This, of course, is now known to be the case—the rods code black-white vision. Another process coded red-green and intermediate colors, and still another process coded the range of colors included in yellow-blue.

Very important recent work by Rushton [1961] permitted determination of the colors selectively absorbed by the cones in the human retina. They found that there appear to be three cone pigments (iodopsins), one most sensitive to red, one to green, and one to blue. In short, they provided strong evidence in support of the Young-Helmholtz three-receptor theory. However, recordings of neural activity from the retina of the cat by Granit [1962] and from the lateral geniculate body of the monkey by DeValois [1965] gave quite a different picture of how color is coded. These investigators found two different general types of responses from different neurons. Some neurons responded to all wavelengths with varying sensitivity and in fact acted like rods; they coded the black-white dimension. In primates there are also two types of color-sensitive neurons. One type changed its activity when red and green lights were presented, and the other type changed its activity when blue and yellow lights were used. Furthermore, they responded in an "opponent" way. One red-green neuron might be excited by red and inhibited by green, whereas another would be excited by green and inhibited by red. Similarly, some blue-yellow neurons are excited by blue

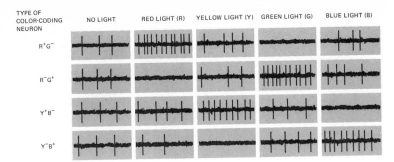

FIGURE 2-6   *Patterns of response of the four types of color-coding neurons in the visual thalamus. The excitatory stimulus causes an increase in the number of spike discharges of the cell, and the inhibitory stimulus causes a decrease; for example, the green⁻red⁺ cell has a given rate of spontaneous discharging which increases when red light is presented but decreases to no discharges when green is presented. [after De Valois, 1965]*

and inhibited by yellow, whereas others are excited by yellow and inhibited by blue. In brief, these color-sensitive neurons respond in an opponent way to red-green and to yellow-blue, just as Hering had postulated. Examples of responses of opponent color neurons are shown in Fig. 2-6.

We seem faced with a direct contradiction. The chemicals in the cones of the eye respond to the three primary colors, but the neurons of the optic nerve and the lateral geniculate body code colors in terms of opponent function. Clearly there must be a conversion process in the retina that transforms responses from the three types of cones into opponent neural processes. Recent evidence from the work of Svaetichin et al. [1961], MacNichol [1964], and others may provide the missing link. Certain types of glial cellular elements in the retina respond to colors in the same way that neurons do—in an opponent manner. It may be that these glial elements somehow modulate the initial responses of the cone receptors so that responses to red, green, and blue interact on neurons to yield the four categories of opponent color neurons. Perhaps the most important point is that the information going into the brain about the color of lights is already coded into the opponent categories. The brain—that is, the visual cortex—can tell what color is being seen by noting what each of the four categories of opponent color neurons is doing. Thus if a pure green light is presented, the green⁺-red⁻ neurons will fire, the green⁻-red⁺ neurons will be inhibited (not fire), and the blue⁺-yellow⁻ and blue⁻-yellow⁺ neurons will not change markedly. Changes in color will be represented to the brain by changes in the relative activity of these four types of color neurons.

In comparing the perception of form and color it is important to note the level of the nervous system where the coding process occurs. Color, as we have just seen, seems to be coded at the retina. The four categories of opponent color cells are present at the optic nerve. However, the coding of form and shape does not occur below the level of the cerebral cortex in mammals. Color is coded at a lower level of the

51

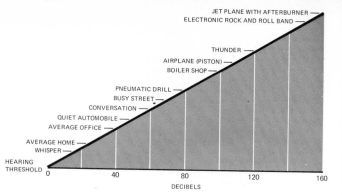

JET PLANE WITH AFTERBURNER —
ELECTRONIC ROCK AND ROLL BAND —

THUNDER —
AIRPLANE (PISTON) —
BOILER SHOP —

PNEUMATIC DRILL —
BUSY STREET —
CONVERSATION —
QUIET AUTOMOBILE —
AVERAGE OFFICE —

AVERAGE HOME —
WHISPER —

HEARING
THRESHOLD   0   40   80   120   160
                        DECIBELS

FIGURE 2-7   *The loudness of various common sounds as measured in decibels.*

nervous system than form and is a much more immediate subjective sensation in both man and monkeys. Perhaps the reason we cannot describe colors in words is that the coding is close to the stimulus, whereas shape is coded at the level of the cerebral cortex, where words are formed.

THE BIOLOGICAL
BASIS OF HEARING

We live in a world of sound. In fact it is rapidly becoming a world of unpleasant noise. Perhaps for the first time in history, ordinary noises in society have reached a level where they can cause permanent impairment of hearing. An electronic rock-and-roll band and a jet engine with an afterburner both produce significant hearing damage (see Fig. 2-7). A less obvious but perhaps more serious problem is the irritating and interfering effects of noise. If you live near an airport, conversation must stop every 2 minutes or so. Tempers flare much more readily in very noisy environments. Our hearing apparatus has evolved over millions of years to detect and analyze faint sounds; we are simply not biologically equipped to deal with loud noise.

Sound is, of course, more than noise. The daily activities of persons with normal hearing are determined by what they hear. Communication is largely verbal. The normal infant learns language in terms of sounds. Most of our responses to sounds are learned, but some are not. A very sudden loud sound produces the same innate startle response in man and mouse. The roll of thunder seems to induce very similar feelings of apprehension in man and other higher mammals. Faint sounds, in contrast, are often intrinsically pleasant [Buddenbrock, 1958, p. 93] :

When you feel an urge to get away from the burden of daily living, from the constant rush and noise of city life, the best escape is to return for a while to nature. Whether you retreat to the solitude of the lofty mountains, to the cool, green forest, or visit the sunlit fields and meadows, you will find everywhere in nature a tonic: the stillness which permits you to listen to the sound of your own breathing. If you are seated at the edge of a forest on a calm, windless summer evening, only now and then will the call of a pheasant, a noise made by a frightened roebuck, the raucous screech of a bird of prey, or the chirping of the crickets in the meadow break the silence.

The physical basis of sound is wave motion in the air. The way a loudspeaker or other sound source generates a sound is shown in Fig. 2-8. In this case a rigid membrane or diaphragm first pushes against the air to create a positive relative pressure and then pulls back to create a relative vacuum or negative pressure. This alternation of positive and negative pressure creates a pressure wave in the air that travels out from the sound source at a relatively slow speed of about 750 miles per hour. All waves have both frequency and amplitude. The frequency of a sound wave determines the tone, or pitch, of a sound—that is, how high or low it sounds to us—and the amplitude of the wave determines how loud the sound is.

Note that pitch and frequency are not the same thing. Frequency refers to a physical characteristic of the *stimulus*—the actual frequency of vibration of the sound waves in the air (commonly expressed in cycles per second or hertz). Pitch refers to the subjective sensation or response to the frequency of a sound—that is, how high or low a tone sounds to us. The relationship of pitch to frequency is not linear, or one-to-one. It tends instead to be logarithmic. For example, middle C on the piano is a tone of 256 hertz. The tone which has a frequency twice as high is C above middle C, 512 hertz. However, 512 hertz does not sound *twice* as high in pitch as 256 hertz; it sounds one octave higher, but much less than twice as high.

A similar difference exists between the physical and subjective scales in the case of sound intensity. The relationship between the amount of physical energy in a tone and the loudness we hear is also approximately logarithmic. This relationship was described a number of

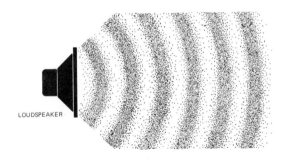

FIGURE 2-8 *Sound waves are pressure waves formed by compression and expansion of the molecules of the air. Below, representative sound waveforms varying in frequency and amplitude.*

LOUDSPEAKER

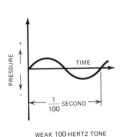
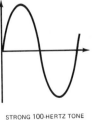
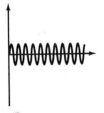
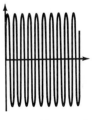

PRESSURE

TIME

$\frac{1}{100}$ SECOND

WEAK 100-HERTZ TONE

STRONG 100-HERTZ TONE

WEAK 1000-HERTZ TONE

STRONG 1000-HERTZ TONE

years ago in terms of the decibel scale for measuring sound intensity. The decibel scale is based on the logarithm of the sound energy level (actually 10 times the logarithm of the ratio of a given sound energy to the lowest threshold of sound energy). Consequently, the judged loudness of sounds corresponds in an approximately linear fashion with the decibel scale of sound intensity. The relationships between pitch and frequency and between loudness and intensity are examples of *psychophysical functions*, the relations between psychological or behavioral judgments of stimuli and physical characteristics of stimuli. We shall discuss some of the more general aspects of psychophysical relationships later in the chapter.

In contrast to the million or so fibers in the optic nerve of man, each auditory nerve has only about 28,000 fibers. Nevertheless, the total number of single tones discriminable on the basis of frequency and intensity is about 340,000. Curiously enough, this is approximately the same as the total number of single visual stimuli discernible on the basis of frequency (wavelength) and intensity of light. The nature of the mechanisms underlying the efficiency in the auditory system has puzzled investigators for many years. Historically there have been two major theories of auditory pitch discrimination—Helmholtz's *place theory*, which assumes that each tone frequency activates a different portion of the auditory receptor, and Rutherford's *frequency theory*, which proposes that the frequency of the tone is reflected in the frequency of auditory-nerve-fiber discharges. Recent developments in the field, particularly from the work of von Békésy, Davis, Tasaki, and Stevens, have shown that the more correct view lies somewhere in between these extremes.

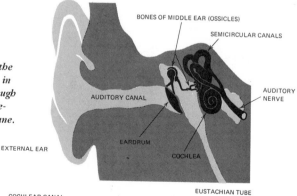

FIGURE 2-9 *General structure of the ear. The actual receptor mechanism is in the coiled cochlea. Below, a view through one coil of the cochlea, showing the receptor hair cells of the basilar membrane.*

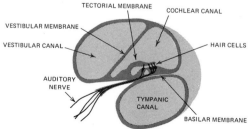

The anatomy of the auditory receptor system is rather complicated. In brief, the external ear canal ends in the eardrum. This connects through three small bones (*ossicles*) of the middle ear to a membrane covering the end of the *cochlea*, which is a coiled tube shaped much like a snail shell. The tube is filled with fluid and contains within it a smaller tube, the *cochlear duct*, which in turn contains the sense organ proper. A cross section through the tube of the cochlea is shown in Fig. 2-9. Sound vibrations transmitted through the ossicles cause movement of fluid, which in turn produces vibrations of the *basilar membrane*. This rather stiff membrane bends relative to the *tectorial membrane*, thus bending and activating the *hair-cell* receptors lying between. These receptors are innervated by fibers of the auditory nerve, whose cell bodies lie in the *spiral ganglion* embedded in the skull. Axons of these fibers enter the central nervous system and synapse in the *cochlear nuclei* in the brain stem.

THE CODING OF AUDITORY STIMULI

Identification of the particular aspects of receptor and neural processes that determine various aspects of sensory experience or behavior is one of the fundamental goals in the analysis of sensory processes. The absolute loudness threshold is a good case in point. In man the total range of audible frequencies is from 15 to 20,000 hertz. However, the ear is most sensitive to tones between 1000 and 4000 hertz. As frequency is increased or decreased away from this region of maximum sensitivity, increasingly greater sound energy is required to make the tone audible. The curve relating absolute threshold and frequency is shown in Fig. 2-10.

FIGURE 2-10　*Sensitivity curve for the human auditory threshold as a function of tone frequency. The approximate frequency and amplitude region of normal speech is indicated.*

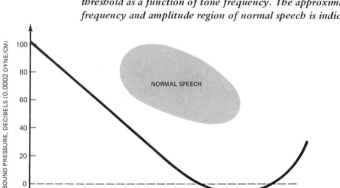

55

The acoustical and mechanical properties of the ear canal, eardrum, and the middle ear bones determine the efficiency with which sounds of various frequencies are converted to mechanical vibrations and transmitted to the cochlea. Because the absolute-threshold curve is determined by the physical properties of these accessory auditory structures, it might be expected that the size of an animal—that is, the size of its external and middle ear structures—would influence its threshold curve. In general this seems to be true. Among mammals elephants are sensitive to the lowest frequencies, and small animals such as rats and mice are sensitive to very much higher frequencies. Man, incidentally, has a relatively "middle"-frequency range. Cats can hear sounds ranging from about 30 to 70,000 hertz. There are some important exceptions to this general rule. Both bats and porpoises can hear sounds of up to about 100,000 hertz. However, these animals are exceptional in that they make use of a very specialized echo-location, or sonar, system; they emit very-high-frequency pulses of sound and determine the position of objects in space by the characteristics of the reflected sound pulses.

The degree of sensitivity of the human ear is quite remarkable, at least in the frequency region of best threshold (around 2000 hertz). A movement of the eardrum of less than one-tenth the diameter of a hydrogen atom can result in an auditory sensation. If the ear were more sensitive than this, the random brownian movements of air molecules would produce a constant roaring sound, which would tend to mask auditory stimuli. Thus, paradoxically, if the ear were more sensitive it would be less sensitive. As a matter of fact, persons with very good hearing are able to detect brownian noise under ideal listening conditions.

The movements of the basilar membrane of the cochlea in response to auditory stimuli were analyzed in a series of elegant experiments by von Békésy [1956], awarded the Nobel prize in 1962 for his work. In essence, he showed that if a tone of a given frequency is presented, a traveling wave of fluid is set up in the cochlea. The traveling wave causes a maximum displacement in a given region of the basilar membrane. The location of this maximum displacement on the membrane is related to the frequency of the tone (see Fig. 2-11). Some rather complex mechanical effects occur because of the differential stiffness of the membrane. The net result is that high-frequency tones selectively distort regions of the basilar membrane close to the base of the cochlea, intermediate tones distort a portion of the membrane in an intermediate region, and low-frequency tones tend to distort the entire membrane.

The findings of von Békésy actually seem to offer some support for each of the two major theories concerning pitch coding, place and frequency. There is a tendency for a given frequency of tone to produce greatest distortion at a given region of the basilar membrane. The original place theory proposed by Helmholtz assumed that the basilar membrane was a very large series of highly tuned elements, much like tuning forks or the strings on a harp. Von Békésy's data [1956], particularly for high frequencies, support this view with the modification that small differences in degree of distortion of the membrane can serve as "tuned

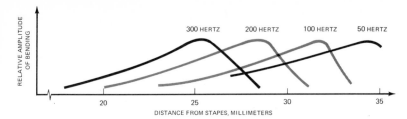

FIGURE 2-11 *The location and amount of distortion (amplitude of bending) of the basilar membrane produced by tones of different frequencies. Distance is from one end (the base or stapes) of the membrane. Note that low-frequency tones cause a broader region of distortion and that higher-frequency tones cause a narrower region of distortion closer to the base. [von Békésy, 1947]*

elements." In general the higher the frequency, the closer the distortion is to the base of the cochlea. However, low-frequency tones tend to activate the entire basilar membrane equivalently, and intermediate tones activate a substantial portion of the membrane. The differential distortion of the membrane does not seem great enough to provide for our very sensitive ability to discriminate pitch, and there is no differential distortion to code low-frequency tones.

If a recording electrode is placed on the cochlea near the auditory nerve, several types of signals can be recorded. The most noticeable of these is the *cochlear microphonic*, discovered by Wever and Bray [1930]. This is an electrical response that follows the frequency and intensity characteristics of the auditory stimulus *exactly*. If a Beethoven symphony is played into the ear of an anesthetized cat and the electrically recorded cochlear microphonic is amplified and connected to a speaker, you will hear the symphony with essentially no distortion. The cochlear microphonic is literally a microphone; sound waves are converted to electrical pulses in exactly the same manner as in a microphone.

The discovery of the cochlear microphonic seemed to provide very strong support for the frequency theory of pitch coding. It was initially believed that the electrical pulses of the cochlear microphonic were spike discharges of the auditory nerve. This would mean that the frequency of discharges in the auditory nerve exactly follows the input frequency of any sound. However, it soon became apparent that the cochlear microphonic can follow sound frequencies up to 70,000 hertz, which is a great deal faster than any nerve fiber can respond (2000 hertz is about the highest frequency recordable from a nerve fiber). It appears that the cochlear microphonic is produced by the hair cells in the cochlea and may represent a generator potential. The hair cells are bent with a frequency that follows the input sound frequency. The cochlear microphonic seems to result from a transducer action of the hair cells quite analogous to the conversion of mechanical vibrations into electrical pulses by the crystal in a phonograph cartridge. It has been suggested that the same kind of piezoelectric effect may be involved in both. Although the cochlear microphonic has been considered by some as merely an accidental electromechanical byproduct resulting from bending of the hair cells, many other authorities [Davis, 1959; Tasaki and Davis,

57

1955] favor the view that the terminals of the auditory nerve fibers are directly activated by the flows of current associated with the cochlear microphonic—that is, it acts as a generator potential.

Individual nerve fibers in the auditory nerve can follow low-frequency sounds up to about 1000 hertz. Each nerve fiber fires a spike each time the sound pressure wave activates the cochlea—that is, 1000 times per second. When the sound frequency exceeds 1000 hertz an interesting "volley" effect occurs. Different groups of fibers fire out of step. If a 2000-hertz tone is given, for example, one group of fibers may discharge 1000 times per second and another group 1000 times per second, out of phase with the first group; thus if we look at the activity of the entire auditory nerve, it is firing 2000 times per second, the same frequency as the tone, even though no individual fiber is firing more than 1000 times per second. This is another remarkable example of the adaptability of the nervous system. Consequently low frequencies of sound can be coded by the frequency of discharge of auditory nerve fibers.

It appears that both the place of excitation on the basilar membrane and the frequency of nerve responses are important in coding tone frequency. For high frequencies place is most important, but for lower frequencies (below 4000 hertz) synchronous discharges in nerve fibers also play a role. Intensity may be coded both by total number of fibers activated and by activation of high threshold fibers (nerve fibers that require considerable bending of the hair cells to be stimulated). The nerve fibers are stimulated by the bending of the hair cells, possibly as a direct result of the cochlear microphonic.

The auditory pathways from the cochlea to the auditory area of the cerebral cortex are rather complex, involving several relay stations. An important point to note is that the system is bilateral. Both ears

FIGURE 2-12   *Tonotopic representation on the auditory cortex of the dog (brain facing to the left). Low-frequency tones activate the most posterior region of the auditory cortex and higher-frequency tones activate progressively more anterior regions. Each line is a best-frequency line, indicating the region of auditory cortex most activated by a given frequency. [after Tunturi, 1952]*

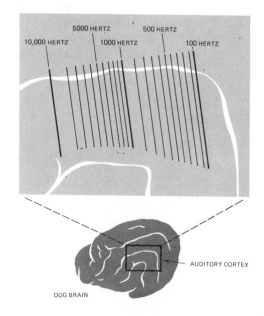

SENSORY-MOTOR INTEGRATION

contribute input to the auditory system on each side, although at the level of the cerebral cortex the ear from the opposite side contributes more. At the cerebral cortex, the auditory receptor surface, the basilar membrane, is sorted out again. In fact, a complete representation of the basilar membrane is laid out along the auditory cortex. Remember that high-frequency tones bend one end of the basilar membrane and lower tones bend the membrane farther toward the other end (see Fig. 2-12), but low tones bend the entire membrane. At the cortex, these effects have been converted into *place* representation along the auditory area. This is termed *tonotopic representation* [Tunturi, 1944]. As indicated in Fig. 2-12, a high-frequency tone activates neurons at one end of the cortex, and progressively lower tones activate a progressively more distant region of the cortex. Thus tone frequency is mapped out along the cortex. In addition to this general mapping of tone frequency, individual cells in the auditory cortex code frequency. For any given neuron there is a best frequency, a tone frequency that produces greatest activation of the cell. Many neurons in the auditory cortex also have best intensities; for a given frequency range a particular intensity of tone will cause the cell to fire more than will either a weaker or a stronger tone.

In summary, at the level of the auditory cortex, tone frequency is coded both in terms of a spatial representation on the cortex and by single neurons, and tone intensity is also coded by single neurons. It is likely that our perception of complex sounds is mediated by the auditory cortex. Of course, understanding the *meaning* of sounds, as in language, entails far more than merely perceiving sounds. This process involves other higher functions and association areas of the cerebral cortex.

THE SOMATIC SENSORY SYSTEM

The somatic sensory system, particularly the skin senses, provides one of the most important avenues of social interaction. In many higher mammals, nuzzling and mutual grooming are common social expressions; monkeys are often seen picking imaginary fleas from a fellow. In man skin stimulation provides some of the most pleasurable sensations. Even more to the point, it is essential to the fundamental process of sexual interaction.

The opposite sensation, pain, is also a part of the somatic sensory system. The sensation produced by damage to skin and deep tissues is one of the most compelling and intense of our subjective experiences. The immediacy of this sensation is such that, like color, pain is impossible to describe in words. The best the early introspectionist psychologists were able to do was to distinguish between fast, sharp, "bright" pain and slow, dull, aching pain. Society has long exploited the fact that avoidance of pain is among the most primary drives or motives. Torture or the threat of it has been used since time immemorial to shape and control human behavior.

The major types of somatic sensory sensation are light touch, deep pressure, awareness of limb position (where your legs, arms, and fingers are in space or in approximation to other body parts), heat, cold, and pain. It has often been assumed that there are specific receptors for each type of sensation, but this does not seem to be the case. There are special pressure receptors close to the surface of the skin that could provide some information about light touch, there are well-known special deep-pressure receptors (the pacinian corpuscles), and there are pressure receptors in the joints that provide us with information about the position of our limbs in relation to the body. The muscles themselves provide us with a complete array of information, via muscle-stretch receptors, about the degree of stretch and rate of contraction of every muscle in the body. This input serves to regulate such reflex activities as standing and moving, but it plays no role at all in our awareness of where our limbs are; this is provided entirely by pressure receptors in the joints. However, it has also been shown that light touch, warm, cold, and pain can all be experienced in the absence of specialized receptors other than free nerve endings [Lele and Weddell, 1956]. Although the cornea of the eye has only free nerve endings and contains no specialized pressure or other receptors, with careful and appropriate stimulation of the cornea, subjects can be made to experience light touch, warm, cold, and pain.

THE CODING OF SOMATIC SENSORY STIMULI

The major differentiation in our somatic sensory experience seems to be between specific sensations of touch, pressure, and limb position on the one hand and pain and temperature sensation on the other. Sensory nerves from skin and deep tissues separate into two separate pathways when they enter the spinal cord. One of these, which we will call the *discrete system*, mediates touch, pressure, and limb position, and the other, which we will call the *nonspecific system*, mediates pain and temperature. A simplified schematic of these two pathways is shown in Fig. 2-13. The details of these pathways are not important here; the major difference between them is that the discrete system goes directly from the lower brain stem to the thalamus in a pathway called the *medial lemniscus*, and then is relayed to the primary somatic sensory area of the cerebral cortex. The nonspecific system does not have a direct pathway to the thalamus, but instead relays into and through the ascending reticular activating system.

The discrete somatic sensory system is a more recent development in the evolution of the nervous system. It provides us with precise and specific information about stimuli and allows us to analyze the nature of adaptively "neutral" stimuli. The nonspecific system is much older and more primitive. It provides feelings and sensations that are vague in terms of our ability to analyze stimuli, but overriding in terms of adaptive survival value. Pain and temperature sensations, for example, are essential to survival. A higher animal that is deprived of these sensations has no awareness of, and hence no protection against, tissue damage and infection that may be fatal. There are certain types of neurological diseases that selectively destroy the pain and temperature pathways in man. Such patients constantly develop serious infections because they are unaware of minor cuts and bruises that the rest of us avoid.

The fact that two different sensory pathways are involved is apparent in the action of general anesthetics such as ether. If a general anesthetic is administered slowly, the patient passes through several stages of anesthesia. In the lightest stage, called *analgesia*, he is still conscious and can respond to questions and can report auditory and visual stimuli. He also responds to tactile stimuli—but he has no awareness of pain. It appears that general anesthetics act first on the ascending reticular activating system (see Fig. 1-7). This very ancient nonspecific system is activated or influenced by many types of stimuli and is the major relay system for the nonspecific sensory pathway mediating pain. It has many synaptic relays and seems to be particularly sensitive to anesthetics.

In summary, there are two separate somatic sensory pathways—a more recent precise discrete system that permits analysis of stimuli in terms of touch, pressure, and limb position and a much older and more

FIGURE 2-13   *Simplified schematic of the two major somatic sensory systems. In the discrete system, which mediates light touch, pressure, and limb-position sense, the sensory nerve fibers enter the spinal cord and ascend to the lower brain stem, where they synapse in relay nuclei which in turn project to the thalamus and on to the cerebral cortex. The nonspecific system, which mediates pain, temperature, and diffuse touch, synapses in the spinal cord and then ascends and relays through the brain stem reticular system to the thalamus and on to the cerebral cortex.*

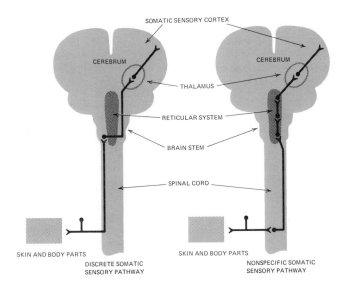

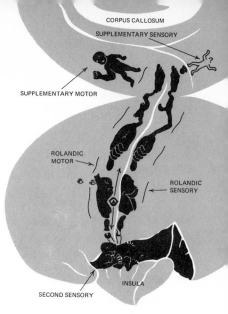

FIGURE 2-14 *Location and approximate representation of the somatic sensory and motor areas on the cerebral cortex of man. The drawings indicate the relative amount of cortex devoted to each region of the body. There are two major sensory areas, rolandic and second, and two motor areas, rolandic and supplementary. The brain is facing to the right, and a portion has been removed below to show the second sensory area. In the upper region, bounded at the top by the corpus callosum, the cortex in the middle of the hemisphere is shown folded up. The foot representation in the primary (rolandic) areas actually bends over the top of the hemisphere and down onto the middle side. [Penfield and Jasper, 1954]*

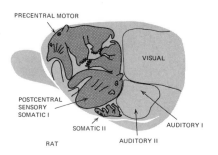

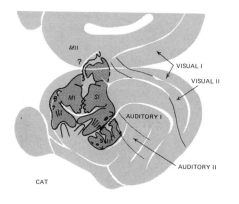

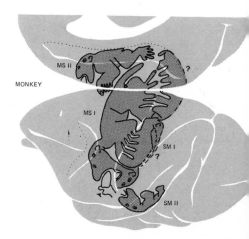

primitive system that is concerned with pain and temperature and is much more related to biological survival.

As with the visual and auditory systems, the somatic receptor surface is mapped out along the somatic sensory area of the cerebral cortex. In this case, of course, the receptor surface is the skin surface of the body. The entire body surface is laid out in representation along the somatic sensory cortex (see Fig. 2-14). The fact that the relative amount of cortex devoted to a particular receptor region is proportional to the behavioral importance of that region is nowhere more evident than in the somatic sensory system. The form of the representation on the cortex is termed a *homunculus*. In animals like the rat there is relatively less distortion of the homunculus on the cortex, although the nose area is somewhat enlarged. The cat has greater enlargement of forepaws and face, and monkeys have enormous enlargement of the hands and feet. Comparisons of somatic sensory homunculi on the cortex in these animals are shown in Fig. 2-15. The amount of cortex devoted to a given region of the body surface is directly proportional to the use and sensitivity of that region. In so far as the cerebral cortex is concerned, man is clearly a creature composed largely of hands, lips, and tongue.

Studies of the manner in which single neurons in the somatic sensory cortex code sensory stimuli indicate that this coding is extremely precise and detailed. A most important finding is the columnar organization of cells in the somatic sensory cortex [Werner and Mountcastle, 1968]. If a very small electrode is pushed down through the cortex at a right angle to the surface, so that it goes directly down through the cortex, it might first encounter a cell that responds only to light touch. As it moves down through the cortex it will encounter additional cells, all of which respond only to light touch. In other words, the light-touch cells form a minute functional *column* down through the cortex. If the electrode is removed, moved to the side a fraction of a millimeter, and pushed down into the cortex again, it might encounter cells that code joint position; all cells in that column will code joint position. Still another column will code deep pressure. Thus each different modality of the discrete system is coded by separate columns of cells. Each small region of skin representation on the somatic sensory cortex is filled with these small columns which code the different modalities. This is true, incidentally, only for the discrete, or lemniscal, system. The older non-

FIGURE 2-15   *Homunculi of the sensory and motor areas for monkey, cat, and rat. Note that on the rat cerebral cortex the sensory and motor representations look rather like the rat, except for the large nose and mouth. The cat has greatly enlarged forepaws and face. In the monkey the representation becomes grossly distorted and is mostly hands and feet (SM I, somatic sensory area I; SM II, somatic sensory area II; MS I, primary motor area; MS II, supplementary motor area). Note from Fig. 2-14 that in man a much greater amount of primary somatic and motor cortex is devoted to lips and tongue, and less is devoted to feet. [Woolsey, 1958; Schaltenbrand and Woolsey, 1964]*

63

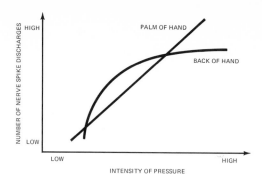

FIGURE 2-16   *Coding of tactile pressure by receptors on the palm and the back of the hand. The rate of spike discharge increases with pressure; on the palm this increase is linear, but on the back of the hand it is not. [data from Werner and Mountcastle, 1968]*

specific system does not have a separate or distinct representation on the cerebral cortex.

The neurons that respond to touch and pressure exhibit incredibly precise coding of the intensity of a stimulus; they discharge spikes in direct proportion to the intensity of pressure on the skin (see Fig. 2-16). In primates and man there is a most interesting difference in the way intensity of touch pressure is coded on the palm and back of the hand. For the palm or fingertips the number of spikes fired as a function of pressure on the skin is a direct linear (straight-line) relationship. For the back of the hand the relationship is direct, but it is not linear. As pressure increases, the proportional increase in number of spikes decreases toward a limit. What this means is that neurons activated by the fingertips and palm are more sensitive to differences in pressure at strong pressures, whereas neurons activated by the back of the hand cannot discriminate among strong pressures. This probably has adaptive significance in that higher primates must discriminate among relatively strong pressures when they grip objects.

COMMON FEATURES OF SENSORY SYSTEMS

In reviewing the major sensory systems we have noted several common principles of how the brain codes sensory stimuli. The first is the receptotopic organization of the cerebral cortex. The receptor surface—the retina of the eye, the basilar membrane of the inner ear, and the skin surface—is mapped out on the cortex in such a way that activation of different regions of the receptor surface leads to activation of differing groups of neurons in the cerebral cortex. This results in coding of location of objects in space for the visual system, tone frequency in the auditory system, and location of touch on the body surface for the somatic sensory system. Furthermore, that aspect of sensory experience that has the greatest functional importance for us, such as center of gaze for vision and fingertips for touch, has relatively greater cortical representation.

A much more fine-grained analysis of sensory quality is provided by individual nerve-cell coding. Colors and forms are coded by various neurons in the visual system; tone pitch and loudness are distinguished by neurons in the auditory system; and type of tactile stimulus is differentiated by neurons in the discrete somatic sensory system.

Coding relationships such as those shown in Fig. 2-16 for pressure of stimulus versus number of nerve spike discharges are psychophysical functions. Psychophysical studies in which human subjects are asked to judge the relationship between stimulus pressure and their subjective experience of pressure yield identical results. Stevens [1961], who has analyzed such psychophysical relationships between physical stimuli and subjective experience in great detail for tactile, auditory, and visual stimuli, has shown that all these functions exhibit a particular kind of mathematical relationship between stimulus and response. It is called a *power function* and has the general form $\Psi = k\Phi^n$, where Ψ is the psychological response of the subject (his subjective judgment of how strong the stimulus is), Φ is the actual stimulus intensity, k is a numerical constant, and n is an exponent whose value depends on the type of stimulus used. In the curves of Fig. 2-16, for example, the palm stimulus yields a function with an exponent of 1, but the back-of-the-hand stimulus yields an exponent of about 0.3. Different forms of psychophysical curves are shown in Fig. 2-17.

It thus appears that for essentially all stimuli, the relationship between physical stimulus intensity and our subjective experience of stimulus intensity is a power function. A question of fundamental importance is where the transformation from the physical-stimulus scale to the

FIGURE 2-17   *Relationship between stimulus intensity (abscissa) and sensation of stimulus magnitude for three different types of stimuli. For length (of lines) the relationship is linear; perceived length corresponds exactly to stimulus length. For brightness, relatively large increases in actual stimulus intensity are perceived as small increases, permitting us to perceive a wide range of stimulus intensity. For electric shock it is just the opposite; above a certain point (about 30 on the scale) small increases in shock intensity are perceived as very large increases. This is at about the point where shock causes pain and tissue damage. [Stevens, 1961]*

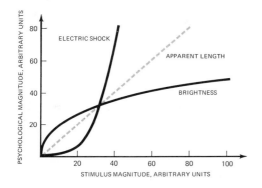

65

subjective-experience scale takes place. Detailed studies of various levels in the somatic sensory system indicate that this transformation is actually at the receptors [Werner and Mountcastle, 1968]. This means that we do not experience the world as it is; we experience it only as a power function of what it is. In other words, the entire sea of subjective experiences by which we guide our lives is not a direct reflection of the real world, but bears only a mathematical relationship to that world. Things are even less as they seem than you think.

In recent years it has been demonstrated that the brain itself can exert some control over incoming sensory information by means of certain descending neural systems. In the visual, auditory, and somatic sensory systems fibers project down from higher regions of the brain to sensory receptors or early central relay stations for sensory input to exert direct control over sensory input. For this reason electrical stimulation of a number of regions of the brain, particularly the reticular formation of the brain stem, will alter the nature of incoming sensory information.

The potential significance of these descending sensory control systems is considerable. The amount and kind of incoming sensory information can be controlled, or "gated," at the level of sensory input. Sensory information might even be prevented from reaching higher levels of the brain. Thus some aspects of selective attention, where we concentrate on one type of sensory input to the exclusion of others, may involve these systems. It is not yet clear just what role the descending control systems play in behavior; it is currently a research area of great interest.

MOTOR RESPONSE

Essentially all aspects of behavior that we can observe in other people and animals are muscle movements—walking, running, fighting, tightrope walking, ballet dancing, piano playing. All of these are simply sequences of skeletal-muscle contractions and relaxations. To the extent that psychology is the study of behavior, it is really the study of muscle movements. However, an understanding of the muscular actions themselves, and even the immediate neuronal mechanisms controlling the muscles, does not provide us with an understanding of behavior. A complete recording of all the finger-muscle actions made by a novelist as he types a novel will tell us nothing about the novel he has written; we would do far better to read it. To understand behavior we must learn about the higher-order systems involved in the control of movement.

The number and variety of brain structures that have something to do with the control of movement are large and somewhat bewildering, to say the least. The English neurologist Hughlings Jackson stated many years ago that the basic function of the nervous system is movement.

SENSORY-MOTOR INTEGRATION

The motor systems of the central nervous system contain some of the most elegant and complex examples of feedback control systems known. In a sense the motor systems are a progressively more complex series of interlocking feedback systems, ranging from the exquisitely tuned gamma motor system of the spinal cord up through the basal ganglia and cerebellum to the pyramidal and extrapyramidal systems of the cerebral cortex. Most of these systems are concerned with the more immediate control mechanisms of movement, and the details are not of direct relevance [see Thompson, 1967].

The most complex aspects of movement control that we know about are mediated by the cerebral cortex. As we noted in Chapter 1, the cerebral cortex is essential for the most important movements we make—those of the tongue, lips, and throat associated with speech. Handwriting, typing, and even reading are really secondary to vocal movements. It is likely, in fact, that most thought processes have as an essential component some degree of movement of the vocal apparatus.

The role of the cerebral cortex in movement is graphically illustrated in the following protocol from a brain operation described by Penfield and Jasper. The patient was a right-handed woman of thirty-nine whose symptoms suggested a tumor in the left hemisphere of the brain. The motor region of the left hemisphere was exposed, and various points of the cerebral cortex were stimulated electrically to aid in locating the abnormal tissue. The patient was under only local anesthesia, so that she could respond and describe her sensations and feelings. The numbers at the left in the protocol are simply arbitrary designations for the specific points on the brain that are being stimulated [Penfield and Jasper, 1954, p. 97]:

Stimulate 17   Patient made a vowel sound which was repeated rhythmically. After electrode withdrawn she explained that she thought she was starting to say something but "it" [the stimulation] had forced her to repeat.
Stimulate 17   Repeated while patient was counting. Stimulation arrested speech completely. Patient added, "It [the stimulus] raised my right arm." The arm had actually raised itself.
Stimulate 18   Patient counting. Stimulation caused her to vocalize in a continuous sound. She explained afterward that she was sorry she could not count. There was some movement in the right arm also.
Stimulate 19   Patient counting. She made an exclamation and then was silent, but the whole body moved. This movement caused the head to turn a little to the right. There was not much movement of the arm. When asked whether she had felt as she did before one of her attacks, she said "Yes." When asked why, she replied "Because I repeated my speech."
Stimulate 20   Patient counting backward. Stimulation caused the counting to stop. Two or three seconds after withdrawal she continued

counting backward. The observer noted no change during her silence except that she looked surprised.

Stimulate 19   Approximate repetition of 20. Vocalization was produced, somewhat rhythmical. There was some movement of both arms and both legs.

Stimulate 18   Repeated without warning. Stimulation produced vocalization which sounded like "da, da, da."

Stimulate 21   Stimulation while patient was counting. She hesitated and then continued. There was movement of right arm, the shoulder being drawn posteriorly. The right leg was extended and raised off the table. When asked what she had noticed, she said her right arm. When asked if she could prevent the movement, she said, "No."

Stimulate 22   Patient said, "Oh." There were generalized movements. When asked what she noticed, she said her body seemed to rise up but she did not seem to be doing it.

The motor area of the human cerebral cortex represents both muscles and movements. In fact it contains a complete mapping, or homunculus, of the body. Using the technique just described, Penfield et al. mapped out the representation of movement on the human cerebral cortex (see Fig. 2-14); this representation is essentially a mirror image of the somatic sensory projection that lies just posterior to it. Similar maps of the motor areas of a variety of mammals and particularly primates obtained by Woolsey [1958] have provided us with a comparative view of the development of the motor cortex (see Fig. 2-15). As in the somatic sensory cortex, man has become largely lips, tongue, and hands. Results of these studies indicate that the motor cortex is indeed a high-order control system. In both man and other higher mammals movements elicited by electrical stimulation of the motor cortex are not random twitches, but are well-integrated movements, even to the point of producing recognizable vocalizations in man. People seem to have no control over these electrically induced movements; in the example above the stimulus preempted the patient's voluntary control of her movements. Of equal importance is the fact that patients do not describe any experiences, memories, or even strong sensations other than the movements themselves that result from the stimulus. The motor cortex is the region that controls complex integrated movements.

Our discussion of motor cortex has thus far been concerned primarily with the kinds of movements elicited by electrical stimulation. Such a technique by itself will not necessarily tell us what the essential role of the motor cortex is in the control of movement. Removal of the primary motor cortex in man produces loss of the most delicate and skilled movements, particularly those of the fingers and hand. However, it has little or no permanent effect on the movements produced by electrical stimulation, which consist largely of flexion and extension of the arms and legs, opening and closing of the fist, and vocalizations. These movements have the same character in a child of eight, a man of sixty, a skilled pianist, and a manual laborer. This would seem to be a paradox. According to Penfield and Jasper [1954, p. 65]:

68

The movements which are said to be "represented" in the precentral gyrus [motor cortex] because they are produced by stimulation of that gyrus are not abolished when the gyrus is removed and, on the other hand, the acquired skills of the contralateral extremities [hand and foot], which do not seem to be "represented" in the gyrus at all, are abolished forever by gyrectomy [removal of the motor cortex].

Apparently what happens is that electrical stimulation activates the cortex to play on subcortical motor systems already "wired up" at birth and under the ultimate control of the motor cortex. Thus the stimulus simply activates portions of this prewired system to produce certain types of unskilled and infantile movements. Movements such as closing the fist and vocalization are in no sense simple muscle contractions, but they fall far short of the complex skilled movements for which the motor cortex is essential. In normal development the motor cortex serves to coordinate highly complex and skilled movements resulting from complex actions on the motor cortex from other regions of the brain. The electrical stimulus cannot duplicate such complex patterns of activation. As Penfield and Jasper put it [1954, pp. 65–66]:

The succession of motor units in the Rolandic (motor) cortex is like a keyboard. Each key is connected to a different peripheral resounding wire. Music results only when the keyboard is played upon according to a pattern that has its localization elsewhere in the central nervous system.

The crucial question is, of course, the nature and organization of the higher-order central control systems that play on the motor cortex. We cannot even begin to answer this question at present; essentially nothing is known about such systems.

SENSORY—MOTOR INTEGRATION

It is not necessary to tell you how the world looks to you; your perceptions of the world are your own immediate experience. We have considered how the major sensory systems code stimuli into sensations and at least simple perceptions such as form, color, pitch, and touch. Your own experience of the world is somehow compounded out of these sensations into a relatively integrated flow of awareness. We know very little about how this happens, but we are beginning to have some idea of how the complex perceptions of the adult human develop. Many aspects of perception, such as the ability to see form and depth, may well be innate. Primates which have been raised in the dark from infancy have very poor vision. For a time it was believed that this was because the animal was unable to learn from visual experience and hence to develop the neural circuits to code pattern vision. However, more recent studies suggest quite a different interpretation. Hubel and Wiesel [1963] determined the characteristics of single neurons in the visual cortex of the newborn animal and found the same types of edge-, line-, and form-coding cells present at birth as in the adult animal.

69

Furthermore, they found that when an animal was raised for a period in the dark, or with one eye covered, cells in the cortex that were thus deprived of visual experience lost the ability to code complex forms. In other words, form perception may be present in the brain at birth, but if the system is not activated by form stimuli during growth and development after birth, form coding is lost.

These findings do not imply that there is no perceptual learning after birth, but they do demonstrate that significant aspects of perception may indeed be innate. In fact there is growing evidence that even complex visual perception is wired into the brain at birth.

We do not yet know the limits of predetermined sensory-perceptual experience. It may even be that certain types of complex perceptions or experiences are transmitted genetically. The Swiss psychoanalyst Karl Jung once proposed a theory of "archetypes," suggesting that certain types of symbolism, such as upright objects representing a penis, are inherited by man as a species and hence represent archetypical perception common to the human race. Of course there is no experimental evidence for this idea, but, at least in theory, it is possible. We do know that many aspects of perception are learned as a result of our responses to the perceptual world. This is particularly true in relation to the consequences of stimuli—that is, their significance in terms of reward or punishment. For a child the sight of candy means "candy to eat," and the sight of the strap means "run." The issue that concerns us here, however, is the extent to which the perceptual organization of our experiential world is influenced by learning. Several recent studies by Held, Hein, Hess, and others have shown that actual behavioral responses are essential for plasticity of sensory-motor integration. Both the normal development of visual perception and visual adaptation apparently require an opportunity to make some motor response to visual stimuli. The fact that motor response is essential for visual "experience" indicates that "perceptual learning" may be fundamentally a motor plasticity rather than a literal reorganization of the sensory input.

The idea that learning in sensory-motor integration is more in the motor response than in the sensory input is entirely consistent with our general position concerning the predetermined coding of sensory stimuli by the sensory systems of the brain. Even very complex and abstract aspects of physical stimuli seem to be coded by preexisting, genetically determined neural circuits. What we normally learn during growth and development, then, is not how the world looks, but rather how to respond to it.

SUMMARY

Much of our understanding of sensation and perception, our sensory responses to stimuli, come from detailed analyses of the sensory systems. The particular sensory modality activated by a stimulus depends not on the nature of the stimulus, but on the sensory receptors that it activates and the sensory area of the brain to which these receptors are connected. The most direct type of stimulus coding is the transduction of stimulus energy into neural impulses by the rods and cones in the retina of the eye, the hair cells in the cochlea of the ear, and the specific and nonspecific nerve endings of the somatic sensory system.

One feature common to all sensory coding is that the receptor surface is mapped out on the corresponding area of the cerebral cortex, the retina on the visual cortex, the basilar membrane along the auditory cortex, the skin surface on the somatic sensory cortex. Single neurons in each of these areas code finer stimulus quality such as color, form, pitch, and type of touch. Stimulus intensity also appears to be coded by single neurons. For essentially all stimuli the relationship between actual stimulus intensity and our subjective experience of it is a power function of the general form $\Psi = k\,\Phi^n$. The brain itself may also exert some control over incoming sensory information through descending neural pathways, but this effect is not yet clearly understood.

The motor area of the human cerebral cortex is perhaps the most important of the various structures involved in the control and integration of movement. The results of electrical stimulation of motor cortex indicate that it represents both muscles and movements. Its removal in man causes a loss of delicate and skilled movements but does not affect the motor gross aspects of movement flexion and extension of limbs.

Sensory-motor integration appears to be innate in some simple organisms in the form of rigidly predetermined behavioral responses to specific sensory stimuli. Many aspects of perception may also be predetermined in higher organisms, including man. The single cells that code form are found in newborn animals. Evidence that motor response to visual stimuli is necessary for normal perceptual development indicates that the learned aspects of perception lie in the response to perception rather than in the perceptual processes.

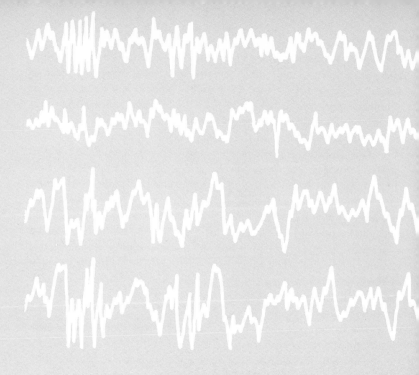

CHAPTER THREE

SLEEP AND WAKEFULNESS

Perhaps the most evident or pervasive experience which we have is the sense of our own existence, an awareness of our own consciousness. From a philosophic point of view man has long sought to understand the nature of his mental existence, and even to use it to "prove" his physical existence, as exemplified by the sixteenth-century philosopher Descartes: "I think, therefore I am." During the nineteenth century, as scientific phychology began to emerge as a discipline separate from philosophy, the problem of consciousness became the topic of "objective" methods of scientific analysis, principally the method of introspection. This consisted of "looking within" one's self and reporting the "contents" of one's own mind. It soon became evident that this method could never yield generally reliable data, for there was no way for one investigator to validate the contents of another's consciousness. Even the presentation of the same simple stimulus to several subjects simultaneously could result in widely different introspective reports of their various consciousnesses.

Although the contents of consciousness could not be agreed on, there was general agreement on the existence of different states of

72

SLEEP, DREAMING, AND ATTENTION

consciousness, principally wakefulness and sleep. "Attention" was generally conceived to be a property of waking, but as we will see recent research suggests that we can also be attentive during sleep. In addition, intensive research into the state of sleep during the past 20 years has shown that sleep is not a unitary state, but consists of separate phases, and that dreaming may constitute, with waking and sleep, a third major state of consciousness. Interest in the "contents of consciousness" has not flagged, although this expression is no longer widely used. Developments in this area have relied on innovations in methods of behavioral measurement, to a large extent in the field of discrimination learning, in order to determine the stimuli or strategies which organisms use to solve particular problems.

One contemporary theory of the universe, the "big-bang" theory, holds that the universe which is now expanding eventually will start to contract until all matter comes together, at which time an unimaginable explosion will once again send matter hurtling outward until the next contraction begins. The time required for one complete pulsation, or cycle, has been estimated to be 80 billion years. This ultimate cycle is still a matter of speculation. The slow but unceasing rotation of our own pinwheel Milky Way galaxy is more firmly established; each cycle

73

of rotation requires 200 million years. Near our galaxy's rim a tiny star carries with it nine planets; they in turn circle this sun in periods ranging from 88 earth days to 247 earth years. Satellites periodically circumnavigate the planets (except Mercury, Venus, and Pluto), and each planet periodically rotates on its axis. We could continue to list cycles or periods of regularly repeating events down to those of the electrons, which spin around atomic nuclei, miniature mimics of star systems. It would be strange indeed if life forms were exempt from the periodicity which characterizes their universe. Life on earth is not. The alternation of sleeping and waking is a manifestation, in our lives and those of other animals, of this pervasive periodicity.

BIOLOGICAL RHYTHMS

The sleep-wakefulness cycle occurs daily, that is, it has a period of approximately 24 hours. Such biological rhythms are called circadian (after the Latin *circa* "about" and *dies* "a day"). However biological rhythms are by no means limited to periods of about 24 hours. They span a wide range, from yearly migrations, hibernations, and matings, to monthly menstrual cycles, to twice-a-day changes in the activity level of marine animals in coastal intertidal zones, down to heart beats on the order of several per second and wingbeats of several hundred per second in the locust.

What is the source of biological rhythm? It might seem that periodic behaviors such as sleeping and waking are controlled by the physical rhythms of the universe, in this case the daily rotation of the earth with its periodic day-night cycle. Indeed, there has been a great amount of controversy about whether such rhythms are controlled by external forces or are due to some process intrinsic to the organism. The truth seems to lie between these two extreme positions. For example, rats which have access to activity wheels will spontaneously enter the wheels and run enthusiastically for varying periods of time (this may be to compensate for limited opportunities for activity within their home cages, but the actual reasons are unknown). Daily activity records over a period of 47 days show one period of activity and one period of inactivity during each 24 hours, with the active period largely confined to the dark or night (Fig. 3-1). These findings support the notion of external control, presumably by changes in light as a result of the earth's rotation. However, this is not the entire story.

If illumination cues are eliminated by housing rats in constant light or darkness, the wheel-running behavior continues to exhibit periodicity. Furthermore, under such constant conditions the activity rhythm is still approximately 24 hours (circadian), with normal ranges from about 40 minutes shorter to 30 minutes longer than 24 hours. Because this "free running" cycle is not exactly 24 hours, it drifts with

74

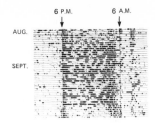

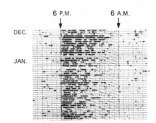

FIGURE 3-1 *Activity cycles for two normal rats over a 47-day period. Each horizontal line represents a 24-hour day, and each dark mark indicates spontaneous running activity. The rats were in total darkness each night from 6 P.M. to 6 A.M. [Richter, 1967]*

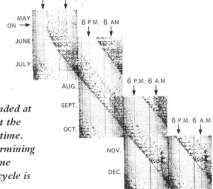

FIGURE 3-2 *Activity cycles for a rat blinded at ON (optic nerves were destroyed). Note that the period of activity drifts with respect to real time. In October this animal, with no way of determining whether it is light or dark, runs in the daytime rather than at night. However, this activity cycle is always nearly 24 hours. [Richter, 1967]*

respect to real time (Fig. 3-2) but it is still remarkably persistent and accurate over the long course of the experiment.

Since cyclic behavior continues in the absence of changes in light, it might be argued that some other physical phenomenon, such as humidity or atmospheric pressure, might be responsible. However, extensive studies by Richter [1967] have unearthed no evidence to support this "externalist" position. Rats housed next to each other may have rhythms that differ by almost 1 hour, so that after 12 days one animal is active while the other is not, although all external phenomena should be identical for both rats. Even more remarkably, Richter has found that the internal clock still runs even when the animal does not. For example, rats subjected to electric shock followed by nine days of inactivity resumed running at the predicted time. Also, the clock is impervious to almost every conceivable manipulation of internal environment, ranging from starvation to extensive brain lesions (Tables 3-1 and 3-2).

These and similar studies reveal that normal circadian rhythms are not controlled exclusively either by external stimulation, such as the day-

TABLE 3-1   *Endocrinological interferences that had no effect on clock.*

GLAND	MANNER PRODUCED	NO. OF RATS
Gonads	Gonadectomy	15
	Mating	17
	Pregnancy and lactation	15
Adrenals	Total removal	25
Hypophysis	Total removal	15
	Posterior lobectomy	8
Pineal	Total removal	26
Pancreas	Partial removal	4
	Alloxan injection	6
Thyroid	Thyroid powder in food	12
	Antithyroid compound	7
	Injection of I-131	4

TABLE 3-2   *Disturbances of the nervous system that had no effect on the clock.*

CONDITION	MANNER PRODUCED	NO. OF RATS
Anoxia	Nitrogen	8
Convulsions	Electroshock	18
	Caffeine—fourth ventricle	23
Tranquilization	Chlorpromazine	6
Poisoning	Lysergic acid diethylamide	11
	Serotonin	8
Anesthesia	Ether	20
	Pentobarbital	11
	Carbon dioxide	5
	Nitrous oxide	7
	Urethane	5
Intoxication	Alcohol	14
Deep sleep	Phenobarbital	5
	Barbital sodium	9
Acute stress	Forced swimming	32
	Restraint	5
	Electric shock	2
Hypo- and hyperactivity	Atropine	7
of autonomic nervous	Acetylcholine	5
system	Epinephrine	4
	Superior cervical ganglionectomy	16
Analgesia	Colchicine	8
Catalepsy	Bulbocapnine	7

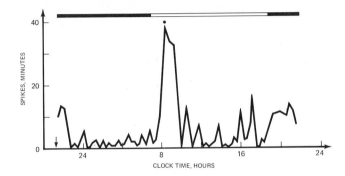

FIGURE 3-3   *Spike discharges generated by a circadian-rhythm neuron in the sea snail Aplysia. The animal had been conditioned previously to regular cycles of 12 hours light and 12 hours darkness, indicated by bar above. Note that although there was no light-dark cycle during the observation period, the cell's activity continued to follow the cycle to which it had been conditioned. [Strumwasser, 1965]*

night cycle, or by a "clock" located in the brain. It appears that each organism does indeed possess an internal clock which has a period of about 24 hours, but this clock is reset each day by external stimulation such as the day-night cycle. Thus the normal active period of a rat is during the dark, but the internal clock continues to cycle in the absence of light-dark cues (accomplished in the laboratory). In other words, circadian rhythms are the result of an interaction between an internal clock and external stimulation.

We know a great deal about the external forces which reset the biological clock, but where is this remarkable internal clock located? In extensive studies, Richter systematically destroyed various parts of the rat brain without affecting activity cycles. However, he did discover that lesions only in the hypothalamus, a tiny bit of tissue at the base of the brain (see Chapter 2), stopped the clock from running. Presumably some specialized group of nerve cells in this region comprise the clock. In fact even isolated single neurons possess the capability of exhibiting precise circadian rhythms. Strumwasser [1965] has found such cells in the marine snail *Aplysia californicus*. The intrinsic metabolic processes of such cells result in periodic changes in the rate of production of neuron firings (see Fig. 3-3). Such cells may act as "pacemakers," controlling the firing rates of large aggregates of other neurons so that their behavior mimics that of the pacemaker. A similar mechanism exists in heart tissue. Indeed, we owe our very lives to a relatively small number of cardiac pacemaker cells. Biological rhythms, then, have their origins in single cells, and circadian periodicities may be produced ultimately by pacemaker cells in the hypothalamus.

The most conspicuous of the circadian rhythms in man is the alternation between sleeping and waking. Many other circadian periodicities accompany this cycle. Body temperature drops to a low between 1 and 7 A.M.; oxygen consumption is highest during normal peak hours of activity whether or not the activity actually occurs; the heartbeat is lowest between 10 P.M. and 7 A.M.; adrenal gland secretion is lower during sleep and rises prior to normal awakening; blood count, the number of red and white corpuscles, is minimal during the morning hours. These and other physiological rhythms exert a profound influence on behavior. The modern air traveler, who finds himself having to adjust to a time zone several hours different from that of his place of origin, may not only feel hungry at inappropriate local times, but he may also be somewhat sluggish and unable to perform well during waking hours even if he has had a good night's sleep. There has been real concern that pilots of intercontinental jets perform at less than peak efficiency in a new time zone and suitable precautions are now routinely employed. The physiological systems require a few days to adjust or be reset, and pilots may not fly again until the passage of two days.

It is apparently possible, although somewhat difficult, to alter the circadian period in man. Researchers have lived in caves for many days isolated from normal day-night cues. In one well-known study, two investigators attempted to live on a 28-hour day for a month. Richardson, the younger of the two, was able to reset his internal clock and adjust to the 28-hour day; Kleitman, 20 years his senior, had much more difficulty. Although the internal clock responsible for cyclic behaviors may be reset or entrained to some extent by external factors, this intrinsic mechanism acts autonomously in the absence of such factors. It is conceivable that in the early stages of evolution cyclic behavior was entirely governed by external forces such as the tides and day-night cycles and that these external rhythms were gradually internalized in the form of pacemaker cells. Whatever the origin of the biological clock, it is clear that the pervasive periodicity of the physical universe also characterizes the biological universe, and that behavior is inextricably intertwined with the periodicity of biological functions.

AROUSAL LEVEL

We generally think of sleeping and waking as distinct and separate states. However, at what point does a sleeping person become a waking person? Is drowsiness part of the waking or the sleeping state? There is now general agreement that a spectrum or continuum of arousal level spans the states of sleep and wakefulness, from a level of very high excitement or emotion down to the level of deep sleep. Thus there are various gradations of sleeping and waking. For example, a person who is poised to deal with an expected event, such as dashing across a busy street between onrushing cars, is far more than merely awake; he is highly aroused. If in crossing it appears that he may in fact be hit, arousal would increase to a state of intense emotional excitement.

Other gradations of arousal include alertness, relaxed wakefulness, drowsiness, light sleep, and deep sleep. We should bear in mind that

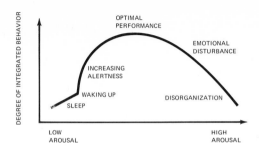

FIGURE 3-4   *Hypothetical relation between the degree of integrated behavior—the effective level of function—and the level of arousal. Note the characteristic inverted-U shape. [Hebb, 1966]*

these states of arousal are not distinct one from the other, like steps in a staircase, but rather, are adjacent positions along a ramp, with intense emotional excitement at one end and deep sleep at the other. We can easily move from one level to the next, as when we slip from relaxed wakefulness to drowsiness. Larger, sudden changes, as from quiet waking to deep sleep, do not occur except in unusual situations.

The relationship between arousal level and ability to perform in a well-integrated manner vis-à-vis the environment is not linear. Obviously our performance is poor when we are drowsy and much better when awake, but performance during the highest states of arousal or emotional excitement is not necessarily better than during quiet wakefulness. In fact there seems to be an optimum range of arousal for the performance of well-integrated behavior. This range consists of levels of moderate arousal during wakefulness. For example, on a task which requires the detection of a signal presented at unpredictable times performance is poor at both the low and high ends of the arousal continuum. This relationship is often referred to as the *inverted-U* function (see Fig. 3-4).

What is responsible for this odd relationship? The disorganizing effect of extreme arousal levels is apparently not a motor problem, for while it is true that the musculature of the sleeper is relaxed, that of an emotional person is well capable of particular discrete behaviors. We do not yet know to what extent the sensory systems are responsible, but physiological studies have indicated that sensory system processing of stimuli continues during sleep and, of course, high arousal. It is possible that sensory information processing is altered during extreme levels of arousal. However, there is more reason to believe that central integrative mechanisms in the brain which intercede between stimulus processing and motor behavior are responsible for the disorganizing effects of arousal-level extremes.

THE CEREBRAL CORTEX

The activity of the brain is reflected in actual minute electrical phenomena which are produced by the natural physiochemical processes that constitute brain functioning. The electroencephalogram (EEG) is one of these phenomena, and although its basis is still imperfectly under-

79

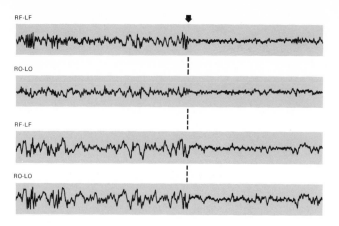

RF-LF

RO-LO

RF-LF

RO-LO

FIGURE 3–5   *EEG records showing the transition from sleep to wakefulness. The arrow indicates spontaneous awakening in the upper two tracings,
and awakening caused by an imposed stimulus (sound) in the lower two
tracings. RF-LF (right and left frontal) tracings were recorded over the
frontal region of the brain; RO-LO (right and left orbital) tracings were taken
over the posterior region.*

stood, it has proved to be a very valuable tool in the study of sleeping
and waking (Chapter 1).

The EEG is recorded from the human cortex via scalp electrodes;
in animals it can be recorded directly by electrodes placed on the cortex
or in other brain regions. The EEG is characterized by somewhat rhythmic
fluctuations in electrical waves which may range from very slow waves
of a few tenths of a hertz (cycle per second) to faster waves in the range
of 20 to 50 hertz. Biological periodicity is thus seen in the brain as well
as in behavior. In general the slower brain waves are of greater amplitude
than the fast waves, and the two types of EEG are described as *high-
voltage slow* and *low-voltage fast*. However, the EEG is characterized by
a single frequency only under restricted conditions; most records consist of a mixture of frequencies. The point is that there is a close relationship between the EEG and behavioral arousal level. Higher levels of
behavioral arousal are accompanied by lower-voltage faster activity,
while reduced arousal level, culminating in sleep, is associated with
higher-voltage slower activity. This relationship between arousal and the
EEG holds for mammals; less is known about nonmammals.

The human EEG differs from that of other animals, especially non-
primates, in having a "richer" diversity. The alpha rhythm, characterized
by a highly "pure" rhythm of 8 to 12 hertz, is a particularly interesting
example. It occurs only during relaxed wakefulness, often only if the
eyes are closed. It is easily blocked by an increase in arousal level produced simply by opening the eyes to admit visual stimuli, or by thinking
about a simple addition problem, without any correlated overt behavior.
When it is blocked, the alpha wave is replaced by lower-voltage faster
waves, in accordance with the general principle that increased arousal is
accompanied by low-voltage fast activity.

The transition from sleep to wakefulness is also accompanied by a shift from pronounced high-voltage slow activity to low-voltage fast activity, whether the awakening is caused by an imposed stimulus or is spontaneous (Fig. 3-5). This shift is often termed *cortical activation* or *desynchronization*. The transition from wakefulness to sleep occurs in stages which are characterized by differing EEG patterns. At stage 1, as waking merges into drowsiness, the alpha rhythm fades, and lower-voltage faster activity predominates. This stage is usually brief, and is an exception to the principle that low-voltage fast activity accompanies heightened arousal. At stage 2 short bursts of "spindles" invade the record. In stage 3 there are no spindles; the record is mainly slow waves in the range of 1 to 3 per second. Stage 4 has even larger and slower waves and constitutes a deep level of sleep. Body temperature and heart rate continue to decline, as they have since stage 1; respiration is slow and even, and wakening requires a fairly loud stimulus. The various sleep stages are summarized in Fig. 3-6.

The fact that the EEG of the cerebral cortex has a high correlation with behavioral arousal might indicate that the cortex itself is responsible for or constitutes the neural substrates of arousal level. One test of this hypothesis is to determine whether it is possible to dissociate the EEG and behavioral arousal. Can we demonstrate a "sleeping" animal with a "waking" EEG? As we shall see later, dreaming is an actual case in point; the EEG pattern is desynchronized, as is characteristic of the waking state. It has also proved possible to dissociate the EEG and arousal level by the use of drugs. The drug atropine, for example, produces a sleeplike

FIGURE 3-6   *The EEG record characteristic of the different stages of arousal in the human adult [Hartmann, 1967; Penfield and Jasper, 1954].*

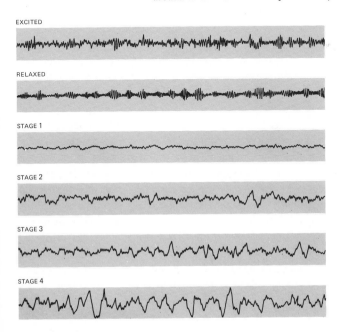

EXCITED

RELAXED

STAGE 1

STAGE 2

STAGE 3

STAGE 4

81

EEG dominated by slow waves while the animal is clearly awake and moving. Conversely, the drug eserine produces a behaviorally sleeping animal which has an activated or low-voltage fast EEG. These findings indicate that the cerebral cortex is not a likely candidate as the substrate of arousal level. One possibility is that the EEG of the cortex reflects the action of some subcortical arousal mechanism, and that the control of the cortical EEG by such a mechanism is disrupted by such pharmacological agents as atropine and scopolamine.

THE RETICULAR FORMATION
OF THE BRAIN STEM

For many years the neural bases of sleep and wakefulness were considered to be controlled only by sensory stimulation received by the brain. This position seemed reasonable, for sensory stimulation is reduced during sleep because the eyes are closed and the body is reclining. It was thought that wakefulness was maintained by sensory "bombardment," which produced a sort of cerebral "tonus." This conception was changed overnight by a dramatic discovery.

Moruzzi and Magoun [1949] were investigating the action of subcortical mechanisms on spinal motor activity by stimulating the central core area of the brain stem, generally known as the *reticular formation* (see Chapter 2). They were also monitoring the cortical EEG of their subject, a lightly anesthetized cat. To their astonishment, stimulation of the reticular formation produced cortical desynchronization—that is, it changed the brain waves from high-voltage slow to low-voltage fast, mimicking the normal EEG changes from sleeping to waking. In a follow-up study Lindsley et al. [1949; 1950] found that lesions which destroyed portions of the reticular formation in cats caused them to remain asleep or in a coma, with accompanying sleeplike high-voltage slow cortical activity. Subsequent study indicated that the reticular stimulation and lesions had not impinged on the classical sensory systems, whose pathways lie in the lateral aspects of the brain stem. Here, then, was strong evidence for a subcortical arousal mechanism that was independent of the sensory systems.

However, since it is well established that sensory stimulation, such as a sudden noise, produces changes in arousal level, what about the role of the sensory systems? Lindsley found that when the sensory paths in the brain stem were destroyed without disturbing the reticular formation, this operation, which greatly reduced the amount of sensory input to the forebrain, did not produce sleep. Although such animals do not behave normally, their sleep-waking cycles are not grossly disrupted. Thus wakefulness does not depend on sensory input. Rather, it seems to depend on intrinsic brain mechanisms, including the reticular formation. How, then, does sensory stimulation normally cause arousal? The answer seems to be that while sensory information is processed in the sensory systems, if the sensory system analysis of the environment reveals a need for arousal, signals are then sent to the reticular formation to trigger arousal. If there is no need for arousal—as with repeated unimportant sensory events such as the ticking of a clock—arousal signals are not sent to the reticular activating system.

Both extrinsic (sensory) and intrinsic (reticular formation) forces interact to produce arousal or determine arousal level, but like the internal biological clock, the intrinsic mechanisms can act in the absence of extrinsic control. This is to be expected if the reticular formation constitutes the neural substrate of arousal, whether arousal is indexed by wheel running, as in our rat studies above, or simply by observation of normal animal activity. At present, however, we still do not understand the relationships between the presumptive hypothalamic internal clock and the reticular formation. The evidence discussed above indicates that the reticular formation sustains the waking state; its stimulation causes awakening and its destruction produces coma or permanent sleep. Does this mean that sleep is produced by decreased activity of the reticular formation? In other words, is sleep simply the absence of waking, or, like waking, does it possess some neural substrates of its own? Extensive work during the past 20 years indicates that sleep is not at all a passive phenomenon, but has active neural substrates. One major finding has been that the reticular formation is not a unitary arousal system. Certain regions, principally the anterior portions, are especially important for increased arousal. Other, more posterior portions located just above the beginning of the spinal cord seem to be concerned with dearousal, or inducement of sleep. Electrical stimulation in this latter region can slow the cortical EEG from low-voltage fast to high-voltage slow and also produce behavioral sleep in cats. The same effects have been produced by stimulation of a region of the brain outside the reticular formation, just in front of the hypothalamus. Lesions of both these dearousing areas can produce insomnia or even complete inability to sleep, which culminates in death.

It has also been found that the onset of sleep can be conditioned. Wyrwicka et al. [1962] presented a tone followed by stimulation of the anterior hypothalamic "sleep" zone to waking cats. As expected, the brain stimulation produced sleep. However, after many pairings of the tone followed by stimulation, it was found that the tone alone, without brain stimulation, also produced sleep. However, this type of conditioning procedure is not necessary for sensory stimulation to produce sleep. The sleep-producing zones seem to be particularly sensitive to any rhythmic, periodic, or unchanging and highly predictable sensory events. Thus exposure to a monotonous environment to which we are not actively attending, such as a droning voice or the unchanging visual stimulation of a long drive on a superhighway, enhances sleep. So too does the steady rocking of a young child, which produces rhythmic vestibular input to the brain. Conversely, the arousal regions seem to detect surprising, unexpected, or suddenly changing aspects of the environment. Let the lecturer call a name or the mother suddenly stop rocking, and arousal is instantaneous.

83

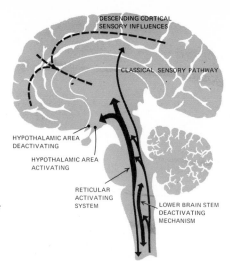

FIGURE 3–7   *Locations of the activating and deactivating regions in the hypothalamus and the reticular formation of the brain [Murray, 1965].*

Thus there are active sleep-producing regions in the brain as well as areas concerned with wakefulness. These occupy various regions of the primitive brain stem, from its lowest levels in the medulla to its highest levels in the hypothalamus, and appear to interact or balance each other in such a way as to determine arousal level from one moment to the next. If the higher region of the reticular system predominates then arousal level will increase and waking may be sustained; otherwise drowsiness and sleep may ensue. Both arousing and dearousing brain regions may be influenced by environmental stimuli, but in the absence of external stimulation they constitute wholly intrinsic mechanisms which regulate the degree of arousal at any given moment. These relationships are summarized in Fig. 3-7.

DREAMING

Dreams constitute vivid and intense experiences for many people. Other people believe that they never dream at all. Almost everyone is intrigued by the meanings of dreams, and dream interpretation has had a long and colorful, if somewhat varied, history. One of the most famous interpretations appears in the Old Testament, where Joseph took the king's dream of seven fat and seven lean cows as a sign that seven years of good harvest would be followed by seven years of famine. His premise was that dream content is symbolic, and that in this case cows symbolized years and the health of the cow symbolized the projected harvest. Freud also subscribed to the theory of symbolism. However, he considered dreams to be not a sign of future events, but an expression of wish fulfillment. According to his classical theory of dreams, we dream in symbolic terms in order to disguise a variety of anxiety-provoking wishes, ranging from minor discomforts to extremes,

84

such as the hope that a parent or sibling will suffer some misfortune [Freud, 1938, p. 211]:

> It is quite as simple a matter to discover the wish-fulfillment in several dreams which I have collected from healthy persons. A friend who was acquainted with my theory of dreams, and had explained it to his wife, said to me one day: "My wife asked me to tell you that she dreamt yesterday that she was having her menses. You will know what that means." Of course I know: if the young wife dreams that she is having her menses, the menses have stopped. I can well imagine that she would have liked to enjoy her freedom a little longer, before the discomforts of maternity began. It was a clever way of giving notice of her first pregnancy. Another friend writes that his wife had dreamt not long ago that she noticed milk-stains on the front of her blouse. This also is an indication of pregnancy, but not of the first one; the young mother hoped she would have more nourishment for the second child than she had for the first.

A series of controlled studies conducted by Hall [1959] showed little support for Freud's contention that dream symbols are disguises for anxiety-producing thoughts. However, Hall did conclude that dreams constitute thinking of a simplified nature, with symbols serving in place of words. Murray [1965] has suggested that complex mental activity cannot take place during sleep, and in his view Hall's conceptions are more likely correct. At the present time there is no general agreement on the approach to interpretation of dream content. However, there is considerable information on the dream state itself. In contrast to previous conceptions, we now know that dreaming is of biological importance and that everyone dreams every night.

THE REM SLEEP STATE

How can dreaming be studied objectively? As with studies of arousal level, the EEG has proved invaluable, particularly in conjunction with other measures such as eye movements and muscle tonus. It has long been known that the depth of sleep varies during the night. Aserinsky and Kleitman [1953] reported that during certain times, when the EEG has ascended to stage 1 (see Fig. 3-8), subjects often made many rapid movements of their eyes beneath closed lids, and that this activity occurred periodically throughout the night. Careful study revealed that the subjects were not briefly awake at these times, for among other indices these periods of rapid eye movement (REM) were accompanied by a complete loss of the slight muscle tonus which is ordinarily present during sleep and is always present during the waking state. When subjects were awakened during a REM period, in most cases they reported a dream. When they were awakened during other stages of sleep, in the absence of rapid eye movements, a significantly lower percentage of dreams were reported.

85

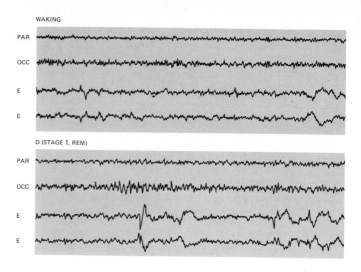

WAKING

PAR

OCC

E

E

D (STAGE 1, REM)

PAR

OCC

E

E

FIGURE 3–8   *Comparison of EEG activity and eye movements (E) during wakefulness and dreaming (REM sleep). The top two tracings of each set are EEG records from parietal (PAR) and occipital (OCC) locations on the scalp. Note in the lower two tracings of each set that the eyes move together (conjugate eye movements).* *[Hartmann, 1967]*

Further studies indicated that all subjects were in a REM state during sleep and that the REM periods occurred more than once. But what of the many people who apparently do not dream? Goodenough et al. [1959] compared people who considered themselves to be habitual dreamers with those who seldom if ever reported dreams. Both groups exhibited REM sleep periods. When awakened during REM periods the habitual dreamers reported dreams 93 percent of the time, and the non-dreamers 46 percent of the time. When awakened during non-REM periods the dreamers reported dreams on 53 percent of the occasions and the nondreamers on 17 percent. Thus, although there is a real difference in the amount of dreaming done by the two types of people, even "nondreamers" do dream. Why then, do some people believe that they do not dream? Apparently dreams may be forgotten during sleep, so that by the time they awaken the recollection may be gone. One significant point is that dreaming is much more likely to occur during the REM state. As it was also found to some extent during slow-wave sleep, it would seem that the REM state is not absolutely necessary for dreaming to occur. However, dream reports during non-REM periods may be due to the recall of dreams that occurred in preceding REM periods. This possibility needs to be explored.

The occurrence of the REM state during a night's sleep appears to follow a general sequence. Deep slow-wave sleep (stage 4) is usually reached soon after falling asleep, but about an hour later the progression of sleep from stage 1 to stage 4 is reversed; body movements are seen, and there is a short period of stage 1 sleep accompanied by rapid eye movements, lasting perhaps 10 minutes. This is generally followed by a progression back down to stage 4 sleep, but in an hour or so the cycle

86

repeats itself. Generally the second and subsequent REM periods are longer than the first, lasting as long as 40 minutes. Stage 4 sleep may not occur again during the night, but stage 3 will be reached between REM periods. These events are summarized in Fig. 3-9). The long duration of REM periods strongly suggests, contrary to many popular beliefs, that dreaming does not occur in a mere instant of time.

Overall, adults spend about 20 percent of a night's sleep in the REM state; this amount decreases slightly after age fifty. Surprisingly, REM sleep is present in the newborn and is actually more prevalent during early childhood than during maturity. Infants spend up to 80 percent of their sleep in the REM state; young children up to the age of four are in REM sleep about 40 percent of the time; thereafter the adult pattern appears. If newborns spend most of their sleeping hours in the REM state, it follows that they must dream more than adults. But what do they dream about? Their cognitive capacity ought to be too unformed to sustain so much apparent visual imagery during sleep. We have no way of answering this question directly at present, but research with both human and nonhuman subjects has provided some clues about the function of dreaming and the REM state.

Asking whether animals dream is a bit like addressing the same question to the newborn; neither can verbalize his answer. Anyone who has closely observed a pet dog or cat during sleep has noticed occasional twitches of the limbs and vibrissae, as well as eye movements, perhaps accompanied by a few vocalizations. Studies, primarily with cats, have revealed that this behavior occurs during the REM state, which as in the human is accompanied by a complete loss of general muscle tonus and a change in the EEG from slow-wave sleep to a more desynchronized pattern. In fact the EEG in a sleeping cat appears identical to that when it is highly aroused during waking. Because of this odd conjunction of a "waking" EEG in a sleeping animal, it is termed *paradoxical sleep*. Paradoxical or REM sleep has been found in all mammals investigated, including apes, monkeys, sheep, dogs, and opossums; it has also been reported to appear for brief intervals, less than 1 minute, in birds.

Since the REM state is so prevalent in all mammals and manifests itself throughout life, it is bound to be of some biological significance.

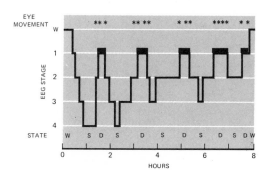

FIGURE 3-9 *A typical night of sleep— an average of many all-night recordings— in a young adult. Heavy lines indicate the dream (D) periods, characterized by a stage 1 EEG pattern and the presence of rapid conjugate eye movements. [Hartmann, 1967]*

87

Studies of REM deprivation have indicated that it is in fact quite important. In both human and nonhuman studies subjects were selectively deprived of REM sleep by awakening them as soon as muscle tonus fell, which occurs just before the EEG changes (this is particularly easy to do in rabbits, because the only time that a rabbit's ears flop is during the REM state). Control subjects were awakened an equal number of times during slow-wave, non-REM sleep. This procedure was followed for several consecutive nights, and sleep patterns on subsequent recovery nights were then carefully analyzed. A universal finding was that REM deprivation resulted in a compensatory increase in the amount of time spent in REM sleep on subsequent nights. For example, Dement [1960] found an increase of about 60 percent in the amount of compensatory REM sleep. He also reported that many subjects deprived of REM sleep exhibited depression, anxiety, and other signs of disturbance, despite the fact that they had obtained 6 hours or so of normal slow-wave sleep per night. It is hoped that additional work will reveal possible relationships between some forms of behavioral pathology and sleep or disturbances in REM sleep.

THE REM AND SLOW-WAVE SLEEP STATES

It was earlier intimated that the state during which dreaming occurs might constitute a separate organismic state, quite distinct from the sleep state with which we are more familiar. The existence in animals of the REM state has permitted investigations of its neural bases and comparison with the substrates of slow-wave sleep. For example, the relative amount of time spent in REM and slow-wave sleep can be selectively altered by discrete brain stem lesions. Two separate areas appear to be involved—a portion of the central reticular formation and the raphé nuclei, which lie in the midline in the brain stem (see Chapter 2). Lesions of the central reticular region reduce or abolish REM sleep but not slow-wave sleep. Destruction of the raphé nuclei produces the opposite effect; it reduces slow-wave sleep without disturbing REM sleep. Electrical stimulation of the reticular region can produce the REM state if the animal is in slow-wave sleep. Thus the central reticular region seems to underlie the REM state, while the raphé nuclei are associated with slow-wave sleep.

Additional evidence comes from studies of brain amines and their manipulation by pharmacological agents. As mentioned in Chapter 2, discrete brain amine systems have been found by the use of elegant histochemical techniques. At this point we are particularly interested in two systems—a *catecholaminergic system* which originates in the central reticular region and contains large amounts of norepinephrine (noradrenaline) and a *serotonergic (5 HT) system* which originates in the raphé nuclei. Drugs which are known to increase the amount of available

88

norepinephrine also increase the amount of time spent in the REM state. Thus injection of a precursor of norepinephrine, such as DOPA, produces more REM sleep. Conversely, drugs which increase the available serotonin also increase the amount of slow-wave sleep and reduce the amount spent in REM sleep. Thus injecting 5 HTP, a precursor of serotonin, produces an increase in the amount of slow-wave sleep. If both norepinephrine and serotonin are reduced by the injection of reserpine, which depletes reserves of all brain amines, then both the REM and slow-wave states are reduced resulting in a chronic waking state until the reserpine has been metabolized.

If REM differs from slow-wave sleep, is it "lighter" or "deeper" sleep? Animal studies have shown that the level of brain activity is much higher during REM than slow-wave sleep. In fact the number and rate of single-neuron activity approaches that seen during excited wakefulness. There are other indications that REM is a period of intense inner arousal; blood pressure rises, heart and respiratory rate increases, and in males of all ages penile erection occurs. This is not related to dreams having sexual content, but is part of a state of general high excitability. We have already noted that the EEG during the REM state tends to be desynchronized as in waking. From these indices it would seem that REM is "light" or "aroused" sleep, but in contrast to these indices of increased arousal, there are indications that the subject is quite deeply asleep. The threshold for awakening by auditory stimulation or direct stimulation of the reticular formation in cats is increased. Most strikingly, low arousal is suggested by the general reduction of muscle tonus, including depression of reflexes.

Actually, the REM state appears to be a condition of intense arousal in which the person is decoupled from his environment. Awakening by environmental stimulation is more difficult than during slow-wave sleep, and the absence of muscle tonus renders the dreamer unable to react to environmental contingencies. Some authorities consider the REM state to represent one of extreme attention or concentration to stored images, etc. Whether one calls the REM state "deep" sleep or "active" sleep, it is qualitatively different from both normal waking and slow-wave sleep.

The study of sleeping and dreaming presents more questions than answers, as is typical in any new field. Such simple questions as "Why do we sleep?" and "Why do we dream?" prove to be simple only in sentence construction. While we have no definitive answers to either of these questions, we have at least learned how to characterize the states to which they refer and how to investigate these states experimentally. It is clear that the understanding of behavior requires an understanding of all states of consciousness. The objective study of sleeping and dreaming promises to shed light on much of our behavior during the one-third of our lives we spend in the nonwaking state. From the general *states* of consciousness, we now turn to a finer level of awareness—attention.

89

ATTENTION

Like sleeping and waking, attention is a common part of our everyday lives. Any attempt to understand behavior must include a consideration of attention. We cannot attend to everything at once, and what we do attend to defines the scope of our behavior at any one moment. Although many people claim to be able to concentrate on several things simultaneously, full comprehension of all of them is extremely rare. There are limits to the amount of information we can process at any one time.

Scientific attempts to cope with attention date back to the middle of the nineteenth century, but they have much older roots in philosophy. The major issue for a long time was how sensory impressions reach consciousness. As we have noted, such introspective approaches proved unsatisfactory, and for many years there was little progress. An additional problem was the use of the term "attention" to refer to different phenomena. Whereas some investigators emphasized the clarity of sense objects in consciousness, others were more concerned about the selective aspects of attention. These differing concepts are evident in statements by the leading proponents of each view. According to Edward Titchener [1908]:

It seems to be beyond question that the problem of attention centres in the fact of sensible clearness . . .

and according to William James [1890]:

Millions of items of the outward order are present to my senses which never properly enter into my experience. Why: Because they have no *interest* for me. *My experience is what I agree to attend to.*

Clarity in consciousness was finally discarded as an important aspect of attention as psychology became more objectively oriented toward behavior. The selective aspects of attention did survive, perhaps because objective methods of determining stimulus selection were developed. Before we consider how attention is measured, however, let us consider the objects of this attention.

THE OBJECTS OF ATTENTION

In his classical consideration of attention William James distinguished two general types of things to which attention could be directed—objects of sense, or stimuli, and ideal or represented objects, our thoughts, ideas, and memories. An objective investigation of the stimulus properties that may be selected has proved to be a far easier task than that of studying ideational attention. This is because stimulus parameters, such as wavelength, shape, and tone frequency, can be directly manipulated by an experimenter; thoughts, ideas, and memories cannot at present be

90

systematically varied and measured as easily. Although objects of sense and objects of the intellect are both valid objects of attention and demand study, we shall restrict our consideration here largely to stimuli as objects of attention.

Any designated stimulus is of necessity somewhat complex. For example, suppose a person is trained simply to press a button whenever he hears a tone pip of 1000 hertz. The occurrence of the tone is made unpredictable, so that when the subject responds correctly we are fairly certain that it is not because of a lucky guess. If he does well—responds correctly most of the time—we may say that he paid attention to the 1000-hertz tone pip. Surprisingly, this interpretation may be incorrect. The subject may in fact have been responding to the change in the ambient stimulus environment rather than specifically to the auditory stimulus. Or even if he had been attending to the fact that the stimulus was auditory, he might not have paid attention to its pitch at all. The problem is that three different stimulus categories are involved in this situation. In the presentation of a 1000-hertz tone pip there is a change in the environment, a stimulus modality (auditory), and a *modality-specific attribute* (tone pitch). Attention to each of these would entail three responses—"Something happened"; "I heard something"; "I heard a 1000-hertz tone."

In addition, two other categories may be noted—locus or the place in the environment from which the stimulus emanated; stimulus pattern, such as shape or tune. Moreover, each of these five dimensions may vary in *intensity* and *duration*. In this case the tone pips must have had a locus in space, and they certainly possessed an intensity and duration. If a sequence of pips had been given, producing a pattern, then *all* of the stimulus categories would have been thoroughly confounded. Unless we untangle these various stimulus categories, we have no way to determine just what particular stimulus attribute constitutes the object of attention at a given time.

There is one last category which might serve as the basis of stimulus selection or attention, stimulus novelty. A novel stimulus may be regarded as one which is different from expected stimulation. Thus novelty is not properly a physical attribute of a stimulus, as are the dimensions above. Rather, novelty is a property of a stimulus in situations in which an organism makes some comparison between the actual stimulus and some memory or representation of other stimuli. Novelty thus involves both of James' categories of the objects of attention, sensory and ideational. As such, it may someday serve as an entrée into investigations of attention to memories, ideas, thoughts, and similar represented objects.

As an illustration of attention to novelty, consider the behavior of a dog placed in a strange environment, such as a new cage or yard. Intense exploration may ensue, indicated by locomotion, sniffing, looking about, and so forth. In this case we cannot be quite sure just what novel aspects are being attended, although we may infer these (perhaps incorrectly) from a casual observation of the animal's behavior.

91

A more systematic approach to novelty is illustrated by a now classical experiment performed by Sharpless and Jasper [1956]. Sleeping cats were presented with a 500-hertz tone, which promptly caused them to awaken. Both behavioral and EEG indices of arousal were measured. After the cats fell back to sleep, the same stimulus was presented again, and again it caused arousal, but of a shorter duration than on the first trial. As the procedure was continued, the cats stayed awake for progressively shorter periods, until after about 30 trials the stimulus produced no effect on either behavior or the EEG. When it was certain that this stimulus had lost its power to arouse, a new frequency, 100 hertz, was presented, and this caused prompt arousal. In this context the 100-hertz tone was considered novel not just by the experimenter, but also by the cats. Novelty was established by noting that the new tone produced arousal in a selective manner, for if the following trial consisted of the original 500-hertz tone, no arousal took place. The cats clearly regarded the 100-hertz stimulus as different from the oft-repeated and expected 500-hertz stimulus. Of course a stimulus that is initially novel will lose its novelty by repeated presentation—that is, through *habituation*. Thus continued presentation of the 100-hertz stimulus also resulted in an absence of response. However, a novel 1000-hertz stimulus could still cause arousal (Fig. 3-10). This procedure was repeated until the cats were not aroused by any tone stimulus and no longer responded to auditory stimulation. Arousal could be induced promptly, however, by lightly touching their fur. Although auditory stimulation was nonnovel, tactile stimulation was novel.

In this case responses to novelty served to determine which of the stimulus categories was being selected by the cats. Selective arousal to the 100-hertz stimulus showed that pitch had been selected. When no auditory stimulus caused arousal but tactile stimulation did, the animals were attending to the stimulus modality, to tactile versus auditory stimulation. Many other tests or measures of the objects of attention, some considerably more elaborate, have been devised.

THE MEASUREMENT OF ATTENTION

We generally believe that someone who "looks" attentive is attentive. By "looks" we are actually referring to general posture, facial expression, and head and eye orientation. Of course if this were an adequate index of attention, we would not be able to succeed in little social deceptions, as when we try to appear interested in the conversation of a bore at a party while thinking of something else (attending to ideational objects). As we all know, these deceptions do succeed. Even if it can be said that the attentive "look" is an index of attention, the object of this attention is clearly an unknown factor. Attempts to measure attention on the basis of the attentive "look" have had the same insufficient and uncertain results in laboratory studies of attention in animals. For example, in a classical study Hernández-Peón et al. [1956] attempted

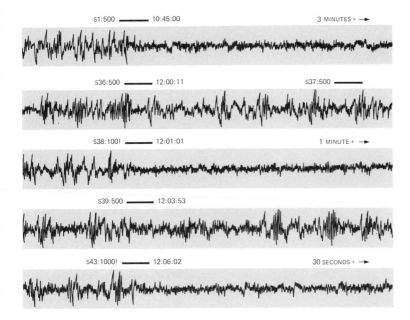

FIGURE 3-10   *EEG from the cerebral cortex of a normal cat showing typical habituation of the arousal reaction to a 500-hertz tone. In the first tracing the response to the first presentation of the 500-hertz tone is S1:500; the solid bar shows the occurrence of the stimulus in hours, minutes, and seconds (10:45:00). The second tracing shows the thirty-sixth (S36) and thirty-seventh (S37) trials and succeeding tracings show responses to a novel tone (!) of 100-hertz (S38:100!), a repetition of the habituated tone (S39:500), and another novel tone (S43:1000!). The duration of the activation in each trial is indicated at the right. [Sharpless and Jasper, 1956]*

to investigate brain processing of stimuli during attention and inattention by placing a jar of mice in front of a cat and noting its clear interest in the mice. They assumed that the cat was paying attention only to visual cues provided by the mice and was inattentive in all other sensory systems since the mice were in an enclosed vessel. However, they failed to consider that the cat may also have been listening intently for mouse noises and attempting to detect mouse odor simply because of the absence of these normal cues. Even in human studies it has been shown that posture and receptor orientation do not guarantee attention to a given stimulus. In studies of visual signal detection it has been demonstrated that even when the signal was clearly focused and fixated, there could be a failure to detect it. Although proper orientation of the eyes may be necessary for attention to a visual stimulus, it does not guarantee such attention; the subject may still daydream.

A more objective index of attention, since it reduces the need for inferences by the experimenter, entails having the subject perform a discrete response in order to be able to view a particular stimulus. These *observing responses* were first employed by Wyckoff [1952], who trained pigeons to press a treadle to produce one of two possible cues—a

93

red or a green light, each of which required different types of responses—in order to obtain a reward of grain. The cue produced by the observing response may also be one that is directly rewarding, as in the case of monkeys who learned to open a panel in order to view laboratory activities [Butler, 1953; Butler and Harlow, 1954]. The observing response can also be used to index stimulus *saliency*, the amount of interest a stimulus has for a particular species. The number of panel openings and duration of viewing on each occasion have been used as such a measure of interest in monkeys. In one study monkeys were found to prefer watching a movie to viewing a moving electric train [Harlow and Mc-Clearn, 1954].

Of course not all attentive behavior includes an overt observing response. For example, particular parts of a stimulus array which is presented for only a few milliseconds (in a device called a *tachistoscope*) can be attended even though the stimulus exposure is too brief to permit a discrete observing response or visual fixation of a given part of the display. Also, it is clearly possible to switch attention from one voice to another without moving one's head. Thus, while the occurrence of a discrete observing response does indicate that the subject is selecting some sensory stimulus, the absence of such a response does not guarantee that he is not appropriately attentive.

In so far as we need not exhibit gross or overt observing responses in order to be attentive, how is the psychologist able to determine the objects of attention? We discussed an appropriate method earlier, the task involving detection of a tone pip which is presented occasionally, on a schedule which precludes correct guessing. Recall that the subject was required to signify the occurrence of the signal by pressing a button—that is, by a discrete behavioral response. This widely used technique is referred to as a *vigilance task*. It requires the subject to monitor his environment continuously. Inattention is indexed by a failure to press the button when the signal occurs. Of course the task can be used with any modality. In one well-known study Mackworth [1950] required subjects to detect a double jump in the movement of the second hand of a clock. This jump of 2 seconds instead of 1 was programmed by the experimenter to occur infrequently, only about 24 times per hour. Mackworth found a performance decrement; there were fewer correct detections after the first half hour. This vigilance decrement has been found repeatedly in a variety of tasks and seems to represent a general loss of attention with time. The implications of these findings are of considerable practical significance, as many industrial and military jobs entail the continuous monitoring of displays and detection of unscheduled signals. In fact much experimental vigilance research grew out of concern about performance decrements exhibited by radar operators.

What causes the loss of vigilance? In a study of radar detection by military personnel it was found that vigilance decrement did not occur if a superior officer entered the radar room at unpredictable intervals. However, this finding does not indicate that vigilance decrements are caused by malingering. Rather, the loss of vigilance is probably due to a

94

lowering of general arousal level during exposure to repetitive monotonous stimuli which have little significance. In the radar task these stimuli were the continuous sweeping of an illuminated beam; in the clock task they were the 1-second hand movements. Any significant change in the subject's environment, whether it is the entrance of an officer or a rest period every half hour, will produce an increase in the subject's general arousal level and a consequent improvement in his detection performance.

Up to this point we have been concerned with attention to relatively simple stimuli and have not asked about the limits of attention. How many things or stimulus dimensions can we attend to at the same time? What is the breadth of selection? One powerful and commonly used technique entails deliberately confounding two stimulus categories during initial training and later separating them to determine whether one, the other, or both were attended. For example, rats may be trained to discriminate between a white horizontal rectangle (rewarded) and a black vertical rectangle (not rewarded). In this situation, stimulus brightness (black or white) is mixed with stimulus orientation (vertical or horizontal). After training to some criterion of correct performance, which may require many sessions, the animal is given a second task in which brightness and orientation are separated; for example, the white horizontal rectangle (still rewarded) may be paired with a black horizontal rectangle. In this way the category of stimulus orientation is removed. If the animal continues to respond correctly to the white rectangle, this clearly indicates that he has been attending to stimulus brightness, not orientation. Should he perform poorly with the orientation cue removed, it would be taken to mean that he had been attending to stimulus orientation more than to brightness. Similarly, other animals trained on the original task could be tested for attention to brightness by pairing a white horizontal rectangle (still rewarded) with a white vertical rectangle. Animals which are tested under both conditions and exhibit a decrement on neither would have been attending to both dimensions (Fig. 3-11).

For this type of discrimination task rats do not attend to both dimensions. In fact it appears that the more an animal attends to one,

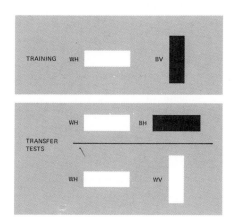

FIGURE 3-11   *Experiments used to determine which aspect of a stimulus is attended by an animal. After training on a horizontal white bar (WH) versus a vertical black bar (BV), the animals are tested on white versus black horizontal bars and horizontal versus vertical white bars. If the animal attends to stimulus orientation during training, he will respond equally to both stimuli in the first test but will respond to the horizontal bar in the second. If, however, he attends to color or brightness, he will respond to the white bar in the first test but equally to the two stimuli in the second.*

the less he attends to the other [Sutherland, 1968]. However, this particular finding does not imply that the rat or any other organism can attend to only one stimulus dimension at a time. The breadth of attention may vary with the situation. For example, Bruner et al. [1955] found that high levels of arousal, caused by extensive food deprivation, reduced the number of cues learned by rats in solving a spatial discrimination problem. Breadth of attention thus may depend on situational variables rather than the particular task and must be determined empirically. It cannot be stated unequivocally that attending to one stimulus dimension necessitates ignoring all others.

The general technique we have been discussing is often referred to as a *transfer test*, because it examines whether or not initial learning transfers to a later task. Complete or extensive transfer of a particular stimulus category is taken as evidence of attention to that stimulus attribute; failure to transfer indicates that the attribute in question was not attended. Note that transfer tests cannot indicate the actual object of attention during the subject's initial response; this information is acquired later during the second transfer task. There is one technique, however, that does provide an immediate index of the object of attention—that in which the subject tracks continuously a stimulus which is moving in space or time. An example of tracking in space might be holding a pointer in contact with a moving target. Tracking in time involves auditory stimulation, as in listening to a recorded message and repeating what is heard. In this case the tracking behavior is referred to as *shadowing*, because the repetition follows the stimulus message.

In research on the limits of human information-processing capacity dichotic selective listening experiments have been used, in which different messages are presented to the two ears simultaneously, and the subject is instructed to shadow the message to one ear. Attention to this message is indicated by success in shadowing. Extensive studies by Treisman [1964] and others have shown that very little, if any, of the unattended message is understood. In fact if the unattended message is given in a foreign language, the subject may not even be aware of this fact. This might suggest that sensory information to the unattended ear does not get processed in the unattended auditory system. However, if the foreign language is actually a translation of the message given to the attended ear, bilingual subjects come to realize this fact, even though subjects unfamiliar with this language will not even realize another language is being spoken. The realization by the bilingual subjects indicates that the unattended message must have been processed, not blocked in the auditory system. Further evidence of this is that words of importance, such as the subject's name or emotion-laden terms, given to the unattended ear in a known language will be recognized and reported. Simple stimuli such as tone pips interjected into the unattended message will also be reported. Moreover, if words appear in the unattended message which have a high probability of appearing in the attended message, they will be incorporated into the shadowed response, sometimes even without the awareness of the subject.

96

All these findings indicate that while information to the unattended ear seems to be blocked, in fact some analysis must take place. Simple or crude stimulus properties, such as tone frequency, are not blocked, and terms of relevance to the person or the attended message get through. It would seem that the meaning of the unattended message and its verbal components is analyzed and then rejected if found to be uninteresting. It is as if the unattended ear does in fact "listen" all of the time, so that interesting items can be attended to by the subject and not get lost. This is similar to the process that seems to be taking place during sleep. Thus it would appear that the sensory systems can continue to process information whether the total information load is low, as during sleep, or high, as during selective dichotic listening. Such a mechanism makes very good sense from an adaptive standpoint, in that it would enable the organism to attend to environmental events of significance even when it is not properly prepared for or expecting them.

We have seen that attention is measured in many ways. In all cases, however, stimulus selection is indexed by allowing the experimenter to determine what stimuli or stimulus aspects are selected by the subject. In other words, the techniques for assessing attention tell us more than the mere fact that a person or animal is attentive; they permit specification of just what he is attending to. For example, in the discrimination-learning experiment it was quite obvious that the rats were attending to some stimulus; the transfer tests revealed whether they were attending to, or selecting, stimulus brightness or stimulus orientation. When a rat selects brightness his behavior may be said to be controlled by that stimulus dimension. Attention to a stimulus, then, is evidenced by the behavior in which it results. In this respect stimulus *selection* is synonymous with stimulus *control*.

We have seen that it is possible to find out what aspects of the environment are selected or attended by an organism. Since an organism may be said to be at some level of arousal at any given moment, how are attention and arousal related? Common sense tells us that

ATTENTION AND AROUSAL

in order to be attentive, to behave quite selectively when presented with the barrage of stimuli which the environment offers, we must be awake, even moderately aroused. Is this actually the case? Does attention imply an existing background of wakefulness? One way to answer this question is to find out if attention is possible during sleep.

Several studies have indicated selective discrimination during sleep. Rowland [1957] conditioned cats to respond to one tone and to ignore a second tone while awake. These two stimuli were then presented while the cats were asleep, with some striking results; even during sleep the cats showed behavioral or EEG changes to the significant tone, but not to the ignored tone. Oswald et al. [1960] found that during sleep

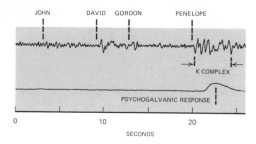

FIGURE 3–12   *Arousal value of a significant stimulus. EEG activity is shown for a sleeping human subject during a period in which names were called out at irregular intervals of 4 to 8 seconds. The names John!, David!, Gordon! have little effect on the subject's EEG and provoke no psychogalvanic responses, while the name of his beloved Penelope! provokes a group of large waves forming a "K complex" in the EEG and a surge of electric potential at the palm. [Oswald, 1966]*

people showed selective EEG responses to their own names versus other names (Fig. 3-12). Granda and Hammack [1961] trained people in the waking state to avoid shock following tone presentation by making some overt response. This behavior, including the pressing of a switch to avoid shock, also occurred during non-REM sleep. In addition, there is the study discussed earlier, in which sleeping cats exhibited selective arousal to novel stimuli. These and other findings support the idea that selective attention during sleep is possible. This is common knowledge to any mother, who may sleep soundly through a thunderstorm, but awakens promptly the minute her child whimpers.

Behavior during sleep is quite crude when compared to the waking state. The body musculature is quite relaxed in slow-wave sleep and actually inhibited during the REM state. Behavior is ordinarily restricted merely to awakening or to an EEG change which indicates a shift to a lighter stage of sleep. Continual integrated interaction with the environment is rare. Drowsiness and sleep, whether caused by boredom or prior sleep loss, invariably result in a performance decrement on vigilance and other tasks which require continuous scanning of the environment (performance during sleep in the Granda and Hammack study could be maintained only by the threat of shock). Learning during genuine sleep is rare, if it occurs at all; the exception is learning not to awaken to repeated stimuli which have no particular significance or urgency—that is, habituation of arousal.

The quality of sleep behavior is clearly lower than that of waking behavior. Nevertheless, the fact that selective attention does occur during sleep indicates that attention is not a property exclusive to one level of arousal, wakefulness. This distinction between arousal and attention implies that they may be served by different brain mechanisms.

98

The simplest encounter that an organism can have with its environment is to be presented with any environmental change—that is, with a single stimulus. If that stimulus is novel, a complex series of physiological re-actions ensues. These constitute the *orienting reflex*, first identified and named by the great Russian physiologist Pavlov [1927]. Changes occur in several systems. The pupils dilate; the head turns toward the source of stimulation; ongoing behavior is temporarily arrested and general muscle tonus rises; there is vasoconstriction in the limbs and concomi-tant vasodilation in the head, which sends more blood to the brain; res-piration and heartbeat are briefly interrupted; and the EEG exhibits activation (lower-voltage faster waves). These changes are illustrated in Fig. 3-13.

The orienting reflex constitutes a physiological syndrome which enhances preparedness on the part of the organsim to interact with its environment. It is not defensive in nature, but neutral. (In fact if the novel stimulus is noxious or too intense, a defensive syndrome will be elicited which differs from the orienting reflex in several ways, including vasoconstriction in both the limbs and head.) The form of the orienting reflex is constant, regardless of the particular nature of the stimulus which elicited it; thus this reflex constitutes a general reaction to un-

FIGURE 3-13   *The orienting reflex. When a sudden, novel, or significant stimulus is presented to a human subject (arrow), the pupil dilates, respiration is temporarily arrested, the heartbeat slows temporarily, muscle tone (EMG) increases, blood flow in the limbs decreases but blood flow in the head increases, the EEG shifts to a low-voltage fast aroused pattern, and the sub-ject turns his head toward the source of stimulation. [after Sokolov, 1963]*

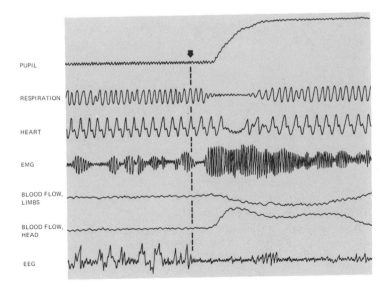

expected or novel stimulation, and as such may serve as an objective index of attention.

We have discussed selective EEG desynchronization in cats in response to different tones. These EEG changes simply constituted one aspect of the orienting reflex. This reflex habituates with repeated presentation of stimuli which lack significance. Thus as an originally novel stimulus recurs, it loses its novelty and also its ability to elicit an orienting reflex. However, habituation does not take place if the stimulus in question bears some particular meaning for an individual: although you have heard your own name called thousands of times, its sight or sound still elicits an orienting reflex. The orienting reflex occurs during both sleeping and waking, and the changes, such as EEG activation, may be very subtle. You may not be aware of all the physiological changes taking place in your body during an orienting reflex, but they are there nevertheless.

In so far as the orienting reflex comprises a basic attentive "attitude" on the part of the body, its neural mechanisms are of particular interest. There is evidence that the part of the reticular formation which underlies increased arousal is responsible. Thus electrical stimulation of the anterior reticular formation produces the orienting reflex. This proposition seems reasonable because both increased arousal and the orienting reflex comprise general, rather than specific, reactions on the part of organisms.

The general sequence which begins with a novel stimulus and culminates in attention appears to be as follows. The stimulus is received and processed by the appropriate sensory system. After the nature of the stimulus is analyzed it is compared with memories of other stimuli in light of the present environment and state of the organism. If the stimulus is found to be either particularly significant or novel, signals are sent to the activating reticular formation, which produces both a general increase in arousal level (as evidenced by EEG changes) and the autonomic and somatic changes of the orienting reflex in preparation for environmental interaction. If the stimulus is found to lack significance, activating signals are not forthcoming. In fact signals may be sent to those parts of the brain stem which produce slow-wave sleep, actually making arousal less probable. This may explain why monotonous or repetitive stimulation often produces drowsiness and sleep.

It might seem from this sequence of events that attention, as indexed by the orienting reflex, and arousal have the same brain mechanisms. However, we have disregarded the selective aspects of attention, including the analysis and decision by sensory systems, which precede and may even initiate general arousal and the orienting reflex. Thus, while it is possible that the reticular formation is responsible for general aspects of attention, it is not the prime mover, but rather, an effector system. The discrete processes which permit us to discriminate among stimuli and attend selectively to particular aspects of our environment must have other brain substrates.

According to the schema outlined above, attention to a stimulus must involve sensory system analysis, but what of inattention or the ignoring of some stimuli? If a child fails to answer his mother's call to the dinner table while he is watching television, has he processed her voice and understood her words? His mother may think so, but some authorities believe otherwise. They hold the position that ignored stimuli can be blocked by inhibition in an unattended sensory modality, and that this blocking can take place at a peripheral level of the sensory system near the receptor, prior to any complex analysis of the stimulus. Evidence for this position comes from two types of studies.

Hernández-Peón et al. [1956] recorded evoked potentials in the cat auditory system which were produced by click stimulation. They found that when the cat viewed a mouse the amplitude of the evoked potentials decreased, and that when it lost interest in the mouse the amplitude was restored to its normal value. They concluded from these findings that when the cat looked at the mouse it was not listening, and was in fact blocking input to its auditory system, evidenced by smaller evoked potentials, and that after the cat lost interest in the mouse auditory function was restored. However, subsequent studies showed that evoked potential was reduced only when the cat *moved* while looking at the mouse, and not if it remained motionless [Dunlop et al., 1965]. Other studies showed that the reduction in evoked-potential amplitude was due to contraction of minute muscles located in the middle ear, rather than to inhibition of the auditory system. These tiny muscles contract during movement, reducing our ability to hear movements produced by our own bodies; they also slightly reduce the intensity of all acoustic stimuli. Since the auditory system evoked potentials were slightly reduced only when the cats moved, this reduction does not indicate that sensory inhibition occurs in one modality during attention to another modality.

The second type of study has concerned habituation of evoked potentials during the repetitive presentation of unimportant stimuli. Once again it was proposed that sensory inhibition occurs during inattention, in this case during inattention produced by monotonous stimulation [Hernández-Peón, 1960]. There has been an active controversy about whether sensory system potentials which are produced by repetitive stimulation do indeed show a systematic decline in amplitude—that is, habituation—and the issue is not yet completely settled. However, in several studies which included careful control of the effective intensity of the stimulus and careful measurement of evoked-potential amplitude, habituation of sensory system potentials has not been found [Worden and Marsh, 1963].

Most studies have not actually measured the attentive behavior of their subjects while evoked potentials were recorded. In one study,

101

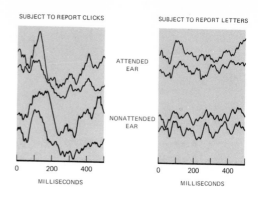

SUBJECT TO REPORT CLICKS

SUBJECT TO REPORT LETTERS

ATTENDED
EAR

NONATTENDED
EAR

0   200   400

0   200   400

MILLISECONDS

MILLISECONDS

FIGURE 3-14   *Average brain potentials evoked by sound (click) stimuli from the scalp of a human subject under various conditions of attention. The subject was given both clicks and letters to each ear and asked to attend to one ear and not the other. In all cases the records show the brain responses to clicks, and each tracing is the average of 50 individual responses. The brain responses to clicks are large in both the attended and unattended ears. The brain responses to clicks delivered to the two ears are much smaller when the subject is asked to report only the letters. [Smith et al., 1970]*

however, auditory system evoked potentials showed no evidence of habituation, but the magnitude of eye movements elicited by auditory stimulation to one ear did show habituation [Weinberger et al., 1969]. Thus there is no evidence in support of the proposal that sensory system habituation underlies behavioral habituation. Much further investigation is needed, but at this point it seems unlikely that sensory system inhibition, particularly at primary sensory nuclei, is responsible for either attending to or ignoring stimuli.

HUMAN EVOKED POTENTIALS

We saw in Chapter 1 that evoked potentials produced by stimuli can be recorded from the human scalp. These differ from the evoked potentials discussed above in that they occur hundreds rather than tens of milliseconds after the stimulus. In addition, these long-latency human evoked potentials probably do not represent primary stimulus processing within one of the classical sensory systems, but are more likely the result of some complex associational analyses. Whatever their neural basis, they are of interest in the study of attention. Unlike the negative findings in nonhuman studies, human evoked potentials recorded during attention have shown that these potentials definitely do change in relation to selective perception or behavior. The human experiments generally employ some type of vigilance or detection task in order to ascertain that the subject is or is not paying attention to a particular stimulus, and evoked potentials are then compared under

102

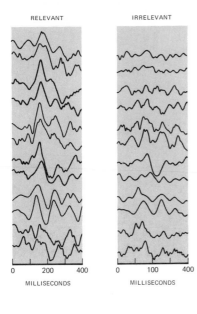

RELEVANT   IRRELEVANT

0   200   400   0   100   400
MILLISECONDS   MILLISECONDS

FIGURE 3–15   *Effects of attention on scalp-recorded brain potentials evoked by visual stimuli (light flash). Flashes are presented to the two eyes, but brain responses are recorded only for flashes given in the left visual field, and each tracing is the average of 100 individual responses. The evoked potentials in this left visual field are substantially larger if the subject is attending to the left flash— he is required to count to himself the number of left flashes to avoid an electric shock (relevant). When he is required to count to himself the number of flashes on the right in order to avoid shock, the brain potentials for the left flashes (irrelevant) are much smaller. [Eason et al., 1969]*

conditions of attention and inattention to that stimulus. The general results, which have been successfully repeated in many laboratories with different types of stimuli, indicate that the evoked potential produced by the stimulus is larger during attention. For example, Smith et al. [1970] studied the effect of attending to clicks in a selective-listening task by having subjects press a button when they heard a click. When they did so a particular wave in the evoked potential was enhanced, but when they failed to attend to the clicks no enhancement occurred (Fig. 3-14). Similar results have been found by Eason et al. [1969] in tasks based on visual stimulation. Some of these effects are shown in Fig. 3-15.

In summary, it appears that the neural substrates of attention include both general and specific components. The general aspects, which include elicitation of the orienting reflex and increased arousal, may be mediated by the activating part of the reticular formation. The specific components, which include analysis and decisions regarding the actual stimuli to be attended or ignored, involve sensory system processing, probably at all levels, from the receptor and peripheral relay nuclei up to and including the cerebral cortex. Evidence to date suggests that there are no significant changes in stimulus processing at peripheral levels of the sensory systems that could account for behavioral attention. However, experiments with human subjects definitely indicate that cortical events, related in some as yet unknown way to sensory system analysis, do change as a function of attention.

103

SUMMARY

The circadian rhythms which pervade the behavior and existence of all living things are determined by both internal factors, the pacemaker cells of the nervous system, and external factors, such as the ebb and flow of the tides and the variation in the light-dark cycle with the seasons. Perhaps the most obvious of the circadian rhythms that characterize man is the sleep-wakefulness cycle. The electroencephalograph (EEG) has been used to identify and classify levels of arousal, particularly the various stages of sleep. From the desynchronized, low-voltage fast activity during wakefulness, an individual might pass into relaxed wakefulness, characterized by the highly synchronized EEG pattern called the alpha rhythm. The onset of sleep stage 1 is signaled by a return to low-voltage fast activity; in stage 2 the EEG shows sleep spindles and higher-voltage lower activity; in stages 3 and 4 the EEG lacks spindles but shows progressively higher and lower voltage variations. Extreme values on the arousal continuum are accompanied by a disorganization in behavior which appears to be neither a motor nor sensory deficit, but a deficit in their integration.

Although there is good correlation between the characteristics of the cortical EEG and behavioral arousal, the cortical area apparently is not the neural basis of arousal, since the EEG and arousal level can be dissociated through the use of drugs and during the rapid-eye-movement (REM) state. The neural substrates of arousal seem to involve activity of the reticular formation and certain portions of the hypothalamus. The anterior portions of the reticular formation appear to be important in the production of behavioral and electrophysiological signs of arousal, while the more posterior portions of the reticular formation and an area near the hypothalamus appear to regulate the production of sleep. Thus neither sleep nor wakefulness is a passive process.

Dreaming occurs in cycles during the night, primarily during REM sleep periods, which is characterized not only by rapid eye movements, but by a loss of the slight muscle tonus normally maintained during sleep. REM sleep comprises about 20 percent of the normal adult's total sleep time. However, in infants it comprises 80 percent, indicating that they may dream much more than adults.

Whereas the raphé nuclei in the brain stem appear primarily responsible for the production of slow-wave sleep, a portion of the central reticular formation appears to control REM sleep—perhaps by means of the transmitter substances serotonin and norepinephrine, respectively. Although REM is a state of deep sleep, on the basis of the stimulus intensity required for wakening, it is characterized by an EEG similar to that for alert wakefulness.

Attention, which probably plays a role in arousal state, is measured in terms of specific stimulus dimensions. For example, a subject may attend to the mere presence or absence of a stimulus, its modality,

SLEEP, DREAMING, AND ATTENTION

modality-specific attributes, its source, or its pattern, all of which may vary in intensity and in duration. Perhaps the most obvious, but least reliable, determinant of attention is whether an animal "looks" attentive. A more objective measure is provided by a behavioral response to a specific stimulus dimension; this is termed an observing response. Vigilance tasks, transfer tests, tracking, and monitoring some aspect of the environment are other ways of measuring stimulus selection.

Attention to some aspect of the environment elicits an orienting reflex, a complex series of physiological reactions which include dilation of the pupils, vasoconstriction of the limbs and vasodilation of the head, brief cardiac and respiratory arrest, and orientation of the receptors toward the stimulus source. The physiological consequences of inattention are not so clear, but it appears that sensory input is not impeded during inattention. The neural substrates of attention apparently have both general and specific components, and there seem to be no significant changes in stimulus processing at peripheral levels of the sensory system, although cortical events do appear to be involved.

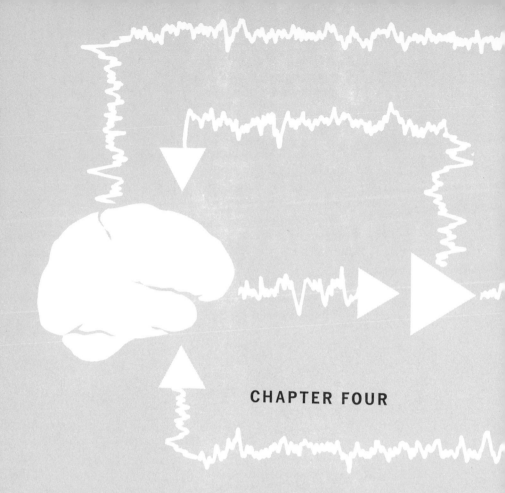

CHAPTER FOUR

THE MOTIVATIONAL PROCESSES

Motivation is the fundamental driving thrust that generates behavior. There are many sources of motivation. Hunger and thirst are elemental forces compelling all animals to act—and in spite of the affluence of Western society, the majority of people in the world today are hungry. Sex, love, and affection—greed, aggressions, and war—exploration, achievement, and approval of our fellows—these are the sources and meaning of motivated behavior. The common definition of motivation as that which causes us to do what we do is true enough, but too broad for scientific purposes. We do not ask what "motivates" a person to give a knee-jerk reflex or why his pupils dilate in strong light.

Certain aspects of motivation may some day be expressed in terms of simple physiological reflexes. At this point, however, the term is generally reserved for particular classes of internal conditions which direct behavior. These background conditions are not directly responsible for the behavior, but they determine whether or not it will be emitted. An animal presented with food is at all times capable of feeding, but the

MOTIVATION

presence or absence of the motivational state of hunger determines whether or not it does so. However, saying that the study of motivation is the study of those states which direct behavior is still not satisfactory. Many would contend that emotion is an essential part of motivation, and that motivational states also have affective, or emotional, components. There have been many theories defining motivation according to scales of pleasantness or unpleasantness; others have insisted that such states "energize," or "drive," the animal, either in general or in specific directions.

Although the theoretical aspects of motivation are not entirely resolved, biopsychologists all agree on the facts of motivated behavior. Much is known about such primary aspects of motivation as hunger, thirst, aggression, and sex, partly because it is easy to observe and measure their behavioral expressions, feeding, fighting, and so forth. We shall examine aggression, hunger, and thirst as elemental forms of motivation, return to theoretical issues concerning the biology of motivation and emotion, and conclude with the more complex aspects of motivation in primates and man. Sex is a topic of particular interest for higher primates and may be treated separately.

107

AGGRESSION AND AGONISTIC BEHAVIORS

It has been estimated that 59 million human beings were killed by other human beings between the years 1820 and 1945. This total, which is almost certainly an underestimate, provides a staggering indication of the extent of human aggression, but no indication of its character. The history of man is in large part a catalog of almost unbelievable cruelty, torture, and brutality. In fact we do other species a great injustice when we describe human actions as brutal or bestial, since we are evidently the only species that deliberately inflicts suffering on its own kind. William James [1890] described man as "the most formidable of all the beasts of prey, and indeed the only one that preys systematically on its own species." In view of contemporary man's unlimited capability for inflicting death, an increased understanding of aggression may well be essential for the survival of the species.

The development of anger and aggression from birth to adulthood in monkey and man has been discussed at length in earlier chapters. Here we are more concerned with the natural history of aggression and the neural mechanisms that produce it in the context of motivation. Aggressive behavior varies enormously among living forms, from species that rarely fight to animals that fight only their own kind, to animals that depend on killing for their survival. It is not surprising, therefore, that a single definition of aggression is likely to be unwieldy. In fact the term *agonistic* (fighting) is probably better in this context, because it has less implication about the origin or nature of the behavior to which it refers. In general there are three types of agonistic behavior—*flight*, in which an animal flees when encountered; *defense*, in which an animal protects itself against attack by fighting; and *attack*, in which an animal initiates fighting behavior.

It is important to distinguish between intraspecies and interspecies fighting behaviors. Most animals other than man do not kill their own kind for food, and it is apparent that intraspecies fighting is not normally related to food-seeking behavior. Intraspecies fighting often takes the form of "stylized" fights, and except in man, it rarely results in death. However, most, but not all, interspecies aggression is on a predator-prey basis and usually does conclude in death.

FACTORS IN AGONISTIC BEHAVIOR

Most theories of fighting behaviors have followed two approaches; one is concerned with the stimulus cues which elicit various agonistic responses, while the other emphasizes the learning history involved in these responses. Arguments have raged over which of these is the more important, although there is general agreement that both factors are involved. However, the relative proportion varies greatly according to the species and situation.

Few vertebrates are more aggressive than the fighting fish, *Betta*

FIGURE 4-1   *Intraspecies aggression in mammals. Both rats are receiving inescapable foot shock. Although the aversive stimulus is not produced by either rat, and a foreign stimulus (the doll) is also present, they attack each other. If only one rat is present he will attack the doll. [Miller, 1948]*

splendons, and it is therefore an excellent subject for analyzing the cues that elicit attack behaviors. On seeing another male the fighting fish goes through a series of complicated but stereotyped behaviors preparatory to attack. These include turning sideways to the intruder and extending the fins, and then turning toward the intruder; this is followed in turn by a sudden attack, culminating in savage biting. These attacks occur primarily when one fish is moving into the "territory" of another fish. What is it that "motivates" the fish to make this response? A sizable body of data suggests that innate responses to particular types of stimuli are involved. In a series of studies with models held outside the fish tank Thompson [1963] demonstrated that the color of the intruder as well as that of the defender fish was one critical variable in determining whether an attack was to be made. Red fish were found to be far more likely to attack green models than blue or red models, whereas blue fish were likely to attack red models and least likely to attack blue models. Other colors were intermediate in their ability to elicit attack behavior. A fighting fish may attack any male fish which appears to be entering its territory, but the probability of an attack apparently follows a strict color code.

Rodents also engage in considerable intraspecies agonistic behavior. When a strange male rat is introduced into the "home" cage of another male rat, the two animals will go through a series of postures which may or may not lead to a fight. The rat who has occupied the cage for some time makes a *threat posture,* in which it arches its back and presents its flank to the newcomer. If the newcomer makes a *submission response,* which usually consists in crawling under the other rat, he is left alone. However, if he adopts the threat posture himself, a fight usually ensues; both animals stand on their hind legs, box with their forepaws, and bite at each other (see Fig. 4-1). The fight stops only when one of the animals adopts the submission position.

Again we can ask what cues are directing these behaviors. Why, for example, does the male not attack female rats? Odors clearly play a

FIGURE 4-2   *Intraspecies aggression in man. Fighting occurs even though, as in Fig. 4-1, the underlying causes are   often not produced by the fighters.* [Los Angeles Times]

major role, since rats with olfactory bulbs removed become considerably more aggressive. Probably more important, however, is the past history of the animal. This was illustrated in an experiment with mice, which engage in agonistic behaviors similar to those of rats [Lagerspetz, 1969]. The number of aggressive responses made by a male mouse when it was caged with randomly selected mice was recorded. The experimental mouse was then caged repeatedly with mice that other studies had established as being very aggressive and successful in their bouts. After several sessions in which the experimental mouse was usually defeated, it was found to be considerably less aggressive. It was then caged repeatedly with nonaggressive mice, and over time it not only returned to but surpassed its previous baseline aggressiveness. This experiment clearly demonstrates the extent to which previous successes and failures in fights—that is, learning—play a major role in aggression in male mice.

Other factors, which are apparently not related to learning, are also intimately involved in the control of aggression. The fact that rats can be bred for aggressiveness, for example, suggests that genetic factors may be related to the role of gonadal (sex) hormones in determining levels of aggressiveness. Environmental variables are also critical; the amount of cage space available to rats and mice directly affects the amount of fighting, as does the quantity of food. We have already seen that animals tend to regard their accustomed living areas as their own territories and will challenge any intruder who enters this space. The presence or absence of females also affects the probability of fighting among male rodents. Finally, the animal's position in the social hierarchy greatly influences his readiness to fight. In short, both the amount and the nature of fighting in rats and mice are determined by a complex interaction of environmental, genetic, and learning variables.

There is also great variation in primate agonistic behavior, both in individuals of the same species and from one species to another. Nearly all primates, however, have a ritualized pattern of behaviors that they follow when faced with conflict. These include facial gestures and radical arm movements, and significantly, vocalizations. Fights do not usually entail serious physical damage in primates (however, see Fig. 4-2). Environmental variables are an important factor in primate agonistic behavior. Southwick et al. [1965] found that decreasing the size of the animals' cages greatly increased the amount of fighting, but surprisingly enough, reducing the amount of food caused a reduction in the number of fights—the reverse of the effect on rodents. He also made the unexpected observation that captive rhesus monkeys were considerably more aggressive than animals found in forests. Again, this is the opposite of what has been reported for rats and nicely illustrates the danger of generalizing from one animal form to another. Factors within the group play a major role in determining primate aggression, but as always, variability is the rule. Thus adult male rhesus monkeys observed in the wild appeared to attack females and juveniles as frequently as other males, while fighting of caged males was usually directed at other males. The social hierarchies of primates are usually formed after an extended series of fights, and struggles to maintain this hierarchy are a major cause of agonistic primate aggression.

THE BRAIN SYSTEMS
THAT CONTROL AGGRESSION

The neural substrates of aggression have been the subject of investigation for some 40 years. Gradually three structures, all part of the limbic system (see Chapter 2) have become isolated as being critically important to the initiation and control of agonistic behaviors. These are the hypothalamus, the amygdala, and the septum (Fig. 4-3).

In the 1930s Bard investigated the effects of cutting the brain at various levels [Bard and Mountcastle, 1948]. A surgical instrument was lowered into the brain, and various amounts of the forebrain were "disconnected" from the remainder of the brain. He found that removal of the entire forebrain in front of the hypothalamus did not eliminate "rage" behavior; in fact it lowered the threshold for its elicitation. To be sure, this rage (attack) behavior was not smooth or well integrated, but there was no doubt that it was attack behavior. However, Bard was not sure that the affective components of rage were truly present in these animals and preferred to call this behavior "sham rage." When the hypothalamus itself was damaged, the rage response disappeared completely.

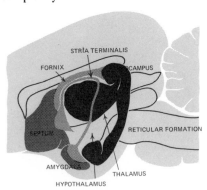

FIGURE 4-3   *Limbic system of the brain. Note the central position of the hypothalamus and the connections to it from the hippocampus and amygdala by way of fiber tracts (stria terminali and fornix). [Fernandez de Molina and Hunsperger, 1959]*

111

Bard's work demonstrated that much of the forebrain is not necessary for the production of attack behavior, and in fact appears to inhibit it, since removal of the forebrain lowers the threshold for the response. The hypothalamus, however, is critical for the generation of rage behavior.

Recent research has attempted to define the ways in which the hypothalamus is involved in the production of rage. Electrical stimulation of the hypothalamus has proved to be a technique of great value. The bare tip of an otherwise insulated wire is inserted into the target brain area (hypothalamus), and after the animal has fully recovered from anesthesia a tiny current is passed through the wire and the effects on its behavior are measured. This procedure elicits various types of agonistic behavior in cats. Most often the flight response is seen, but on other occasions defense or attack responses are elicited. The major factor in determining which kind of agonistic behavior is elicited seems to be the exact location of the electrode in the hypothalamus.

Flynn [1967] has described two very different kinds of attack elicited by stimulation of the hypothalamus in cats. One, *affective attack*, is sudden and resembles what most investigators have called rage (see Fig. 4-4). The cat strikes repeatedly but inefficiently at the attack object, with unusual amounts of accompanying vocalization, hissing, and other signs of rage. *Stalking attack*, the second type of aggression observed after hypothalamic stimulation, resembles the cat's normal mode of attack. The animal stalks the cage and approaches its target with caution. When the attack is made, it is sudden and very efficient. This type of attack behavior is sensitive to the environmental situation and will occur only with appropriate "targets," such as a mouse. In other words, it appears to relate in most details to normal predatory behavior.

FIGURE 4-4   *Two types of agonistic behavior elicited in a cat by stimulation of closely adjacent points in the hypothalamus. Above, rage and attack behavior. Below, quiet biting predation attack. [Flynn, 1967]*

These studies verify Bard's conclusion that the hypothalamus plays a critical role in organizing aggressive behavior. What, then, of his contention that the forebrain suppresses agonistic behavior? One answer to this comes from the functions of the *amygdala* in primates. The amygdala is a large nucleus in the forebrain that is a part of the limbic system (see Fig. 4-3). Primates form intricate social hierarchies, with each animal dominating the animal immediately below him in the social hierarchy. Pribram [1962] found that destruction of the amygdala produced dramatic changes in this hierarchy. When the amygdala was destroyed in a monkey who had been lowest on the social scale, he began to compete with his former superiors and was able to occupy a position at or near the top. When the dominant monkey was lesioned in the amygdala, the picture was reversed; he was no longer able to control the other monkeys and fell in social standing to the bottom of the hierarchy.

This report generated considerable interest and additional work on the role of the amygdala in controlling aggressive behavior, but the only clear finding that has emerged is that the amygdala is involved. It was soon found that electrical stimulation of the amygdala could either produce rage or block it. For example, a great deal more current to the hypothalamus is needed to produce attack behaviors when the amygdala is stimulated concurrently. However, stimulation of the amygdala alone often leads to attack. This suggests that the amygdala may have antagonistic subdivisions which inhibit or facilitate rage. Selective lesioning of the amygdala also suggests the presence of positive and negative systems. Since removal of the entire structure lowers the threshold for rage, it appears that the net effect of these subdivisions is inhibitory.

How does the amygdala control aggressive behavior? A logical approach would be to consider the brain areas to which it is tied. The major fiber connections of the amygdala are with the hypothalamus, which, as we have seen, is crucial for the appearance of rage behavior. Therefore it seems reasonable to hypothesize that the amygdala is working through the hypothalamus. However, this idea is not borne out by experimental evidence. When the hypothalamus is lesioned there are no aggressive responses to electrical stimulation of the amygdala. Lesioning of the amygdala, however, has no effect on hypothalamically induced rage behavior.

The experimental evidence linking the amygdala with aggression has generated considerable interest among neurologists, and there are now a number of reports showing that stimulation of the amygdala in humans can cause attack, while lesions have a calming effect. It is far too early for final evaluation, but it does appear that the amygdala plays a role in controlling aggression in a wide range of mammalian forms.

The third brain region which has been found to be involved in agonistic behavior is the septum. The septum is located between the amygdala and hypothalamus and has extensive fiber connections with both (see Fig. 4-3). The observation that the septal area might be involved in aggression came unexpectedly. During another experiment Brady and Nauta [1953] found that septal lesions caused laboratory rats, which

113

are normally docile animals, to become so irritable and vicious that they would attack and bite animals many times their own size. This dramatic effect has since been obtained in several laboratories, but we do not yet understand the underlying mechanisms.

HUNGER AND FEEDING BEHAVIOR

Feeding behavior represents an area of interest to motivational scientists, whether they are working with behavior, brain, or body physiology. Analysis of feeding can be subdivided into four aspects or concerns—the behaviors which precede it; the feeding bout itself, the cues which start and stop it; the brain systems which initiate it; and the long-term consequences of feeding to body physiology. This sequence is illustrated in Fig. 4-5. Consideration of the long-term physiological consequences includes the question of what bodily variables are monitored by the brain—that is, how the brain "knows" when to initiate another search for food. It should be obvious by now that we cannot simply say that animals eat when they are hungry and stop when they are filled. Since hunger is a subjective experience we must approach it in terms of its observable behavior, feeding.

Let us start our analysis with the behaviors that animals exhibit prior to feeding. The first of these is an increase in motor activity level. In the natural environment this is not a random process but typically becomes directed toward locations in which the animal has found food previously. Here, as in all motivated behavior, we encounter the powerful influence of learning. The effect of learning on food-searching behavior is beautifully demonstrated in studies of the amount of time deer mice will spend digging for food [Hinde, 1966]. Deer mice have a strong taste preference for sawfly cocoons, which they sometimes encounter on or just beneath the surface of the ground. Normally they spend little time looking for this delicacy, but when the experimenter planted several cocoons in the cage, the mouse steadily increased the number of digs it made per day. In other words, as the mouse learned that this desirable food was available, it greatly increased its efforts to obtain it. This study also illustrates the importance of environmental factors in feeding behavior. It was found that the number of digs the mouse made per day was dependent on the other types of food it could obtain without digging. The mouse made fewer digs when the alternate food was sunflower seeds, which is a delicacy to deer mice, than when it was dog biscuits, which they do not especially like. Thus the animal's previous history of successes and failures in finding a particular food as well as what else was available determined its prefeeding behavior. It is important to keep this behavioral flexibility in mind when considering the feeding habits of animals.

The next step, feeding behavior, occurs when the animal encounters food. What determines whether or not he will eat it? The obvious

114

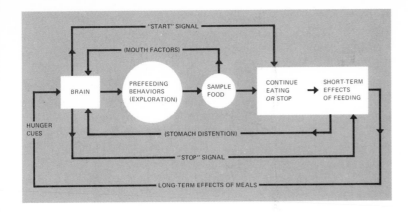

FIGURE 4-5   *Diagram of how the brain might interact with body factors to control feeding behavior. The brain senses bodily signals associated with hunger and organizes a behavioral search for food. When food is found, eating begins and continues until the brain receives sufficient signals to stop. The duration of eating is partly determined by the composition and taste of the food. The long-term consequences (hours) on bodily functions will determine when the brain next receives hunger signals.*

answer is taste, and to a large extent this is correct. The physiological and neurophysiological mechanisms of taste are beyond our present scope. Our main concern here is with the manner in which tastes interact with the underlying motivational states that lead to feeding.

Food preferences seem to have two origins, one learned and the other innate. It appears that animals can associate the long-term effects of a particular food type with its taste; taste serves as a cue that this food contains high concentrations of sugars and fats. This is something that an animal must learn; it does not represent a native ability. Experimental rats have been given a choice between two diets, one of which is low in some substance such as vitamin A. If the diets have the same flavor, the rats choose randomly between them and gradually become sick owing to an insufficiency of vitamin A. If one of the diets is given a distinctive flavor, so that the rats can tell the two diets apart, the rats will gradually eat only from the food supply that contains normal amounts of vitamin A. That is, they learn that a particular taste is associated with a poor diet and come to avoid that taste. This is a remarkable feat when we consider that the taste of food and its digestion and transmission to the blood supply and cells are separated in time by many minutes or even hours.

Many food preferences, however, are not learned. For example, neonatal rats prefer saccharin solutions (which have no nutritional value) to solutions of their mother's milk. This is an important point, because it demonstrates that taste can have motivational value independent of its nutritional value. Even more important, both adult and young, relatively inexperienced organisms tend to select a balanced diet over time if they are given a choice of foods. In one classical experiment human babies aged six months to one year were required to eat all their foods

115

from large trays containing 12 to 20 different foods in separate containers [Davis, 1928]. The experiment resulted in very messy babies, but also very healthy babies. At any one meal an infant might eat only one food, say, all butter, but over the long run each baby selected a well-balanced diet and grew as well as or better than a control group raised on a dietitian's formula. Pioneering cafeteria-type experiments with rats show similar results [Richter, 1942; 1943]. The exotic food cravings expressed by pregnant women provide still another illustration. It appears that specific nutritional needs are translated into rather specific taste preferences, which lead in the long run to a relatively well-balanced pattern of food intake.

PERIPHERAL VERSUS CENTRAL THEORIES OF FEEDING

When a food-deprived animal has found food, sampled it, and found it acceptable, he begins to eat. The next logical question is when does he stop? The intuitive answer to this question is that he stops when his stomach is filled, but this does not appear to be true. Animals, including humans, in which nerves connected to the stomach have been removed appear to be perfectly able to regulate their food intake. Since there is no nervous connection between stomach and brain, the organism has no way of knowing if its stomach is filled or not. Other studies have shown that simple distention of the stomach or loading it with nonnutritive substances does not reduce the hunger drive [Miller and Kessen, 1952]. These and many similar studies show that stomach distention is not the primary satiety cue

These negative conclusions force us to look beyond the stomach for the satiety cue and search for some postingestional consequence which the animal might be monitoring. Two theories which have obtained increasing recognition are Mayer's *glucostatic theory* [Mayer, 1955] and Brobeck's *thermostatic theory* [Brobeck, 1947; 1948]. As the names imply, both these theories are related to the concept of homeostatic functioning. Mayer contends that an animal eats to maintain its blood sugar at an optimal level for utilization. Brobeck is quite direct in stating the contrasting position that "animals eat to *keep warm* and stop eating to prevent hyperthermia." Each theory has in common the idea that a postingestional variable is monitored by the brain, and when certain values for this variable are exceeded or not obtained, the cessation or the initiation of feeding occurs.

According to the glucostatic hypothesis, the difference in blood-sugar concentration in brain arteries and veins provides the clues for the initiation and cessation of feeding. This difference, often called the *A-V difference*, is an indication of the rate of glucose utilization by the brain, so that low A-V values, which signal low utilization, serve as a satiety cue and high values, which signal high utilization, lead to eating.

116

Glucose is the only carbohydrate normally used by the brian, so the extent to which it is being utilized is an indicant of how active the brain is. The evidence for or against this theory has never proved entirely conclusive because of the difficulty in measuring A-V differences across the brain from moment to moment. Nevertheless, there is ample evidence that fluctuations in arterial and venous glucose concentrations are often accompanied by hunger in humans and increased feeding in animals. The most commonly cited evidence in favor of the glucostatic theory is the data obtained with the exotic compound gold thioglucose [Mayer and Marshall, 1956]. Mayer reasoned that if the brain really monitored glucose as its satiety signal, then destruction of these monitoring devices would cause animals to eat continuously. Gold is extremely toxic to living tissue. Consequently, if the hypothetical glucose receptors in the brain absorbed glucose and gold together, the gold would poison the glucoreceptors, leaving the animal no means of measuring glucose and hence no means of sensing satiety. When mice were injected with gold thioglucose, each of these predictions was fulfilled; damage was done to specific brain areas known to be associated with the measurement of satiety signals, and the animals ate ravenously to the point of becoming obese. Later experiments indicate that the brain damage is in fact fairly general and involves numerous regions of the brain which appear to have little to do with the regulation of food intake.

THE BRAIN SYSTEMS
THAT CONTROL FEEDING

The theories we have discussed have in common the idea that there are brain centers which monitor some blood variables—glucose, temperature, or circulating fats—and use these as cues for the starting or stopping of food intake. One of the major concerns of research has been to locate these receptive areas. For years it has been observed that brain damage in the area surrounding the pituitary glands often causes obesity in man. However, research conducted in the 1930s and 1940s showed that removal of the pituitary in experimental animals did not produce overeating obesity. This led to the thought that the critical areas were the brain regions immediately adjacent to the pituitary, the hypothalamus. Subsequent work showed that destruction of a nucleus in the medial region of the hypothalamus does produce chronic overeating, or *hyperphagia* (see Fig. 4-6). This suggested that the medial nucleus might normally suppress food intake, since its removal resulted in increased eating (see Fig. 4-7). However, it was not until the 1950s that satisfactory data were available on the brain areas which normally facilitate food intake. Anand and Brobeck [1951] reported that lesions in the lateral region of the hypothalamus, immediately adjacent to the medial hypothalamus, caused animals to stop eating (*aphagia*). It was later shown that electrical stimulation of the lateral hypothalamus region caused

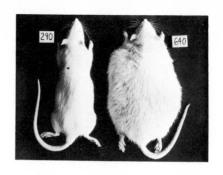

FIGURE 4-6   *Left, a normal rat. Right, a rat that has become fat by overeating (hyperphagia) after destruction of a small region in the medial hypothalamus of the brain. The same effect can be produced by feeding gold thioglucose. [Teitelbaum, 1964]*

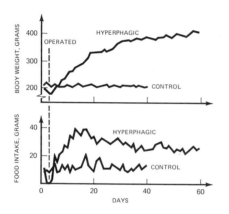

FIGURE 4-7   *Body weight and daily food intake of a hyperphagic animal with a lesion in the medial hypothalamus [Teitelbaum, 1961].*

previously satiated rats to begin eating voraciously and stimulation of the medial region caused starving rats to stop feeding. These results indicated that the hypothalamus contains antagonistic systems—one which causes animals to begin feeding and a second system which inhibits the first, thus producing cessation of feeding. This demonstration that the medial and lateral regions serve opposite functions in the regulation of food intake excited a great deal of interest and led to much additional experimental research.

One difficulty with the hypothesis that the medial region plays a role in the production of satiety is that experimental animals (usually rats) with medial hypothalamic lesions are finicky eaters. They will not eat bad-tasting foods but will overeat when foods that taste pleasant (to a rat) are available. At an intuitive level this does not make sense; if the medial region does produce the neural signals we interpret as satiation and thus makes animals rabidly hungry, we would expect such animals to be *less* selective in their diets. In fact, however, starved animals are more selective in their diets than normal ones, and in this sense the correlation between medial hypothalamic damage and hunger is very good.

Drinking behavior follows much the same sequence as feeding behavior. The brain recognizes some state which is perceived as thirst and initiates behavioral activity which continues until water is encountered; the animal then samples the water, drinks, and stops

drinking. Presumably some effect of the water eliminates the cues which the brain had originally sensed and acted on. Therefore the problem can be broken down into more manageable portions—the cues which initiate drinking, the cues which result in the cessation of drinking, and the brain regions which sense these cues. The general view is that a single mechanism produces both these cues—that is, an animal starts drinking when some physiological variable falls below a certain point and stops when the proper level is restored.

PERIPHERAL VERSUS CENTRAL THEORIES OF DRINKING

As with feeding behavior, there are two general theories about the origins of thirst. According to *peripheral theories*, prolonged water deprivation causes a physical change in bodily organs, such as dryness of mouth, and this change is recorded by the brain via the peripheral nervous system. The *central theories* are based on the contention that water deprivation changes blood factors, such as salt concentration, this change is recorded by the brain via the circulatory system, and the brain monitors the blood factors directly.

The strongest proponent of a peripheral interpretation of thirst was Cannon, who argued that thirst resulted from decreased saliva flow into the mouth causing the mouth dryness associated with thirst. The saliva, or *parotid*, glands dry out because of low water content of blood during prolonged water deprivation. In support of his idea that saliva flow is the cue for thirst, Cannon showed that saliva flow was inversely proportional to degree of thirst in man. From this model it could be argued that drinking is an attempt to substitute water for saliva. Other studies have cast serious doubt on the dry-mouth idea. Bernard had demonstrated years earlier that animals would show essentially normal cessation of drinking when water was placed directly into their stomachs (via an implanted tube called a fistula), without passing through the mouth and throat. Thus wetting a dry mouth cannot be the sole mechanism which controls drinking. Moreover, removal of the parotid glands does not eliminate or even drastically increase drinking. These findings pose severe difficulties for the dry-mouth theory. It is possible, of course, that mouth sensations interact with other factors in the control of thirst. However, they cannot be the only or necessary thirst cue.

Central theories have emphasized the obvious physiological effects of prolonged water deprivation on blood supply and body cells. The human body, for example, is about 75 percent water. Body water is

119

found both inside cells and outside cells (in the blood supply) as extracellular water. Since cell membranes are semipermeable, water moves back and forth across them according to relative concentrations. If water concentration is unusually low in the blood, water will tend to move from the cells out to the blood. Hence changes in extracellular water levels have a direct effect on the water content of cells—including neurons in the brain—and it is more likely that this serves as a direct cue for drinking behavior.

THE BRAIN SYSTEMS
THAT CONTROL DRINKING

The hypothalamus is also critically involved in the control of drinking. The central theories postulate that there are receptors somewhere in the body that monitor blood factors, and there is evidence that these receptors are to be found in the brain. Minute injections of hypertonic saline, high-salt-content water, into the carotid arteries, which lead directly to the brain, result in immediate drinking. Injections elsewhere in the body do not have this effect. This led to the idea that the brain had receptors for monitoring blood salinity—that is, cells responsive to a drop in salt concentrations below the level needed to influence normal cells [Grossman, 1967]. A major step in the development of a hypothalamic theory of thirst came with the work of Andersson [1953]. He carried the carotid injection experiments one step farther and showed that direct application of hypertonic saline to the hypothalamus produces prolonged drinking behavior. In fact he was able to isolate the anterior, or front, portion of the hypothalamus as the area in which the saline was effective; application elsewhere did not have the same effect. Andersson concluded that this area sensed the blood factor which was the physiological correlate of thirst and was thus involved in the behavioral response of drinking—an impressive example of the linking together of physiological, neurological, and behavioral variables to derive an explanation for a motivational phenomenon.

There is another aspect of the anterior hypothalamus that must be mentioned in the context of drinking. Located in this region is the *supraoptic nucleus*, which contains neurosecretory cells that synthesize and release the antidiuretic hormone (ADH). This hormone causes the kidneys to remove less water from the blood for excretion as urine. During conditions of water need ADH secretion is high, and the body conserves water. Moreover, the electrical activity of cells in this area is extremely sensitive to saline injections and they show a physical response to osmotic pressure. Thus this particular brain region contains cells that are responsive to blood factors related to imbalances in body water. Some of these cells organize a physiologically appropriate defense response, the secretion of ADH, while others produce an appropriate behavioral reaction. Additional evidence of hypothalamic involvement in drinking comes from lesion and electrical-stimulation studies. Briefly,

120

it has been shown that lesion of the lateral hypothalamus eliminates drinking. However, we are only beginning to differentiate contributions of the various parts of the hypothalamus to the control of drinking behavior.

There are only scattered reports on the roles of other brain structures in the control of drinking behavior. Not surprisingly, various parts of the limbic system have been shown to be involved, especially the septum. The most consistent model for limbic involvement in drinking comes from chemical-stimulation studies.

THE NEUROCHEMISTRY
OF FEEDING AND DRINKING

It is obvious from our discussions of the neural substrates of feeding and drinking that there is a great overlap between the two systems throughout the limbic system. It is not possible to separate them with standard lesioning and electrical-stimulation techniques because these procedures are relatively nonspecific; they destroy or stimulate everything—axons, dendrites, synapses—at the tip of the electrode. However, since the synaptic transmission involved is a chemical process (see Chapter 1), it was reasoned that if the drinking and feeding circuits used different neurotransmitters, they could be selectively stimulated (or blocked) by drugs directly related to one or the other transmitter substance. To some extent this goal has been realized; it is in fact possible to produce eating or drinking from a particular brain locus by chemical stimulation.

The first successful application of this technique in motivational studies was injection of drugs into the lateral hypothalamus. Injections of norepinephrine caused rats to eat voraciously; injections of carbacol, a synthetic form of acetylcholine, produced prolonged drinking behavior. This is the pattern found throughout the limbic system. The sites at which carbacol produces drinking are more extensive than those at which norepinephrine-induced eating can be obtained, but much of the limbic system—the hypothalamus, septum, amygdala, and hippocampus—are involved in both. Not all regions are involved in the same fashion. The amygdala, for example, appears to modulate feeding and drinking behavior rather than to initiate it directly.

A similar and relatively simple overall picture emerges of feeding and drinking behavior. Deprivation leads to activation of certain neural receptor mechanisms—glucose receptors for hunger and fluid salt content for thirst—which in turn activate specific brain systems, particularly in the hypothalamus. Peripheral factors such as stomach contractions and dryness of mouth may enhance these effects but are not crucial for them. Increased activity in certain hypothalamic and related limbic regions of the brain leads to increased activity level and increased goal-directed activity—the seeking of food and water. Both innate and learned preferences and behavior patterns are important at this point. As the needed substance is ingested the balance of neural activity in the hypothalamus and related brain regions shifts toward a net pattern of satiation, and ingestion ceases.

The control of feeding and thinking, and their underlying motivations of hunger and thirst, are elegant examples of homeostatic systems designed to maintain the organism át a stable normal level of nutrition and water balance. The fact that higher animals seem to derive considerable enjoyment from these activities is both an added benefit and an essential aspect of feeding and drinking behavior.

MOTIVATION: THEORY AND BIOLOGY

Feeding and drinking are particularly easy aspects of motivated behavior to analyze in terms of their underlying mechanisms. These behaviors serve to maintain an optimum state of physiological stability and fit beautifully in the general framework of homeostatic-balance theories of motivation. During the middle of the nineteenth century physiologists became aware that the internal environment of the body exists in a remarkable state of balance. For every action or change there appears to be a response which restores the original equilibrium. The French physiologist Claude Bernard coined the phrase the *internal milieu* for the internal environment of the body and with great foresight suggested that much behavior might represent attempts to maintain the optimal balance for this system. This idea has had great appeal for behavioral scientists because it places behavior on the same continuum with physiological responses; for example, feeding occurs when internal defenses against low blood sugar are no longer adequate.

The value of the balance theories of behavior was apparent in the work of Richter and Cannon. Cannon's classical book *The Wisdom of the Body* [1932] elaborated the notion of homeostasis. According to this theory, the body senses changes from an optimal point for a given physiological process and then initiates physiological and behavioral responses appropriate to restoring the proper level. Building on Bernard's ideas, Cannon provided an explanation of specific physiological and, more important for our purposes, behavioral responses as defenses of internal balance. Thus for Cannon and many who followed him the study of motivation was a search for bodily imbalances and the physiological cues associated with them.

The most extensive behavioral formulation of motivation is the *drive theory*, developed by Clark Hull [1943] and subsequently expanded by Neil Miller [1963] and Judson Brown [1961]. According to this theory, which has its roots in the homeostasis approach, sources of motivation such as deprivation of food or water result in internal states that drive the animal to act. Appropriate actions such as eating and drinking reduce this drive. Since drive reduction is rewarding, the organism learns to respond to the stimulus cues present during reduction of drive. Sources of motivation have a dual function; they generate the

122

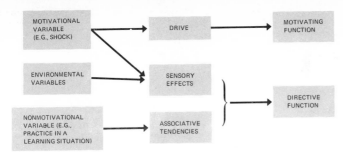

FIGURE 4–8   *Diagram of the hypothetical dual effects of a motivational variable such as food deprivation or painful electric shock. This results in an increased general drive level which is motivating, and also in sensory cues which interact with other stimuli in the environment and with innate and learned factors to produce directed behavior such as obtaining food or avoiding shock. [Brown, 1961]*

drive to act and they provide cues for appropriate action, as schematized in Fig. 4-8. Thus food deprivation leads to an increase in general drive state and also leads to a variety of internal cues which interact with other environmental stimuli and with learned behaviors to lead to food-seeking behavior. Drive itself is *nonspecific*; food deprivation and water deprivation together do not lead to a hunger drive and a thirst drive, but to a greater degree of general drive plus food-seeking and water-seeking behavior.

Drive theory is the most well-developed and consistent theoretical analysis of motivation, but other points of view have played important roles. Late in the nineteenth century William James and Herbert Lange developed an intriguing formulation that motivated states followed the occurrence of particular types of responses. This hypothesis, known since as the *James-Lange theory*, is best illustrated by the example of the man who encounters a bear and runs. A common-sense notion of the sequence of events is that sight of bear elicits the state of fear, which leads directly to the response of flight. The James-Lange model, however, suggests a less obvious sequence: sight of bear leads to the learned response of flight, which in turn results in the innate state of fear. This thesis has certainly not received the intense experimental interest generated by homeostasis and drive theories, but enough experimental data have been produced to suggest that the theory, or a near cousin of it, may contain a significant truth. The experiments by Sheffield are particularly relevant in this regard [Sheffield and Roby, 1950; Sheffield et al., 1951]. Sheffield's theory that rats will work to "induce" a particular central state is nearly a mirror image of the drive-reduction model. One of his more striking demonstrations was that male rats will continue to copulate almost indefinitely even if they are never allowed to ejaculate. It is difficult, though not impossible, to fit these results into a drive-reduction framework, since the behavior is continued despite the fact that it does nothing to reduce the presumed sexually derived drive state. The results are, however, explained by a hypothesis that the animal works to produce a state which, unlike that produced by flight from a bear, is pleasant.

123

The concept of arousal provides a unifying bridge between drive theory and other approaches to motivation. We have already noted that the behavior of a rat toward food is not the same when it is hungry as when it has recently fed, but how would a hungry animal behave if no food was present? Rats in this situation become very active; they explore their environments and become very sensitive to stimulus areas that they might previously have ignored. In short, they become very excited or *aroused*. A similar phenomenon is observed in the female rat in the estrous state, or heat; her activity becomes greatly heightened, and she will pace her cage incessantly. This excitability appears to accompany most, and possibly all, motivational states. It even finds expression in theories of human motivation; for example, in Freud's psychoanalytic theory this nonspecific activation is related to the libido. In short, behavioral arousal may be considered the outward reflection of internal drive state.

In our discussion of drive theory it was emphasized that motivational states may have two aspects, one leading to general drive and the other interacting with environmental cues to result in goal-directed activity. Campbell and Sheffield [1953] demonstrated that the amount of activity exhibited by rats during starvation was directly dependent on richness of the environment in which they were placed. Rats housed in sensory-isolation chambers showed little or no increase in activity during prolonged food deprivation, while those whose cages were located in more normal environments showed great increases in activity. Later experiments have further dissociated the specific motivational effects of need states from their nonspecific arousal changes. For example, it has been shown that destruction of the frontal cortex in rats greatly augments the generalized activity caused by hunger without increasing bar-pressing behavior for food, an indicant often used to measure drive state [Campbell and Lynch, 1969]. Thus we can see that a motivational state is accompanied by two types of behavioral change—an increase in activity and responses to the environment (arousal) and a set of specific responses appropriate to the motivational state.

The greatest theoretical interest in the significance of arousal in motivation has to do with its effect on performance. One view is that behavioral efficiency is dependent on arousal level, which in turn reflects level of motivational state. We explored this view at some length in Chapter 3. The relationship between level of arousal—that is, level of motivational state or drive—is an inverted U (see Fig. 3-4). Up to a point, as motivational level increases, behavioral performance increases. Beyond that point behavior becomes disrupted and the organism shows increasingly severe signs of emotional disturbance. For example, Malmo [1959] measured heart rate as an indicant of arousal level in rats and found that it increased steadily over 72 hours of water deprivation. Bar pressing for water, however, increased only for the first 36 hours and then de-

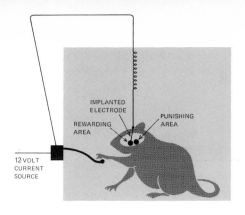

FIGURE 4-9   *Brain self-stimulation. An animal (including man) with an electrode implanted in "rewarding" areas of the brain, such as the lateral hypothalamus, will learn to press a bar in a Skinner box to turn on a mild electric current to that brain area. [after Olds, 1955]*

creased. Various controls established that this decrease was not due to physical weakness. Many other studies have demonstrated similar relationships in various species, including man, and across various types of performance tasks. A motivated, and hence aroused, animal performs better than a nonmotivated one.

We saw in Chapter 3 that one region in the hypothalamus activates or arouses behavior and the cortical EEG and another deactivates both cortical activity and behavior (see Fig. 3-7). Similarly, there is an activating system in the more anterior reticular formation and a deactivating system in the more posterior region. Recent work indicates that other regions of the limbic system, such as the hippocampus and frontal cortex, play critical roles in regulating these arousal effects. Finally, there is considerable evidence that the brain arousal system involves the action of a particular chemical synaptic transmitter substance, norepinephrine. This substance is found in high concentrations in the reticular formation and the limbic structures, and is particularly concentrated in the hypothalamus. Recall from Chapter 1 that drugs which increase brain levels of norepinephrine, such as amphetamines, tend to produce behavioral and EEG arousal.

Lindsley [1951] first suggested that the brain arousal system forms the neural basis of behavioral arousal, and Hebb [1955] proposed the specific hypothesis that the brain arousal system is the neural basis of generalized drive. This approach provides a unifying theme for much of the material we have considered, relating drive theory to the brain arousal system and to the mechanisms involved in such primary motivational behaviors as aggression, feeding, and drinking. The hypothalamus is a critical link. Motivated behavior has two aspects, a generalized drive or arousal component and a goal-directed component. Activation of the hypothalamus can elicit both aspects—arousal and specific activities such as stalking, eating, and drinking. Limbic forebrain structures *modulate* the actions of the hypothalamus (and reticular formation) in arousal and in specific activities such as agonistic behavior and food seeking.

If this general view is correct, then it ought to be possible to intervene directly in the brain motivational system. The discovery of Olds and Milner [1954] that rats will work very hard simply to receive an electrical stimulus to the brain motivational system seems to provide this evidence (see Fig. 4-9). By far the most critical region for self-

125

stimulation is the lateral region of the hypothalamus in the vicinity of the feeding center. Rats will press a lever hundreds of times per minute if they receive a weak electric shock in the lateral hypothalamus by doing so. The other effective brain areas are in the limbic system, particularly the septal area and hippocampus. Interestingly, electrical stimulation of these regions in conscious man has similar effects. Reported sensations include vague but intense feelings of well being and extreme euphoria.

COMPLEX MOTIVES

The monkey looking out at you in Fig. 4-10 has learned to push one of two panels from inside his prison cage for no other reward than to look out. Curiosity and its satisfaction seem almost as basic a motivation as hunger, aggression, and sex in higher animals, particularly primates. Theorists have argued at length about which aspects of motivation are primary and which are secondary. Primary motives are said to be "built in" to the organism without learning, and secondary motives are learned. One view limits primary motivation to tissue needs, such as the need for nutrition, water, and avoidance of tissue damage; all other motivation is held to be learned through associations rewarded by food, water, and avoidance of pain. However, there is considerable evidence that motivated behaviors ranging from activity, manipulation, and curiosity to affection and social behavior are not learned from eating, drinking, and avoidance of pain. In fact many of these more complex motivations have significant aspects that are not learned at all.

MANIPULATION AND CURIOSITY

Rats will learn to press a bar for no other reason than to turn the lights in their cages on or off. Kavanau [1963] showed further that rats will not run in an exercise wheel which is externally powered even if it is turning at a speed they normally select for themselves, but if they can turn the wheel themselves, they run for several hours a day. In both these instances the rats apparently are motivated merely to manipulate their environment. Experiments with primates are more dramatic. In order to prove that monkeys have basic motivation to manipulate or be curious it is necessary to show that they will work for long periods with the manipulatory behavior itself as the only reward, that the motivation to manipulate will produce learning in the same way as food reward, and that no motivation other than curiosity has a significant influence on the animal's behavior. A series of experiments by Butler and Harlow [1954], Harlow and McClearn [1954], and Butler [1954*a*; 1954*b*] have demonstrated all these points.

126

FIGURE 4-10   *A curious monkey peers out of his prison cage to watch the watchers watching him [Harlow, University of Wisconsin].*

FIGURE 4-11   *Monkeys will work on mechanical puzzles for no reward other than to work on the puzzle. This interest is apparent at a very early age. [Harlow, University of Wisconsin]*

The first issue, whether monkeys will manipulate for the sake of manipulation, was demonstrated in monkey puzzle experiments. A mechanical puzzle was devised that had three interlocking objects, a metal pin, a hook-and-eye, and a hasp. The three objects could be taken apart only in one order—by removing the pin, taking the hook out of the eye, and lifting the hasp (see Fig. 4-11). After a few sessions on this problem the monkey's score was nearly perfect. The puzzle was then made more difficult by adding other devices and was arranged to be reset every 6 minutes. Under these conditions the monkey kept on disassembling it for 10 hours. At this point the experiment was terminated because of experimenter fatigue; the monkey was still going strong.

Another set of manipulation experiments was designed to be analogous to ordinary visual discrimination learning, in which one of two different stimuli is rewarded with food when chosen. Here, however, no food was used; the only reward consisted in obtaining the object to play with. Ten screw eyes were mounted on a metal panel. Five were green and could not be removed; the other five were red and could be removed. They were arranged in a random order on the panel. The monkeys soon learned that the red screw eyes could be removed to play with and did not touch the green ones.

In an elegant series of experiments on play and manipulation of objects by chimpanzees Welker [1956] demonstrated that if a chimp is given a choice between a movable and a fixed object, he much prefers the movable object and will play with it for periods up to 30 minutes before losing interest. If series of different objects are given in succes-

127

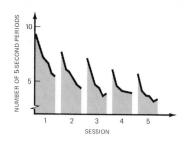

FIGURE 4-12 *Curiosity in chimpanzees as measured by the number of 5-second periods in a daily 6-minute session during which the chimpanzee made some response to a novel set of objects. "Boredom," or habituation, occurs each day (decrease in each curve) and from day to day (each successive curve starts at a lower point.)* [Welker, 1956]

sion, each for a few minutes, the animal will play with each for a decreasing period of time. As indicated in Fig. 4-12, the chimp plays most with the first object in the series and shows increasing boredom, both for each object and across objects. These results are particularly clear examples of habituation of curiosity behavior, both in response to each object and in response to the series. This phenomenon is familiar in young children with new toys. Whether the toy costs 10 cents or 10 dollars, the child will play with it happily for a short time and then lose interest.

The monkey peering out of **Fig. 4-10** is an example of curiosity motivation. The animal learned to push the correct panel inside the cage for no other reward than being able to look out. Butler originally discovered this phenomenon by accident. He was testing a monkey on a food-reward learning problem and wanted to observe the monkey without being seen. Normally the monkey and experimenter are separated by a screen and cannot see one another. Butler drilled a small peephole through the screen to watch the monkey. Unfortunately the monkey soon found the hole and spent all his time peeking out at Butler. He then tried observing the monkey through a mirror, but the monkey outsmarted him again and kept an eye on him in the mirror.

These frustrating experiences led Butler and Harlow to the significant discovery that monkeys are strongly motivated to explore the world visually. In a typical experiment on visual curiosity animals are first familiarized with the box and are given an opportunity to peek out the open door. Then the doors of the box are closed; one door, identified with a yellow card on the inside, is locked, and the other, identified with a blue card on the inside, is left unlocked. If the monkey pushes against the blue card, the door will open for 30 seconds to allow the monkey to look out. In one experiment animals were tested 45 minutes per day for 57 days. Their curiosity was so persistent that they never tired of opening the door to look out.

These experiments indicate that motivation to manipulate and explore the world visually is fundamental and primary in monkeys and man. Under ordinary laboratory conditions visual curiosity is a much stronger motivation than food reward. In tests of visual curiosity where the door was closed each time 30 seconds after the monkeys had opened it, the animals worked continuously for up to 19 hours, far longer than they would work for a food reward.

128

The development of the infant's love and affection for his mother is considered by many psychologists to provide the initial foundation for more complex social motives. This early attachment can form the basis for the subsequent development of interpersonal relationships with other people. Love and affection were investigated extensively by Harlow (1959) and he showed that the strong bond of affection the infant monkey develops for his cloth surrogate mother has nothing whatever to do with where he obtains his food. When the infants had two surrogate mothers, a nonnursing terrycloth mother and a nursing wire mother, their only source of food was the wire mother. According to the more extreme version of drive-reduction theory, the infants should have become attached to the wire mother; affection should have developed as a secondary or derived motive through hunger reduction associated with the wire mother. Freudian theory would also predict development of affection for the wire mother, on the basis of oral gratification associated with feeding. The results were quite different; the infant monkeys became attached to the cloth mother.

Another significant fact is that the infant monkey's attachment for his cloth mother develops only during the critical period of the first 30 to 90 days. Furthermore, if the infant does not form such an attachment, his later social behavior is markedly retarded and incompetent. These observations support the general view that social motivation is basic and innate and develops from an early critical experience of an affectional relationship.

COMPLEX HUMAN MOTIVATION

Let us consider a young man just entering college—full of bright hopes and great expectations. Why has he decided to spend four years of his life reading books, writing papers, and listening to lectures when he could get a job, get married, and provide for all of his physiological motives? Going to college cannot be explained on the basis of hunger, thirst, or even sex.

It is possible of course, that the student is motivated by an intrinsic curiosity motive—an unquenchable thirst for knowledge. This may be true for some, but most students have had this intrinsic motivation inhibited by years of dreary schooling or the general cultural antagonism to intellectual pursuits. Therefore, intrinsic curiosity cannot explain the intense, sometimes desperate, desire to go to college [Murray, 1964, pp. 83–84].

The reasons that we as moderately adult human beings behave as we do are obviously complex. A complete discussion of human motivation would be tantamount to a complete discussion of human behavior. Much that we have learned about the basic factors in human motivation comes from controlled laboratory experiments on infrahuman animals.

129

Everything we have said about primary motivation and its neurological foundations is approximately true for man. The human hypothalamus is not much different from the hypothalamus of the rat or cat. Hunger, thirst, aggression, sex, curiosity, and affection are powerful motives in rat, monkey, and man.

There are other potent aspects of human motivation that we may not be aware of in ourselves—*unconscious motivation*. A simple example is provided by the sexual symbolism in stories written by college students. Clark [1952] had groups of male students write stories as they viewed neutral pictures after having been shown pictures of attractive nude females. One group of students was tested in a classroom and another group was tested at a fraternity beer party. The stories written at the beer party, although they may have been somewhat less coherent, had more examples of overt sexual imagery than the classroom stories. However, imagery that the experimenters judged to be indirect or symbolic expression of sexual fantasies was more prevalent in the stories by the classroom group.

Basic biological factors can go a long way toward explaining certain aspects of human behavior. However, they fall short of providing an adequate account of normal human motivation, particularly in our affluent Western society. Hunger, thirst, aggression, curiosity, and probably even sex are not the dominant motives in our own ordinary daily life. Achievement of success in school or work, recognition and approval from peers, popularity, these are some of our more common motives and are *social*; they derive in part from our relations with other people.

A representative approach to the study of complex human social motivation is McClelland's work in achievement motivation. He uses the Thematic Apperception Test (TAT), a type of projective test in which the subject views neutral pictures of scenes involving people and writes stories about them. The stories are then scored by several raters in terms of the strength of the subject's desire to achieve success. Although this is a somewhat difficult procedure, good agreement among raters is usually obtained. The following is an example of a strong achievement story [Smith and Feld, 1958, p. 717]:

This young boy [in the picture] is dreaming of the day he will have completed his training and become a great and famous doctor. Perhaps this portrays someone already famous for research. He has been asked by his father or relative what he wants to do when he grows up and he is trying to tell them the mental picture that he has in his mind of himself in thirty years. The boy is thinking of the great thrill that must be experienced by a doctor when he performs a delicate operation saving someone's life. The boy will go on through college and eventually become a world-famous doctor.

McClelland et al. [1953] have studied the ways in which an individual's desire to achieve success affects speed of learning, performance efficiency, situational stress, and task complexity. The extent to which high and low achievers differ in these situations is truly remarkable; high achievers are substantially better. To no one's surprise, it turns out that high achievers are ambitious, hard-working, and work toward personal standards of excellence rather than extrinsic rewards. Developmental studies have shown that the difference between high and low achievers in some part reflects parental attitudes, particularly maternal attitudes. Low achievers tended to come from homes where the parents insisted on dependence on the family, while those with high achievement motivation had backgrounds which encourage independence [Murray, 1964].

In addition to eating, reproducing, exploring, and socializing, we also think. In view of the fact that we spend much of our waking and sleeping time in thinking activity of one kind or another, it would be surprising if thought processes themselves did not provide a source of motivation. This cognitive approach to human motivation has been developed by Festinger [1957], with particular reference to the effects of contradictory thoughts or ideas. According to Festinger's theory of *cognitive dissonance*, if a person has two or more aspects of information or opinion that are inconsistent or mutually contradictory, a state of dissonance occurs which is uncomfortable and motivates an attempt to resolve it. Festinger's view is related to the old idea that people have logic-tight compartments, such as simultaneous beliefs in God and in science, but it goes one step farther and assumes that people do not *like* to have logic-tight compartments, a somewhat optimistic view of human nature.

Festinger cites cigarette smoking as an example [1957, p. 2] :

> ... the person who continues to smoke, knowing that it is bad for his health, may also feel (*a*) he enjoys smoking so much it is worth it; (*b*) the chances of his health suffering are not as serious as some would make out; (*c*) he can't always avoid every possible dangerous contingency and still live; and (*d*) perhaps even if he stopped smoking he would put on weight which is equally bad for his health. So, continuing to smoke is, after all, consistent with his ideas about smoking.

The data shown in Fig. 4-13 provide support; the more heavily a person smokes, the less convinced he is that smoking is linked to lung cancer.

Festinger et al. have attempted to isolate and define the various techniques people use to reduce dissonance. One of the most common is a *selective* search for information. The person seeks out material which supports one idea and ignores information that supports dissonant ideas. Our cigarette smoker might spend a great deal of time watch-

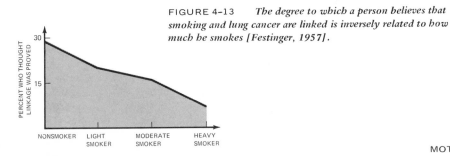

FIGURE 4-13   *The degree to which a person believes that smoking and lung cancer are linked is inversely related to how much he smokes [Festinger, 1957].*

ing television ads for cigarettes but avoid reading newspaper articles about lung cancer. In another commonly cited experiment purchasers of new cars were shown a series of ads for various makes of cars. The most commonly read ads were for the car the subject had just bought, while ads for competing models were relatively ignored.

Dissonance theory has obvious parallels with the drive-reduction theory of motivation we discussed earlier. Absence of cognitive dissonance is equivalent to maintenance of internal balance, cognitive dissonance serves the same purpose as drive, and reduction of dissonance is comparable to drive reduction. The dissonant person who learns to reduce dissonance through rationalization is like the hungry rat who learns to press a bar for food.

Our discussion of motivation has ranged from the brain mechanisms of hunger, thirst and aggression, through manipulation, curiosity, and the development of affection, to complex social and cognitive motives. Arousal was introduced as a behavioral and biological concept that can serve to unify various approaches to motivation, particularly for basic states that reflect innate tissue needs. What about the more complex aspects of motivation? Curiosity and manipulation, at least, have obvious parallels. Hunger provides tissue-need cues to the hypothalamus. The eyes, ears, and hands could provide analogous need cues to the central nervous system regarding exploration and manipulation. All these inputs can serve to modulate and regulate behavioral and neural arousal toward an optimal level. Social and cognitive factors can similarly influence arousal.

The distinction between primary and secondary sources of motivation may be more apparent than real. A case could be made that all major sources of motivated behavior are primary. Man is a social animal; he is one of a number of social species. Hence the ultimate source of his need for social approval may be found in the genes, just as is the tissue need for food. Perhaps what is learned is the behavioral expression of these needs. We need food, and even certain types of food, but we learn to like particular flavors. We need social interaction, and even certain types of it, but we learn to prefer particular forms of social interactions and activities.

SUMMARY

One important aspect of motivation that is observable in all species is aggressive, or agonistic, behavior, which takes the three general forms flight, defense, and attack. Intraspecies fighting is usually a pattern of threat and submission and rarely results in death. This is in contrast to interspecies fighting, as between predator and prey. In many species agonistic behavior is triggered by specific stimulus cues, such as color or shape. Fighting is further influenced, at least among rodents, by environmental factors, such as amount of living space available, amount of food, or presence of females. Genetic variables and the *history* of previous successes in fighting also play a role. Agonistic behavior appears to be controlled by the hypothalamus and the amygdala, which are critical in the appearance of rage and attack, and the septal area, which seems to suppress rage.

Hunger and thirst have been studied in terms of the behaviors that precede eating and drinking, the actual consumatory responses, the brain systems that control eating and drinking, and the long-term consequences to the internal environment. Peripheral effects of food or water deprivation, such as stomach contractions or dryness of the mouth and throat, are not sufficient to explain hunger and thirst. Actually, food deprivation leads to activation of hypothalamic glucose receptors and water deprivation to activation of hypothalamic osmoreceptors, which produce an increase in general activity or arousal, plus an increase in appropriate goal-directed behavior. Ingestion causes a cessation of neural activity, and hence cessation of the behavioral response, so that homeostatic balance is maintained.

The drive theory of motivation postulates that sources of motivation generate a drive to act and provide the cues for appropriate behavior. Drive reduction is presumed to be rewarding, and behavior which reduces drive is therefore learned. Another theory of motivation, the *James-Lange* formulation, proposes that motivated states *follow* the occurrence of particular behavioral responses rather than *precede* them. Both theoretical approaches have proved useful in the analysis of motivated behavior. Other types of motivation, such as manipulative needs and curiosity, do not appear to fit well into current theoretical frameworks.

There are also more complex aspects of motivation, particularly in primates, which biological analyses do not yet explain. The early infant-mother attachment may be the basis of later social motives for achievement, approval, etc. Formulations such as Festinger's theory of cognitive dissonance may be a first step toward understanding the substrates of complex motivation.

CHAPTER FIVE

NATURE AND NURTURE

For thousands of years man has had a general understanding of heredity. It takes no great insight to see that dogs give birth to dogs and cats give birth to cats. Nor is it difficult to see that the offspring of big dogs tend to be big, while the offspring of little dogs tend to be little. At a very general level the facts of heredity are obvious: like begets like. Our ancestors utilized these obvious facts to develop breeds of cattle, sheep, dogs, and cats long before there was any understanding of the underlying genetic principles. As early as the sixth century B.C. the Greek scholar Theognis noted that while great care was exercised in selecting rams, sheep, and horses for breeding, men and women readily marry an unworthy partner simply for money.

It is important to note that by selecting animals for breeding our ancestors were able to influence their behavior as well as physical characteristics. The domestication of dogs, for example, required the selection of behavioral tendencies such as docility and the reduction of tendencies such as aggressiveness and excessive fear of man. A dog is not just a tame wolf. The dog has been domesticated through countless generations of

HEREDITY

selective breeding. Clearly, heredity influences behavior as well as physical structure. This is true for man as well as the other animals. Although we may not all have an explicit understanding of the exact nature of hereditary influences, we all have some general understanding that behavior is influenced by heredity. Intelligent parents expect to have intelligent children. Musicians expect to have musically talented children. Whenever a child is not a "chip off the old block," it is because of "something that came from *your* side of the family." However, expectations based on common-sense knowledge of heredity are not always fulfilled. Bright parents often have dull-witted children, and musically talented parents can have tone-deaf offspring.

The question of how heredity influences behavior is admittedly rather baffling on first consideration. Behavior seems to be so insubstantial. How can a pattern of thought or a personality trait be subject to the same forces of inheritance as those that influence body height or shape of the nose? The first scientific investigation of the hereditary basis of behavior was undertaken in the nineteenth century. It was not until this time that the sciences of biology and psychology had developed sufficiently to support systematic studies in this area.

135

EARLY FAMILY STUDIES

Studies of genetic influences on human behavior grew out of observations of family resemblances in behavior. Early thinking on the matter was necessarily based on folklore and anecdote. Particular cases of "like father, like son" were obvious. It was widely accepted that behavioral as well as physical characteristics tended to "run in families." Some families had many smart members. Others had had problems with alcohol for generations. Some families were blessed with good singers and others with strong backs. Less fortunate families were burdened with "queerness."

GALTON'S STUDY OF EMINENCE   The first systematic attempt to study family resemblances in psychological characteristics was conducted in 1865 by Francis Galton, who was a cousin of Charles Darwin. Since "greatness" obviously ran in his own family, Galton wanted to know whether this was generally true for other families. To investigate this problem he studied the relatives of selected men renowned for their accomplishments in a variety of fields, including science, law, literature, military service, politics, and the ministry. When Galton tabulated the number of eminent relatives of these selected men and arranged them according to distance of relationship, two facts became apparent. First, the number of eminent people in these families vastly exceeded the number to be expected on the basis of pure chance—that is, if everyone in the population were equally likely, or more accurately, equally *unlikely*, to become eminent. In short, eminence definitely did run in families. Second, those relatives closest to the most renowned member of the family (brothers, sons, fathers) were more likely to be eminent than were the more distant relatives such as cousins and uncles. The greater the proportion of genetic material shared with an eminent man, the greater the chances for eminence. Thus the evidence, viewed in this way, indicated that eminence is biologically based.

It is obvious, of course, that environmental influences are also involved. Close relatives share similar environmental influences as well as heredity. The privileged relatives of illustrious people have many educational and social advantages not available to relatives of the less illustrious. Such benefits might well be the critical factors in the development of eminence. Galton noted, however, that men had sometimes risen from low social rank to high positions. Moreover, although education was universally available in the United States, the proportion of eminent scholars was no greater than in Great Britain, where education was at that time a function of social class. Consequently Galton concluded that social advantage did not explain eminence. Subsequent studies by others attempted to show that musical talent was an inherited trait in the Bach family, and that such traits as obstinacy and love of scholastic pursuits were transmitted through heredity in the royal families of Great Britain. However, these studies did not resolve the problem of distinguishing the contributions of heredity from those of privilege.

The next important family studies dealt with the opposite side of the coin—immorality, criminality, and pauperism. These studies were so dramatic and became so widely known that the fictitious names of the families, the Jukes and Kallikaks, have come to represent the essence of dereliction and vice. The Jukes were a New York family who in a period of 130 years had contributed slightly more than 2000 citizens to the state. Over half the members of the Jukes family were committed to state institutions, either for feeble-mindedness or because of conviction for various criminal acts. The advocates of the view that behavior is influenced by "nature" interpreted this sordid family history to be proof of a "morbid inheritance." The patrons of "nurture" maintained that the high incidence of these undesirable characteristics in the family demonstrated the unwholesome effects of the miserable environmental circumstances in which the family had found itself. The study of the Jukes posed a problem but failed to solve it.

The Kallikak family had two branches. One was allegedly begun by a young Revolutionary War soldier, Martin Kallikak, who had an affair with a tavern girl who was reportedly feeble-minded. The members of this branch of the family were much like those of the Jukes family. They excelled only in dereliction and stupidity. After his return from military service Martin Kallikak married a girl from a "good family." The second branch of the Kallikak family, which resulted from this legal union, comprised people of good reputation and solid accomplishment.

These early family studies had a number of shortcomings. Of particular importance is that the standards of evidence were lower than we would require today. Galton based his judgment of eminence on biographical accounts and similar sources which are subject to bias in reporting. The paternity of the tavern girl's son was attributed to Martin Kallikak solely on the basis of the girl's testimony. Furthermore, the girl's condition of mental retardation was diagnosed after the fact on the basis of hearsay evidence. The evaluation of Kallikak family members, living or dead, was based largely on interviews by a field worker. The reports make lively reading, as can be seen in the following example [Goddard, 1914, pp. 28–29]:

> The field worker accosts an old farmer—"Do you remember an old man, Martin Kallikak (Jr.), who lived on the mountain-edge yonder?" "Do I? Well, I guess! Nobody'd forget him. Simple, not quite right here (tapping his head) but inoffensive and kind. All the family was that. Old Moll, simple as she was, would do anything for a neighbor. She finally died—burned to death in the chimney corner. She had come in drunk and sat down there. Whether she fell over in a fit or her clothes caught fire, nobody knows. She was burned to a crisp when they found her. That was the worst of them, they would drink. Poverty was their best friend in this respect, or they would have been drunk all the time. Old Martin could never stop as long as he had a drop. Many's the time he's rolled

off of Billy Parson's porch. Billy always had a barrel of cider handy. He'd just chuckle to see old Martin drink and drink until finally he'd lose his balance and over he'd go!"

However interesting they may be, such reports are of very limited scientific value. The findings do not lend themselves well to quantification or objective replication, and so there is no way to be certain that the reports are reliable. The fundamental weakness of the family approach to the study of hereditary influences on behavior is that the influences of heredity cannot be disentangled from environmental influences. Although the Kallikak family was considered by some as a neatly balanced natural experiment, since the two branches derived from a single male ancestor and two very different female ancestors, it was subjected to the same important criticism we have noted in the case of the Jukes—the families differed in environmental circumstances as well as in hereditary background.

Although the Jukes and Kallikak family studies must be judged deficient by current standards, it is well to keep in mind the context in which this work was done. At the time of Galton's study and the early investigations of the Jukes family the basic facts of genetics were not yet known. Moreover, there were no standardized objective tests for measuring behavioral characteristics. When the Kallikak study was under way the first discoveries of modern genetics had been published, but their implications and generality were not understood, and at this time only the very earliest, primitive devices for assessing intelligence had been developed. These classic studies must now be regarded as providing very little information of value to modern behavioral genetics. However, they played an important role in stimulating debate, in motivating further research, and in providing the background for contemporary research on the problem of hereditary influences on behavior.

TWIN STUDIES

One of the most widely used methods in studies of hereditary influences on behavior is the *twin study*. This method was introduced by Galton 20 years after his study on the inheritance of eminence. Since that time it has been modified and refined, and it is now an important approach to the problem of inheritance of behavior in human beings. The method is based on the fact that identical (monozygotic) twins develop from a single fertilized egg and thus are *exactly alike* in hereditary endowment, whereas fraternal (dizygotic) twins develop from separate eggs and are no more alike in heredity than are ordinary siblings. In both cases twins share the same basic enrivonment. They share a uterus in prenatal development, they are the same age at the same time in their families (unlike ordinary single-born siblings), and they tend to be treated alike by parents, teachers, and other children.

Thus the two kinds of twins appear to provide a naturally occurring simple experiment. One influence (genetic similarity) varies, while the effects of others (environmental influences) are held fairly constant.

Of course the situation is not quite this simple. For example, it is possible that individuals who are identical twins may be treated more alike than individuals who are fraternal twins. If this is so, then it becomes difficult to tell whether the differences between fraternal twins, in comparison with the differences between identical twins, are caused by heredity or environment. When both factors vary, the results cannot be easily interpreted. Although this is an interesting problem, it is not a serious one. Many studies of twins have provided results which are quite clear cut.

HERITABLE TRAITS

PHYSICAL CHARACTERISTICS   The basic twin method is illustrated by a study of body height [Newman et al., 1937] of 50 pairs of identical twins and 52 pairs of fraternal twins. The standing height was measured. The individuals of each identical-twin pair were not exactly alike in height; on the average, the members of a pair differed by 1.7 centimeters. This difference cannot be hereditary in origin, since the members of an identical-twin pair have identical heredity. The only possible source is environment. Although twins do receive very similar treatment, their environments cannot be exactly equivalent. There is evidence, for example, that different positions in the uterus can have detectable effects on body size. Differences in eating habits, diseases, or accidents suffered can also contribute to size difference.

Fraternal twins are, of course, subject to the same kinds of environmental forces, in addition to the fact that they differ from each other in heredity. Although they have the same parents, each received a different sample of hereditary material from their parents. If heredity also influences body height, we would expect the average height difference of fraternal-twin pairs to be larger than 1.7 centimeters. In fact it is over twice as large—4.4 centimeters. Thus it is clear that heredity does play a role in body size. We might further enquire if the relative similarity of environments of a pair of fraternal twins makes them more alike than ordinary siblings, who are comparable in hereditary similarity but somewhat different in environmental circumstances. The average intrapair difference for ordinary siblings, measured at the same age, is 4.5 centimeters—almost exactly that found with fraternal twins. Thus the differences between the environments of ordinary siblings and the environments of fraternal twins do not seem to be important in influencing body height.

INTELLIGENCE   The twin-study method shows that the same principles hold for intelligence as for physical characteristics such as height. The twins just described were also given the Stanford-Binet IQ test; the results of this assessment are shown along with those for height in

139

Table 5-1. Because different scales are employed, the greater intrapair difference for IQ is not significant (for example, if height were expressed in millimeters rather than centimeters, the height difference would have been 17 rather than 1.7). The IQ test is not a perfectly reliable test; a difference of about six IQ points is to be expected if a single individual is given the test twice. However, the average difference in IQ of identical-twin pairs is 5.9; in other words, identical twins are as much like each other in IQ as a person is like himself. For fraternal twins the average difference in IQ is 9.9. This difference is almost twice as great as that of identical twins, but it is about the same as the difference in siblings.

Since the results for IQ are very similar to those for height, we might conclude, at least provisionally, that IQ is as subject to hereditary influence as is body height. However, detailed studies of mental functioning indicate that some aspects of intelligence are more influenced by heredity than are others. For example, in one study traits labeled "verbal reasoning," "clerical speed and accuracy," and "language use" all showed evidence of substantial hereditary determination, whereas "numerical ability," "abstract reasoning," and "mechanical reasoning" showed little or no hereditary component [Vandenberg, 1968a]. These results clearly illustrate the important fact that some characteristics are more heritable than others. This is true, of course, for physical traits as well; body weight, for example, is somewhat more influenced by environment than is body height.

PERSONALITY TRAITS   Twin studies show that different aspects of personality are also differentially subject to hereditary influences. The evidence from twin studies of personality suggests that traits referred to as "active," "vigorous," "impulsive," and "sociable" are heritable, whereas "dominant," "stable," and "reflective" are not, or at least are much less so [Vandenberg, 1967]. Similarly, the different types of neuroses seem to be subject to different degrees of hereditary influence. One study indicates that neuroses characterized by anxiety, depression, obsession and schizoid withdrawal have substantial hereditary bases, but that those with features of hypochondriasis and hysteria are mostly environmental in origin [Gottesman, 1962].

Perhaps the most dramatic findings of twin studies concern psychoses, particularly schizophrenia. There is a strong indication that heredity plays a role in this disorder. The procedure is as follows: schizophrenic individuals who are twins are identified, and then the other member of each twin pair is studied to see if he or she is also schizophrenic. If the other twin is also affected the pair is termed *concordant*; if only the one twin is affected the pair is termed *discordant*. The results shown in Table 5-2 are typical. The higher incidence of concordance in identical twins indicates that heredity is an important variable in the development of schizophrenia. However, the fact that the concordance in identical twins is only 42 percent, and not 100 percent, shows that heredity is not the only factor involved. There is plenty of room for influences other than heredity.

	HEIGHT	IQ
Identical twins	1.7	5.9
Fraternal twins	4.4	9.9
Ordinary siblings	4.5	9.8

TABLE 5-1 *Average intrapair differences for height (in centimeters) and intelligence (IQ).*

	TWIN PAIRS INVESTIGATED	CONCORDANCE, PERCENT
Identical twins	28	42
Fraternal twins	34	9

TABLE 5-2 *Concordance for schizophrenia in identical and fraternal twins [Gottesman and Shields, 1966].*

STUDIES OF TWINS REARED APART

Sometimes for various reasons, twins are separated and reared in different homes. Studies of identical twins reared apart provide another way of examining environmental influences on intelligence. Since they have identical heredity, any differences must be due to the effects of the different environments. The first major investigation of twins reared apart concerned 19 pairs of identical twins who had been separated and reared in different homes [Newman et al., 1937]. In some cases the twins did not even know of each other's existence until the study was performed. The average intrapair difference in height found in twins reared apart was 1.8 centimeters, almost exactly the same as that found with identical twins reared together (see Table 5-1). The average difference in IQ was 8.2 points. This finding suggests that environment influences IQ score, since a difference of only 5.9 points was found for identical twins reared together. The effect is rather small, however—only slightly greater than two IQ points.

More recently the same problem has been examined in greater detail. The results were reported in terms of an index of similarity called a *correlation coefficient*. The magnitude of this index ranges from .00 to 1.00. A correlation of .00 would mean that identical twin pairs are no more similar than are pairs of people picked at random from the population. A *perfect correlation* of 1.00 would mean that each identical twin had exactly the same score as his twin. For our present purposes we wish to know only whether the correlation for identical twins reared apart is lower than the correlation for identical twins reared together.

Results from several investigations are given in Table 5-3. The evidence is not entirely consistent. One study shows no effect whatsoever of separate rearing, but the other two show some lessened similarity in IQ for twins reared in different homes. However, the high correlation in IQ is still remarkable. Even with varied home and school

			STANFORD
	BINET*	SPECIAL*	BINET*
Identical twins reared together	.88	.76	.92
Identical twins reared apart	.77	.77	.86

TABLE 5-3   *Correlations of intelligence measures of identical twins reared together or apart.*

*Newman et al., 1937; Shields, 1962; Burt, 1966

	FATHER	MOTHER
Foster children	.07	.19
Biological children	.45	.46

TABLE 5-4   *Correlation between IQ of children and their parents.*

circumstances, the twins were highly similar in IQ score. Of course, there is no guarantee that the environments provided by the different homes were particularly different. If they were similar, then there is no reason to expect a different influence on IQ. The environment provided by one middle-class home is not *necessarily* much different from that of another home.

STUDIES OF ADOPTED CHILDREN

The question of the hereditary contribution to the observation "like father, like son" can be examined by studying adopted children. Are they similar to their real parents or to their adoptive parents? It is assumed that a resemblance in IQ found between an adopted child and his adoptive parents results from environmental sources, while a resemblance of an adopted child to its real parents indicates a hereditary influence on intelligence. This assumption is not completely warranted if the adoption agencies attempt to place children on the basis of a similarity of IQ between the child and the adoptive parents. In general the findings of several studies indicate that children resemble their biological parents much more closely than adopted children resemble their adoptive parents. The findings of one representative study are shown in Table 5-4. The resemblance of children to their adoptive parents in IQ is positive but small; the resemblance of children to their biological parents in IQ is substantial.

Comparable results were obtained in a recent study of schizophrenia [Heston, 1966]. Forty-seven children who were born to schizophrenic mothers but adopted within three days of birth were compared to control subjects who were also adopted early in life but were born to nonschizophrenic mothers. Early adoption is important, of course, because if the child had lived with its mother for an extended period, it might be argued that the mother's treatment of the child influenced its later susceptibility to schizophrenia. Five of the 47 children born to schizophrenic mothers subsequently became schizophrenic in later life. In addition to the outright cases of schizophrenia, there was also a significant excess of psychosocial disability of various kinds in about half of the children of schizophrenic mothers. There were no cases of schizophrenia in the control subjects.

Overall the findings of studies of family resemblance provide rather compelling evidence that behavior is influenced by heredity. They also show that family resemblances are to some degree based on environmental influences. Obviously nature and nurture interact in complex ways to produce behavior, and the evidence from these studies is quite general. The findings indicate little about the *nature* of the hereditary influences on behavior, but a discussion of the genetic factors which underlie these influences will shed some light on the reason that like can beget "unlike" as well as "like."

THE GENETIC BASES OF HEREDITY

So far we have presented the problem of hereditary bases of behavior in very broad terms: the general arguments can be comprehended without any detailed knowledge of genetics. In order to proceed, however, we must now briefly examine the nature and function of the genetic material which underlies physical characteristics and behavior. Modern genetics began with the work of Gregor Mendel, a monk in Brunn, Moravia (now Czechoslovakia), in 1865. Prior to Mendel's discoveries there was, of course, considerable information about the resemblance of offspring to parents. For centuries breeds of cattle, dogs, and other domestic animals had been developed with no knowledge of the genetic bases of differences among animals. However, there was no explanation of the diverse and seemingly contradictory observed facts of inheritance. The general assumption was that the hereditary materials of the mother and father were blended in the offspring. Mendel's central discovery was that the hereditary substance is composed of individual elements which exist in alternate forms. Furthermore, they do not blend with each other. We refer to these individual elements as *genes* and to their alternate forms as *alleles*. Genes are located on structures called *chromosomes*, which are found in every cell of the body. An understanding of the biochemical nature of genes is one of the most exciting achievements of modern biology. Although the details are beyond our present scope, in essence a gene can be considered as the unit of heredity. It was at this level of analysis that Mendel contributed to an understanding of the way that individual genes provide the basis for heredity.

The distinction between an individual's genetic composition, or *genotype*, and the observed trait, or *phenotype*, was perhaps Mendel's most ingenious insight. To illustrate, let us represent some particular gene by a circle, where a blue circle distinguishes the *dominant* allelic stage from the alternate *recessive state*. An individual receives one allele

143

from each parent, so that the following genotypes (pairs of alleles) can occur:

●● ●● ●●

Individuals with the pairs ●● or ●◖, where the alleles are alike, are called *homozygotes*; those with the arrangement ●● are called *hetero-zygotes*. The phenotypic value of a heterozygote does not necessarily lie halfway between the phenotypic values of the two homozygotes. In some genes partial or incomplete dominance results in a phenotypic value which is closer to that of one of the homozygotes than the other. In cases of complete dominance, however, the phenotypic value, or appearance, may be exactly the same as that of one of the homozygotes, even though the genetic makeup is not the same. Thus the *appearance* of some trait in an individual gives only an indirect indication of his genetic makeup. The genotype itself can be determined only by appropriate genetic studies.

BEHAVIORAL PHENOTYPES

There are numerous cases of single genes which affect behavioral phe-notypes. A dramatic example is the condition known as phenylketonuria. The normal allele is dominant. Thus individuals who are homozygous for the *dominant* allele, ● ●, are normal. Heterozygotes are also be-haviorally normal, since the normal allele dominates. However, reces-sive homozygotes, ● ●, suffer from severe mental deficit unless this condition is offset by special dietary treatment. A more frequent and less serious condition, red-green color blindness, is also determined by a single gene. Because it is located on the X chromosome it is trans-mitted in a pattern known as sex linkage. One consequence of this mode of transmission is that although females can pass this condition on to their offspring, it actually *occurs* only in males. Some other examples have been found in research with animals. A number of neurological dis-orders in mice have been shown to be due to single genes. One single gene that affects skin pigmentation in mice also influences learning ability, emotionality, and activity level.

Single-gene determination of a phenotype is a restricted case in genetics. Many, if not most, of the traits with which the behavioral geneticist is concerned are influenced by many genes, not just one. For example, a number of years ago it was observed that bees in some colonies are able to control disease by uncapping the cells of diseased larvae and removing the larvae from the hive. It was later found that this highly adaptive behavior is markedly influenced by just two genes. Note that two responses, each of which is quite complex, are required; un-capping of the cells and removal of the larvae. We may depict this situ-ation as follows. Uncapping behavior is carried out by bees that are homozygous for the recessive allele ●; removing is done by bees homo-

144

zygous for the recessive allele ■. Thus bees of the genotype ● ● ■ ■ display a complete sequence of hygienic behavior. Bees that have at least one dominant allele of each gene, ● ● ■ ■, are completely nonhygienic in behavior. Bees of genotype ● ● ■ ■ will uncap the cells but will leave the diseased larvae in place. ● ● ■ ■ bees will do nothing in the absence of assistance; however, if the experimenter does the uncapping for them, they will remove the larvae efficiently [Rothenbuhler, 1964]. Each component of hygienic behavior is discretely recognizable and can be categorized as being either present or not present. In this situation two separate behavioral units, each controlled by separate genes, must be performed in sequence to accomplish a particular end result. This research provides evidence of genetically based division of labor in social animals.

POLYGENIC INHERITANCE

Most behavior is not reducible to such neat all-or-none subdivisions, but is describable only in quantitative terms; that is, it occurs in a greater or lesser *degree*. Inheritance in such circumstances can be understood in terms of a *polygenic* system, in which each of a number of genes makes a small contribution to the level of expression of the behavior. Several important aspects of polygenic inheritance can be illustrated by means of a three-gene model. For example, a person who is a heterozygote for all three genes might be depicted as

●● ■■ ▲▲

When this individual generates *gametes*, or sex cells, half will receive an ● allele and half an ● allele. Alleles are not influenced in any way by association with other alleles, and in contrast to the old "blending" notions of heredity, the ● allele in the gamete of an ● ● individual is in no way different from the ● allele in the gamete of an ● ● individual.

 With some restrictions in the case of genes on the same chromosomes, the chances of one gene are completely independent of the chances of other genes in the gamete. For example, of the gametes with ● (instead of ●), half will get a ■ and half a ■, half will get a ▲ and half a ▲, and so on. Thus if our hypothetical triple heterozygote is a male, he can provide eight kinds of sperm with respect to these three genes:

●■▲ ●■▲ ●■▲ ●■▲ ●■▲ ●■▲ ●■▲ ●■▲

If such a male were to mate with a female of the same genotype, who could, of course, generate eggs with the same eight gene arrangements, the situation would be as depicted in Fig. 5-1. Each of these 64 possible genotypes would be equally likely in each offspring from this union. Moreover, only eight of these 64 possibilities are the same as the genotypes of either parent. It is evident that the system by which genes are reshuffled in gamete formation is a powerful mechanism for generating variability.

145

Suppose the mode of gene action were such that a blue allele of any gene added 1 to the phenotypic value; then the phenotypic scores of all the genotypes derivable from this mating would be distributed as in Fig. 5-2. The parents, of course, would each have a phenotypic value of 3. It is obvious that as the number of genes determining a trait increases, the number of possible genotypes rapidly becomes enormous. One important principle emerges from this example. Aside from the obvious influences of environment, there is a regular and systematic biological system for creating individuality in all living organisms. Even if all environmental factors were completely uniform, there would still be a genetic basis for individuality in behavior. Some appreciation for the nearly boundless capacity to generate variability can be gained by noting that each human individual (except, of course, identical twins and other identical multiple births) is a genetically unique creature. For all practical purposes, we can say that no other individual with precisely the same overall genotype has ever lived or will ever live. Of course the genotype of any individual may differ only slightly from a large number of other individuals.

Another extremely important point that can be taken from Fig. 5-2 is that in a polygenic system there are many genotypic ways to arrive at a given phenotypic end result. For instance, there are six genotypes in our model that give phenotypic values of 4. What this means is that different people may achieve the same outcome for quite different genetic reasons.

FIGURE 5-1   *Possible genotypes of offspring of two triple heterozygotes.*

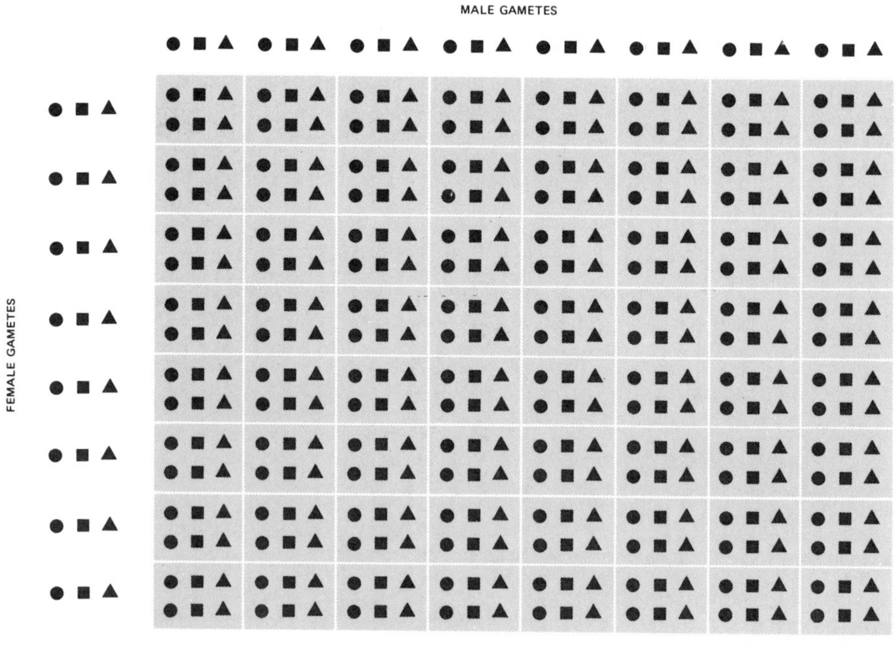

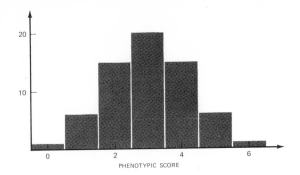

FIGURE 5-2   *Distribution of phenotypes of Fig. 5-1.*

INBRED STRAINS
AND DERIVED GENERATIONS

Degree of genetic similarity among individuals can be experimentally controlled in studies with infrahumans. Through inbreeding it is possible to produce strains of animals in which the genetic variability is virtually eliminated. Such "pure" strains enable us to investigate a great many factors in genetic influences on behavior. In general *inbreeding* means the mating of individuals more closely related than would be members drawn at random from the population and assigned randomly in pairs. In laboratory animals, particularly mice, intensive inbreeding, usually the mating of brothers and sisters, is continued in successive generations to produce a progressive decrease in the amount of genetic heterogeneity. After about 20 generations of inbreeding each animal is very nearly homozygous for all genes and is virtually identical to each other animal of that strain. The chances that two such inbred strains with different origins will have the same genotype are vanishingly small; the exact degree and nature of the genetic difference between any two different inbred strains cannot be specified exactly, but it is certain that they will differ to some degree. Then, if different strains reared and tested under the same conditions exhibit any difference in behavior, the difference must be genetic in origin. Conversely, any variability found among members of the same inbred strain must be due to differences in the environment to which they have been exposed.

The first step in research with inbred strains is to show that the strains differ in behavior—in other words, that the differences in behavior are likely to be due to genetic differences. Mouse strains, for example, have been found to differ in a variety of behaviors such as learning ability in mazes, learning ability in shock avoidance situations, activity level, sexual behavior, food hoarding, susceptibility to sound-induced seizures, and alcohol preference. As an indication of the range of differences among inbred strains, Fig. 5-3 shows the distributions of locomotor activity in a novel situation for six mouse strains. The activity

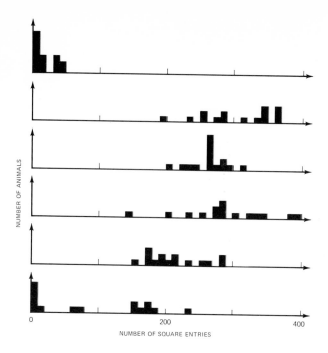

NUMBER OF ANIMALS

0   200   400

NUMBER OF SQUARE ENTRIES

FIGURE 5–3   *Locomotor activity of six mouse strains.*

was measured by placing the animals on a chamber floor which was sectioned off into small squares by a series of rectangular barriers. An animal's activity score was the number of squares it traversed in a 5-minute period. The average differences among the strains on this measure are quite large. Animals from the more active strains cross squares nearly once a second, while animals from the least active strains cross barely four times a minute. However, strain differences in variability also are evident. Since all animals were reared under the same general laboratory conditions, this finding suggests that the strains differ in their susceptibility to environmental variation.

The simple fact of differences, of course, provides no information about the mode of inheritance. Once strain differences have been established, further genetic analysis entails measurement of the responses of the generations derived from the inbred strains. Some information about the average dominance of the genes involved can be obtained from the F_1 generation, the progeny of the two parent strains. However, much more valuable information can be obtained from study of the F_2 generation, which is derived by mating F_1 individuals with each other. Animals of the F_1 generation, like those of each of the parent strains, are alike genetically; each has received half its genes from one parent and half from the other. If two F_1 animals are mated, however, in their offspring the genetic material from either of the original strains may range from zero to 100 percent in any individual. Thus the F_2 generation should be more variable than the F_1. As with the twin studies, where fraternal-twin differences are compared to identical-twin differences, the amount

148

of this excess variability may be taken as a measure of the variability which is genetic in origin. For example, Fig. 5-4 shows the arena activity scores of two inbred strains, the F_1 generation and the F_2 generation. Because our interest here is comparison in variability, the square root of the original activity score was taken in order to provide a scale on which the parent strains are equally variable. As can be seen, the activity of the F_1 animals lies, on the average, between that of the two strains. However, the distribution of F_1 scores is displaced toward one parent, suggesting that, on the average, the genes for higher activity are dominant. The F_2 scores are distributed over a very broad range. In a sample as small as this we would not expect to obtain any animals whose genetic makeup is actually exactly the same as that of either parent strain. Thus it is not surprising that no F_2 animals are actually at the limits of the scale. The scores do, however, spread over a greater range than the F_1 scores. Without going into a detailed analysis, we can conclude from the amount by which the F_2 variability exceeds the F_1 variability that approximately two-thirds of the variability in the F_2 generation arises from genetic differences; the remaining one-third of the variability is attributable to environmental factors. Thus from careful analysis we are able to derive quantitative statements about genetic influences on behavior.

Similar analyses have been performed on a wide variety of mouse behaviors, including hoarding, alcohol preference, and learning. The results all support the general conclusion that in any population some of the variability in behavioral traits is of environmental origin and some is of genetic origin. In very general terms, the proportion of the total phenotypic variance that is due to genetic differences among members of the population is called the *heritability*. Heritability of a trait differs from population to population, depending on the amount of genetic variability present in the population. Within a single inbred strain there is no genetic variability, and hence no heritability. Note that when all animals are genetically identical, heritability is .00; all variation in behavior must be caused by environmental influences. If environmental effects could be made uniform for all members of a genetically *heterogeneous* population, then the remaining variability would be all genetic in origin, and the heritability would be 1.00. Theoretically the complete

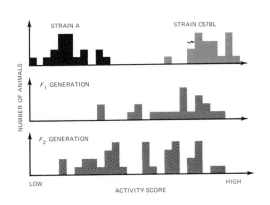

FIGURE 5-4 *Activity scores of two mouse strains and their F_1 and F_2 generations.*

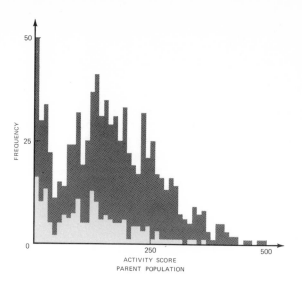

FREQUENCY

50

25

0   250   500

ACTIVITY SCORE
PARENT POPULATION

FIGURE 5-5   *Activity score distributed for a foundation stock of mice and for two generations of selected lines derived from that foundation stock.*

success of programs to provide equal education for all would result in a situation wherein all the differences among individuals would be due to heredity.

SELECTIVE BREEDING

Another major method in animal behavioral genetics research is that of selective breeding. To put it simply, animals who display extreme levels of some behavior are mated together. This procedure is continued over successive generations. If the behavior is genetically influenced, animals selected in the "high" direction will provide their offspring with alleles that make for high values of the behavior, and in successive generations the relative frequency of high alleles would be expected to increase in that line. Similarly, in a line selected for low values of the trait there would be an accumulation of alleles for low phenotypic value. A successful attempt to breed selectively thus demonstrates that the trait for which the selection was performed does indeed have a heritable basis, and the results also permit some estimates of mode of gene action. Animals have been selectively bred for a variety of behavioral tendencies, such as maze brightness and maze dullness in rats, high and low activity in rats, high and low morphine addictability in rats, aggressiveness and nonaggressiveness in mice, positive and negative geotaxis in fruit flies (*Drosophila*), and fast and slow mating speed in *Drosophila*.

Selective breeding is a powerful technique. Within limits, it enables an investigator to tailor-make his research subjects. A graphic example of the effects of selective breeding is given in Fig. 5-5. From a parental population of genetically heterogeneous mice the very active animals were mated together and the very inactive animals were mated together. In order to provide a continuing reference point some randomly selected animals also were mated. After six generations of such selective breeding

150

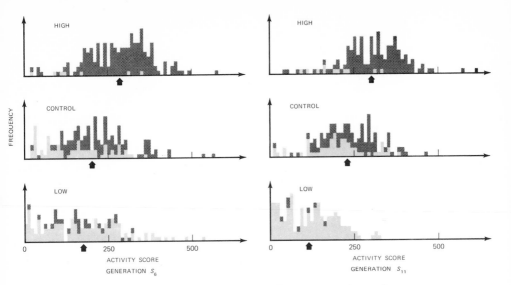

the activity-score distributions of these separate lines were as shown for generation S_6. The average score of each line is indicated by an arrow on the horizontal scale. It can easily be seen that the averages moved in the direction in which selection pressure was applied. There is still extensive overlap, however. After five further generations of selective breeding, in generation S_{11}, the averages are still farther apart, and by this time the most active of the low line is only about as active as the average mouse from the high line. In the control animals, where there has been no selection pressure, the average activity has remained quite stable over time; considerable overlap of the high- and low-line distributions is still evident in S_{11}. The extent to which the variability that results in this overlap is of genetic origin will be indicated by the eventual outcome of this experiment [DeFries et al., 1970]. These results are typical for a trait influenced by many genes.

This study also shows that recognizable single genes may participate in such a situation. In the foundation stock about 25 percent of the animals were albino, as indicated by the light squares in Fig. 5-5. By generation S_6 the albinos had become rare in the high line and the majority in the low line; by generation S_{11} the effect was even more pronounced. Obviously the albino gene has an effect on activity and is one of the genes being sorted out in the two lines by the selection pressure.

MECHANISMS OF GENE ACTION

The studies described above indicate that genes do indeed influence behavior and result in family resemblances in behavior. The basic question, of course, is *how* do genes influence behavior? Biochemical genetics and molecular biology have in recent years revealed the chemical nature of genes and the mechanisms through which they operate. Although we do not yet understand all the details, there is nothing mystical about the

151

way genes operate. Genes influence behavior by affecting all the body systems which are involved in behavior—the central nervous system, the autonomic nervous system, the endocrine glands, the receptors, the muscles, and the digestive system. The genetic material is known to be *deoxyribonucleic acid* (DNA). Genetic information is coded by a sequence of chemical substances, or *bases*, along the DNA molecule. From this molecule, which remains within the cell nucleus, *ribonucleic acid* (RNA) is copied and goes out into the cytoplasm of the cell, where the genetic "message" it transmits is used in establishing the specificity of proteins called *enzymes*, the organic catalysts which are essential to development and functioning of the body.

Although we know that this general description is accurate, we know little about the details of the biochemical path from DNA to behavior. For most behavioral traits little or no concrete information is available. In an increasing number of cases, however, parts of the pathway are being subjected to analysis, and our knowledge is increasing rapidly. Perhaps the best understood mechanism is that involved in the condition of phenylketonuria. The key biochemical deficiency in this disorder is an inability to metabolize phenylalanine, which is an essential amino acid found in normal diet. This inability is related in turn to a deficiency of the enzyme phenylalanine hydroxylase. The failure to convert phenylalanine to tyrosine results in an accumulation of phenylalanine, and also of a number of derivatives of phenylalanine, such as phenylpyruvic acid and phenylacetic acid. It appears that the presence of one of these substances in excess quantities inhibits normal development of the nervous system. The partial understanding of the biochemical basis of the condition has given rise to a rational therapy. A special diet, free of phenylalanine, was developed for afflicted children in 1959. Extensive testing programs of newborn children are now in operation in most of the United States to identify those for whom the dietary treatment should be begun. Although this therapy appears to effect considerable improvement in children afflicted with phenylketonuria, it seems that their development still may not be completely normal.

The success in establishing the nature of genetic determination in phenylketonuria, the discovery of the biochemical defects, and the development of effective therapy has encouraged extensive research on other conditions which involve defects in amino acid metabolism. A number of such conditions have been identified, and mental retardation is usually found to be a feature of the condition. Although none has been shown as clearly to be the consequence of a single gene, we are beginning to learn much about the nature of metabolic defects, and therapeutic diets have been initiated for many of the defects.

In studies using experimental animals there are active research efforts to relate genetically influenced neurochemical differences to learning ability, memory, and aggressiveness; endocrine differences to emotionality, activity, and social and sexual behavior; and enzyme differences to alcohol preference. This is a rapidly developing area of research which holds much promise.

The genes are located in series along the chromosomes in each cell nucleus. In man this genetic material is arranged in 23 *pairs* of chromosomes. One member of each of these pairs is derived from each parent. In the formation of gametes (eggs and sperm) one member of each pair is included, so that each egg or sperm ordinarily contains 23 single chromosomes. When a sperm and an egg unite, the normal situation of 23 pairs is restored. Occasionally, however, an accident occurs during this process, with the result that some particular sperm or egg has an abnormal number of chromosomes. The precise cause of these accidents is unknown, but in some cases we know that maternal age is a factor; chromosome mistakes occur more often in older women. When a gamete with an abnormal number of chromosomes is involved in fertilization, the resulting organism will also have an abnormal chromosome complement. Many of these abnormalities result in early death and account for a substantial percentage of spontaneously occurring abortions. However, some abnormalities are compatible with continued life, and of these conditions, a number have interesting though unfortunate behavioral features.

One of the first conditions shown to be the result of a chromosome abnormality was *Down's syndrome*, more generally known as mongolism. This condition, which is characterized by superficially oriental features, was singled out early for special investigation and had been the focus of active research efforts for a long time. The cause of the condition remained obscure, however, until it was found that affected individuals had 47 instead of 46 chromosomes. Detailed analysis revealed that the extra chromosome is a small one, and according to the classification scheme generally employed by workers in this area, it was designated as number 21. The condition of having three chromosomes instead of a pair is *trisomy*. Not all of the extra genetic material on chromosome 21 is required to cause this condition. Besides the anomaly which results from a complete trisomy for chromosome 21, there is another anomaly in which the extra chromosome 21 is attached instead to the somewhat larger chromosome pair 15—that is, there is a normal pair of chromosome 21 plus an extra fragment. In this case the prospect that a subsequent child of the same parents will also be affected is many times greater than it is for the standard trisomy condition.

Just as extra amounts of chromosome material can produce severe abnormalities, a deficiency of genetic material can also have serious consequences. It appears that the complete absence of a particular chromosome is usually (but not always) fatal. In one situation loss of an end of a certain chromosome is known to produce a condition of severe mental retardation, called the *cat-cry syndrome* because of the distinctive cry of the affected children.

The exception to the generalization that complete chromosomal loss is not compatible with life involves the sex chromosomes. With respect to 22 pairs of chromosomes, the complements of males and females

153

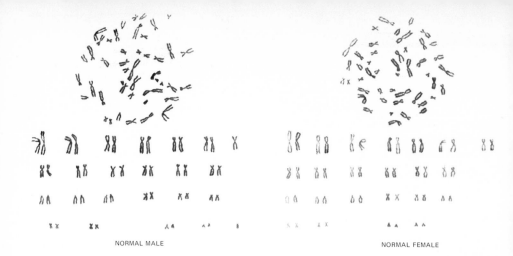

FIGURE 5–6   *Human karyotypes. The top section of each karyotype is a photomicrograph of the chromosomal material of a single cell of the individual. Below this the chromosomes are arranged in pairs in order of decreasing size. The sex chromosomes are shown in the right-hand column adjacent to other chromosomes of about the same size. In the abnormal karyotypes an arrow indicates the anomaly. [Robinson, University of Colorado Medical Center]*

are the same; each has chromosome pairs containing the same genetic loci, with one member of each pair from each of the parents. With respect to the sex chromosomes, it is also the case that one is provided by each parent. However, the sex chromosomes come in two forms—the X chromosome, which is relatively large, and a smaller Y chromosome. An XX pair results in a normal female and an XY pair results in a normal male. A condition called *Turner's syndrome* is frequently found in females who have only a single X chromosome. These individuals are sterile and have a variety of physical anomalies. They are not mentally retarded in the usual sense—in fact, some evidence suggests that their verbal abilities are somewhat higher than average. However, they appear to be deficient in other kinds of cognitive functioning. The defect can best be described as space-form blindness and difficulty in numerical manipulations. In some respects these symptoms are similar to those caused by certain kinds of damage to the parietal lobe of the brain.

Another anomaly of sex-chromosome number in females is the triplow-X situation. This condition has not yet been found to be consistently related to any particular kind of behavioral deficiency. One trisomy of the sex chromosomes in males involves the presence of two Xs and a Y. XXY individuals suffer from *Klinefelter's syndrome*, characterized by retarded sexual development and mental deficiency.

Another male trisomy, XYY, has been the subject of intensive research efforts. A constellation of typical characteristics includes large body size, moderate intellectual dullness, and strong aggressive tendencies. There is strong evidence that XYY males appear in institutions for the criminally insane much more often than would be expected on the basis of their frequency in the general population [Court-Brown et al., 1968]. However, a comparison of close relatives of XYY males and nor-

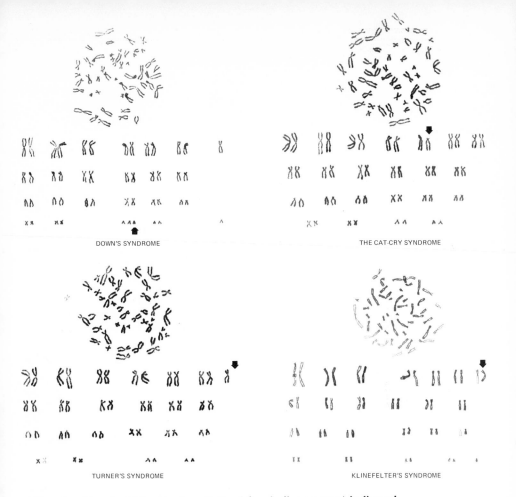

DOWN'S SYNDROME

THE CAT-CRY SYNDROME

TURNER'S SYNDROME

KLINEFELTER'S SYNDROME

mal males (that is, *XY* males hospitalized for similar reasons) indicated that the relatives of the *XYY* males were far *less* likely to have been convicted of a crime. In the control group many more of the relatives had a criminal record. This finding suggests that in an individual whose relatives are not known to be involved in crimes of violence the possession of the extra *Y* chromosome in some way significantly increases the probability of an individual's becoming involved in such crimes [Hirsch, 1970]. The principal unanswered question, of course, is the actual frequency of normal *XYY* individuals in the population at large. The chief problem, of course, is determining their actual frequency in the population at large. Estimates thus far have depended largely on extrapolations from other chromosome anomalies. It is extremely difficult to perform the large-scale population surveys for extra *Y* chromosomes that would be required to make a confident judgment that this syndrome is a reliable consequence of the *XYY* chromosomal constitution. Hence it is too early to say with certainty that there is a genetic basis for criminal behavior.

These cases of chromosome anomalies concern the abnormal presence or absence of whole blocks of genes. Such data do not provide much information about the mode of gene action. For example, we know little about the particular pathways through which extra genes on chromosome 21 lead to mental retardation and the associated symptoms. It is clear, however, that genetic influence on behavior is relevant to the whole array of the social and behavioral sciences, both in terms of our thinking about the causes of behavior and as a powerful research technique for determining specific ways of altering behavior.

As man's biotechnological capacity advances, we come increasingly nearer to the time when we can intervene directly and deliberately to alter the genetic code of given individuals. Furthermore, the crushing population pressures that are foretold will eventuate in a change in our gene pool. Whether we take active steps to curb population growth or just let it happen, the result is certain to be a breeding pattern that is different from what it is now. To even predict the consequences of changed reproductive patterns, let alone influence them in any way, we will need a higher order of knowledge than we presently have. The behavioral sciences in general need more information. One of the critical needs is an understanding of the mechanisms that underlie hereditary influences on behavior.

SUMMARY

Even in the ancient times man employed the general principles of heredity to domesticate dogs and cattle. Interest in the hereditary basis of human behavior led to early family studies such as Galton's classical study of eminence and the famous Jukes and Kallikaks study. These studies demonstrated that certain behavioral traits do run in families, but they did not resolve the question of whether the resemblance was hereditary or due to environmental similarity.

A more recent approach to the study of heredity is based on the fact that identical twins have identical hereditary endowment and fraternal twins are no more alike than ordinary siblings. Comparison of these different types of twins on a number of behavioral and physical traits indicates that such intelligence measures as *verbal reasoning*, *clerical speed* and *accuracy*, *language use*, and *composite IQ* show substantial hereditary influences, while *numerical ability*, *abstract reasoning*, and *mechanical reasoning* show little or no hereditary component. Personality traits such as *active*, *vigorous*, *sociable*, and *impulsive* are heritable, while *dominant*, *stable* and *reflective* are not. In addition, neuroses characterized by anxiety, depression, obsession, and schizoid withdrawal all have substantial hereditary bases, but those with features of hypochondriasis and hysteria are not substantially influenced by heredity. Comparison of identical twins raised together with those raised apart indicates that schizophrenia is strongly influenced by heredity. If one member of a pair of identical twins is schizophrenic, the probability is greater than chance that the other twin will also be schizophrenic.

Modern genetics began with the work of Gregor Mendel, who observed that the elementary genetic units, the genes, exist in pairs of alleles, which may be dominant or recessive. Since the dominant allele governs the outward appearance of a trait, an individual's genetic composition or genotype must be distinguished from the observed trait, or phenotype. Some traits are determined by a single gene, such as the recessive condition of phenylketonuria or the sex-linked characteristic of red-green color blindness. Most behavioral traits, however, are determined polygenetically. The number of genotypes possible from a mating of two triple heterozygotes, for example, provides an important genetic mechanism for actually generating behavioral variability.

Inbred strains and the study of derived generations of experimental animals enable us to relate similarities and differences in genetic composition to differences in behavioral and physical characteristics. Subsequent generations of the inbred strains indicate which traits are heritable, and by selective breeding for particular traits the heritable variability can be distinguished from the variability due to environmental influence.

Genetic information is coded by the chemical constitution of DNA (deoxyribonucleic acid) and a "carbon copy" is transmitted from the nucleus of each cell by RNA (ribonucleic acid). The details of the biochemical path from DNA to behavior are not yet known; however, certain defects in this pathway lead to such defects as phenylketonuria, which, like most of the biochemically based defects, results in mental retardation.

The genetic material in man is carried by 46 chromosomes arranged in 23 pairs, with one member of each pair contributed by each parent. Sometimes an individual will receive more than the required number of chromosomes, which causes a condition of trisomy in one of the chromosome pairs. This anomaly often leads to such behavioral deficiencies as mongolism. The absence of a chromosome is generally fatal, except in the case of the sex chromosomes. There is some evidence that an extra Y chromosome in males may be related to criminal behavior. Further understanding of the genetic bases is important both for the treatment of abnormal behavior and the prediction of genetic makeup in future generations.

BIBLIOGRAPHY

Anand, B. K., and Brobeck, J. R. 1951. Hypothalamic control of food intake in rats and cats. *Yale J. Biol. Med.,* 24, 123.

Andersson, B. 1953. The effect of injections of hypertonic NaCl-solutions into different parts of the hypothalamus of goats. *Acta Physiol. Scand.,* 28, 188–201.

Aserinsky, E., and Kleitman, N. 1953. Regularly occurring periods of eye motility, and concomitant phenomena, during sleep. *Science,* 118, 273–274.

Bard, P., and Macht, M. B. 1958. The behavior of chronically decerebrate cats. *Ciba Foundation symposium, Neurological basis of behavior.* London: Churchill.

Bard, P., and Mountcastle, V. B. 1948, Some forebrain mechanisms involved in expression of rage with special reference to suppression of angry behavior. *Res. Publ. Assn. Res. Nerv. Ment. Dis.,* 27, 362–404.

Brady, J. V., and Nauta, W.J.H. 1953. Subcortical mechanisms in emotional behavior. Affective changes following septal forebrain lesions in the albino rat. *J. Comp. Physiol. Psychol.,* 46, 339–346.

Brazier, M.A.B. 1968. *The electrical activity of the nervous system* (3rd ed. rev.). London: Pitman Scientific and Medical Publ. Co. Ltd., also Baltimore: Williams and Wilkins. (By permission.)

Brobeck, J. R. 1947–48. Food intake as a mechanism of temperature regulation. *Yale J. Biol. Med.,* 20, 545–552.

Brown, J. S. 1961. *The motivation of behavior.* New York: McGraw-Hill. (By permission.)

Bruner, J. S., Matter, J., and Papanek, M. L. 1955. Breadth of learning as a function of drive level and mechanization. *Psychol. Rev.,* 62, 1–10.

Butler, R. A. 1953. Discrimination learning by rhesus monkeys to visual-exploration motivation. *J. Comp. Physiol. Psychol.,* 46, 95–98. (Copyright 1953 by the American Psychological Association, reporduced by permission.)

Butler, R. A. 1954a. Incentive conditions which influence visual exploration. *J. Exp. Psychol.,* 48, 19–23. (By permission.)

Butler, R. A. 1954b. Curiosity in monkeys. *Scient. Amer.,* 190, 70–75.

Butler, R. A., and Harlow, H. F. 1954. Persistence of visual exploration in monkeys. *J. Comp. Physiol. Psychol.,* 47, 258–263.

Campbell, B. A., and Lynch, G. S. 1969. Cortical modulation of spontaneous activity during hunger and thirst. *J. Comp. Physiol. Psychol.,* 67, 15–22.

Campbell, B. A., and Sheffield, F. D. 1953. Relation of random activity to food deprivation. *J. Comp. Physiol. Psychol.,* 46, 320–322.

Canaday, J. 1961. *Main streams of modern art.* New York: Simon and Schuster. (By permission of Holt, Rinehart and Winston, Inc.)

Cannon, W. B. 1932. *The wisdom of the body.* New York: Norton.

Clark, R. A. 1952. The projective measurement of experimentally induced levels of sexual motivation. *J. Exp. Psychol.,* 44, 391–399.

Court-Brown, W. M., Jacobs, P. A., and Price, W. H. 1968. Sex chromosome aneuploidy and criminal behaviour. In J. M. Thoday and A. S. Parkes (Eds.), *Genetic and environmental influence on behavior.* Edinburgh: Oliver and Boyd Ltd.

Davis, C. M. 1928. Self-selection of diet by newly weaned infants. *Amer. J. Dis. Child.,* 36, 651–679.

Davis, H. 1959. Excitation of auditory receptors. In J. Field, H. W. Magoun, and B. E. Hall (Eds.), *Handbook of physiology.* Vol. I, Sec. I, Neurophysiology. Washington, D.C.: American Physiological Society.

DeFries, J. C., Wilson, J. R., and McClearn, G. E. 1970. Open-field behavior in mice: Selection response and situational generality. *Behav. Genetics,* 1.

Dement, W. 1960. The effect of dream deprivation. *Science,* 131, 1705–1707.

DeValois, R. L. 1965. Analysis and coding of color vision in the primate visual system. *Sensory receptors.* Cold Spring Harbor, N. Y.: Laboratory of Quantitative Biology.

Dunlop, C. W., Webster, W. R., and Simons, L. A. 1965. Effect of attention on evoked responses in the classical auditory pathway. *Nature,* 206, 1048–1050.

Eason, R. G., Harter, M. R., and White, C. T. 1969. Effects of attention and arousal on visually evoked cortical potentials and reaction time in man. *Physiol. Behav.,* 4, 283–289. (By permission.)

Eccles, J. C. 1964. *The physiology of synapses.* New York: Academic Press.

Farrell, B. 1966. Scientists, theologians, mystics swept up in a psychic revolution. *Life,* March 25. Reprinted in Life Educational Reprint 22. New York: Time. (By permission.)

Fernandez de Molina, A., and Hunsperger, R. W. 1959. Central representation of affective reactions in forebrain and brain stem: Electrical stimulation of amygdala, stria terminalis, and adjacent structures. *J. Physiol.,* 145, 251–265. (By permission.)

Festinger, L. 1957. *A theory of cognitive dissonance.* Stanford: Stanford University Press. (By permission.)

Flynn, J. P. 1967. The neural basis of aggression in cats. In D. C. Glass (Ed.), *Neurophysiology and emotion.* New York: Rockefeller University Press and Russell Sage Foundation. (By permission.)

Freud, S. 1938. *The basic writings of Sigmund Freud.* Translated and edited by A. A. Brill. New York: Modern Library.

Goddard, H. H. 1914. *Feeblemindedness: Its causes and consequences.* New York: Macmillan. (By permission.)

Goodenough, D. R., Shapiro, A., Holden, M., and Steinschriber, L. 1959. A comparison of "dreamers" and "non-dreamers" eye movements, electroencephalograms, and the recall of dreams. *J. Abnorm. Soc. Psychol.,* 59, 295–302.

Gottesman, I. I. 1962. Differential inheritance of the psychoneuroses. *Eugenics Quart.,* 9, 223, 227.

Gottesman, I. I., and Shields, J. 1966. Schizophrenia in twins: 16 years, consecutive admissions to a psychiatric clinic. *Brit. J. Psych.,* 112, 809–818. (By permission.)

Granda, A., and Hammack, J. 1961. Operant behavior during sleep. *Science,* 133, 1485–1486.

Granit, R. 1962. Neurophysiology of the retina. In H. Dawson (Ed.), *The eye.* Vol. 2. New York: Academic Press.

Grossman, S. P. 1967. *A textbook of physiological psychology.* New York: Wiley.

Haggar, R. A., and Barr, M. L. 1950. Quantitative data on the size of synaptic end-bulbs in the cat's spinal cord. *J. Comp. Neurol.,* 93, 17–35. (By permission.)

Hall, C. S. 1959. *The meaning of dreams.* New York: Dell.

Harlow, H. F. 1952. Functional organization of the brain in relation to mentation and behavior. In *The biology of mental health and diseases.* Ch. 16. New York: Paul B. Hoeber, Inc., Medical Book Dept. of Harper and Brothers.

Harlow, H. F. 1959. Love in infant monkeys. *Scient. Amer.,* 200, 68–74.

Harlow, H. F., and McClearn, G. E. 1954. Object discrimination learned by monkeys on the basis of manipulation motives. *J. Comp. Physiol. Psychol.,* 47, 73–76.

Hartman, E. 1967. *The biology of dreaming.* Springfield: Charles C. Thomas. (By permission of the publisher.)

Hebb, D. O. 1955. Drives and the c.n.s. (conceptual nervous system). *Psychol. Rev.,* 62, 243–254.

Hebb, D. O. 1966. *A textbook of psychology.* Philadelphia: W. B. Saunders. (By permission.)

Hernández-Peón, R. 1960. Neurophysiological correlates of habituation and other manifestations of plastic inhibition (internal inhibition). In H. H. Jasper and G. D. Smirnov (Eds.), The Moscow colloquium on electroencephalography of higher nervous activity. *Electroenceph. Clin. Neurophysiol.,* Suppl. 13.

Hernández-Peón, R., Scherrer, H., and Jouvet, M. 1956. Modification of electric activity in cochlear nucleus during "attention" in unanesthetized cats. *Science,* 123, 331–332.

Heston, L. L. 1966. Psychiatric disorders in foster home reared children of schizophrenic mothers. *Brit. J. Psych.,* 112, 819–825.

Hillarp, N. A., Fuxe, K., and Dahlström, A. 1960. Demonstration and mapping of central neurons containing dopamine, noradrenaline, and 5-hydroxytryptamine and their reactions to psychopharmacia. *Pharmacol. Rev.,* 18, 727.

Hinde, R. A. 1966. *Animal behavior.* New York: McGraw-Hill.

Hirsch, J. 1970. Behavior genetic analysis and its biosocial consequences. *Seminars in Psych.,* 2, 89–105.

Hodgkin, A. L. 1964. The ionic basis of nervous conduction. *Science,* 145, 1148–1154.

Hubel, D. H., and Wiesel, T. N. 1962. Receptive fields, binocular interaction and functional architecture in the cat's visual center. *J. Physiol.,* 160, 106–154. (By permission.)

Hubel, D. H., and Wiesel, T. N. 1963. Receptive fields of cells in striate cortex of very young, visually inexperienced kittens. *J Neurophysiol.,* 26, 994–1002.

Hubel, D. H., and Wiesel, T. N. 1965. Receptive fields and functional architecture in two nonstriate visual areas (18 and 19) of the cat. *J. Neurophysiol.,* 28, 229–289. (By permission.)

Hull, C. L. 1943. *Principles of behavior.* New York: Appleton-Century-Crofts.

Huxley, A. 1928. *Point counterpoint.* New York: Doubleday.

Huxley, A. F. 1964. Excitation and conduction in nerve: Quantitative analysis. *Science,* 145, 1154–1159.

Jaffe, J. H. 1965. Drug addiction and drug abuse. In L. S. Goodman and A. Gilman (Eds.), *The pharmacological basis of therapeutics.* New York: Macmillan.

James, W. 1890. *The principles of psychology.* New York: Henry Holt. Reprinted 1950, Vol. I. New York: Dover.

John, E. R., Herrington, R. N., and Sutton, S. 1967. Effects of visual form on the evoked response. *Science,* 155, 1439–1442. (Copyright 1967 by the American Association for the Advancement of Science, by permission.)

Kavanau, J. L. 1963. Compulsory regime and control of environment in animal behavior. I. Wheel running. *Behaviour,* 20, 251–281.

Lagerspetz, K.M.J. 1969. Aggression and aggressiveness in laboratory mice. In S. Garattini and E. B. Sigg (Eds.), *Aggressive behaviour.* New York: Wiley.

Lele, P. P., and Weddell, G. 1956. The relationship between neurohistology and corneal sensibility. *Brain,* 19, 119–154.

Lindsley, D. B. 1951. Emotion. In S. S. Stevens (Eds.), *Handbook of experimental psychology.* New York: Wiley.

Lindsley, D. B. 1958. The reticular system and perceptual discrimination. In H. H. Jasper (Ed.), *Reticular formation of the brain.* Boston: Little, Brown.

Lindsley, D. B., Bowden, J., and Magoun, H. W. 1949. Effect upon EEG of acute injury to the brain stem activating system. *Electroenceph. Clin. Neurophysiol.,* 1, 475–486.

Lindsley, D. B., Schreiner, L. H. Knowles, W. B., and Magoun, H. W. 1950. Behavioral and EEG changes following chronic brain stem lesions in the cat. *Electroenceph. Clin. Neurophysiol.,* 2, 483–498.

Mackworth, N. H. 1950. *Researches in the measurement of human performance.* MRC Spec. Rpt. 268, HMSO. Reprinted 1961 in H. W. Sinaiko (Ed.), *Selected papers on human factor in the design and use of control systems.* New York: Dover.

MacNichol, E. F. 1964. Retinal mechanisms of color vision. *Vision Res.,* 4, 119–133.

Magoun, H. W. 1954. The ascending reticular system and wakefulness. In J. F. Delafresnaye (Ed.), *Brain mechanisms and consciousness.* Oxford: Blackwell Scientific Publ. (By permission.)

Malmo, R. B. 1959. Activation: A neurophysiological dimension. *Psychol. Rev.,* 66, 367–386.

Mayer, J. 1955. Regulation of energy intake and the body weight. The glucostatic theory and the lipostatic hypothesis. *Ann. New York Acad. Sci.,* 63.

Mayer, J., and Marshall, N. B. 1956. Specificity of gold thioglucose for ventromedial hypothalamic lesions and hyperphagia. *Nature* (London), 178, 1399–1400.

McClelland, D. C., Atkinson, J. W., Clark, R. A., and Lowell, E. L. 1953. *The achievement motive.* New York: Appleton-Century-Crofts.

McGaugh, J. L. 1969. Facilitation of memory storage processes. In S. Bogoch (Ed.), *The future of the brain sciences.* New York: Plenum Press.

Miller, N. E. 1963. Some reflections on the law of effect produce a new alternative to drive reduction. In M. Jones (Ed.), *Nebraska symposium on motivation.* Lincoln: University of Nebraska Press.

Miller, N. E., and Kessen, M. L. 1952. Reward effects of food via stomach fistual compared with those of food via mouth. *J. Comp. Physiol. Psychol.,* 45, 555–564.

Moruzzi, G., and Magoun, H. W. 1949. Brain stem reticular formation and activation of the EEG. *Electroenceph. Clin. Neurophysiol.,* 1, 455–473.

Murray, E. J. 1964. *Motivation and emotion.* Englewood Cliffs, N. J.: Prentice-Hall. (By permission.)

Murray, E. J. 1965. *Sleep, dreams, and arousal.* New York: Appleton-Century-Crofts. (By permission.)

Newman, H. H., Freeman, F. N., and Holzinger, K. J. 1937. *Twins: A study of heredity and environment.* Chicago: University of Chicago Press.

Olds, J. 1955. Physiological mechanisms of reward. In M. R. Jones (Ed.), *Nebraska symposium on motivation.* Vol. 3. Lincoln: University of Nebraska Press. (By permission.)

Olds, J., and Milner, P. 1954. Positive reinforcement produced by electrical stimulation of septal area and other regions of rat brain. *J. Comp. Physiol. Psychol.,* 47, 419–427.

Oswald, I. 1966. *Sleep.* Baltimore: Penguin Books. (By permission.)

Oswald, I., Taylor, A. M., and Treisman, M. 1960. Discriminative responses to stimulation during human sleep. *Brain,* 83, 440–453.

Pavlov, I. P. 1927. *Conditioned reflexes.* London: Oxford University Press.

Peele, T. L. 1954. *Neuroanatomy.* New York: McGraw-Hill. (By permission.)

Penfield, W., and Jasper, H. 1954. *Epilepsy and the functional anatomy of the human brain.* Boston: Little, Brown. (By permission.)

Pribram, K. H. 1962. Interrelations of psychology and the neurological disciplines. In S. Koch (Ed.), *Psychology: A study of a science.* Vol. 4. New York: McGraw-Hill.

Richter, C. P. 1942–43. Total self-regulatory functions in animals and human beings. *Harvey Lect.,* 38, 63–103.

Richter, C. P. 1967. Sleep and activity. Their relation to the 24-hour clock. In S. S. Kety, E. V. Evarts, and H. L. Williams (Eds.) *Sleep and altered states of consciousness.* Ch. 2. Baltimore: Williams and Wilkins. (By permission.)

Riggs, L. A., Ratliff, F., Cornsweet, J. C., and Cornsweet, T. N. 1953. The disappearance of steadily fixated visual test objects. *J. Opt. Soc. Amer.,* 43, 495–501.

Rothenbuhler, W. C. 1964. Behavior genetics of nest cleaning in honey bees. IV. Responses of F_1 and backcross generations to disease-killed brook. *Amer. Zool.,* 4, 111–123.

Rowland, V. 1957. Differential electroencephalographic response to conditioned auditory stimuli in arousal from sleep. *Electroenceph. Clin. Neurophysiol.,* 9, 585–594.

Rushton, W.A.H. 1961. The cone pigments of the human fovea in colour blind and normal. In *Visual problem of color.* New York: Chemical Publ.

Rushton, W.A.H. 1962. The retinal organization of vision in vertebrates. *Biological receptor mechanisms.* Number XVI. Symposia

Soc. Exp. Biol. Cambridge: Cambridge University Press. (By permission.)

Schaltenbrand, G., and Woolsey, C. N. (Eds.). 1964. *Cerebral localization and organization.* Madison: University of Wisconsin Press. (Copyright © 1964 by the Regents of the University of Wisconsin, by permission.)

Schapiro, S., and Vukovich, K. R. 1970. Early experience effects upon cortical dentrites. A proposed model for development. *Science,* 167, 292–294.

Schildkraut, J. J., and Kety, S. S. 1967. Biogenic amines and emotion. *Science,* 156, 21–30.

Sharpless, S. K., and Jasper, H. 1956. Habituation of the arousal reaction. *Brain,* 79, 655–680. (By permission.)

Sheffield, F. D., and Roby, T. B. 1950. Reward value of a non-nutritive sweet taste. *J. Comp. Physiol. Psychol.,* 43, 471–481.

Sheffield, F. D., Wulff, J. J., and Backer, R. 1951. Reward value of copulation without sex drive reduction. *J. Comp. Physiol. Psychol.,* 44, 3–8.

Sholl, D. A. 1956. *The organization of the cerebral cortex.* London: Methuen. (By permission.)

Smith, C. P., and Feld, S. 1958. Appendix I. How to learn the method of content analysis for n achievement, n affiliation and n power. In J. W. Atkinson (Ed.), *Motives in fantasy, action, and society.* Princeton: Van Nostrand. (Copyright © 1958 by Litton Educational Publishing, Inc. by permission of the publisher.)

Smith, D.B.D., Donchin, E., Cohen, L., and Starr, A. 1970. Auditory averaged evoked potentials in man during selective binaural listening. *Electroenceph. Clin. Neurophysiol.,* 28, 146–152. (By permission.)

Sokolov, Y. N. 1963. *Perception and the conditioned reflex.* New York: Pergamon.

Southwick, C. H., Beg, M. A., and Siddigi, M. R. 1965. Rhesus monkeys in north India. In I. DeVore (Ed.), *Primate behavior: Field studies of monkeys and apes.* New York: Holt, Rinehart and Winston.

Stevens, S. S. 1961. The psychophysics of sensory function. In W. A. Rosenblith (Ed.), *Sensory communication.* Ch. 1. Cambridge: MIT Press. (By permission.)

Strumwasser, F. 1965. The demonstration and manipulation of a circadian rhythm in a single neuron. In J. Aschoff (Ed.), *Circadian clocks.* Amsterdam: North-Holland. (By permission.)

Sutherland, N. S. 1968. Outlines of a theory of visual pattern recognition in animals and man. *Proc. Roy. Soc. B.*, 171, 297–317.

Svaetichin, G., Laufer, M., Mitarai, G., Fatehchand, R., Vallecalle, E., and Villegas, J. 1961. Glial control of neuronal networks and receptors. In R. Jung and H. Kornhuber (Eds.), *The visual system: Neurophysiology and psychophysics.* Berlin: Springer.

Tasaki, I., and Davis, H. 1955. Electric responses of individual nerve elements in cochlear nucleus to sound stimulation (guinea pig). *J. Neurophysiol.*, 18, 151–158.

Teitelbaum, P. 1961. Disturbances in feeding and drinking behavior after hypothalamic lesions. In M. R. Jones (Ed.), *Nebraska symposium on motivation.* Vol. 9. Lincoln: University of Nebraska Press. (By permission.)

Teitelbaum, P. 1964. Appetite. *Proc. Amer. Phil. Soc.*, 108, 464–472. (By permission.)

Thompson, R. F. 1967. *Foundations of physiological psychology.* New York: Harper and Row. (By permission.)

Thompson, T. I. 1963. Visual reinforcement in Siamese fighting fish. *Science,* 141, 55–57.

Tichener, E. B. 1908. Lecture V. In *Lectures on the elementary psychology of feeling and attention.* New York: Macmillan. Abridged 1966 as Ch. 2, Attention as sensory clearness. In P. Bakan (Ed.), *Attention.* Princeton: D. Van Nostrand.

Treisman, A. M. 1964. Selective attention in man. *Brit. Med. Bull.*, 20, 12–16.

Truex, R. C., and Carpenter, M. B. 1964. *Strong and Elwyn's human neuroanatomy* (5th ed.) Baltimore: Williams and Wilkins. (By permission.)

Tunturi, A. R. 1944. Audio-frequency localization in the acoustic cortex of the dog. *Amer. J. Physiol.*, 141, 397–403.

Tunturi, A. R. 1952. A difference in the representation of auditory signals for the left and right ears in the iso-frequency contours of the right middle ectosylvian cortex of the dog. *Amer. J. Physiol.*, 168, 712–727. (By permission.)

Vandenberg, S. G. 1967. Hereditary factors in normal personality traits (as measured by inventories). In J. Wortis (Ed.), *Recent advances in biological psychiatry.* Vol. 9. New York: Plenum Press.

Vandenberg, S. G. 1968*a.* Primary mental abilities or general intelligence? Evidence from twin studies. In J. M. Thoday and A. S. Parkes (Eds.), *Genetic and environmental influences on behavior.* Edinburgh: Oliver and Boyd.

van Vogt, A. E. 1940. *Slan.* New York: Simon and Schuster.

vonBékésy, G. 1947. The variation of phase along the basilar membrane with sinusoidal vibrations. *J. Acoust. Soc. Amer.*, 19, 452–460. (By permission.)

von Békésy, G. 1956. Current status of theories of hearing. *Science,* 123, 779–783.

Weinberger, N. M., Goodman, D. A., and Kitzes, L. M. 1969. Is behavioral habituation a function of peripheral auditory system blockade? *Commun. Behav. Biol.,* 3, 111–116.

Welker, W. I. 1956. Some determinants of play and exploration in chimpanzees. *J. Comp. Physiol. Psychol.,* 49, 84–89. (Copyright 1956 by the American Psychological Association, reproduced by permission.)

Werner, G., and Mountcastle, V. B. 1968. Quantitative relations between mechanical stimuli to the skin and neural responses evoked by them. In D. R. Kenshalo (Ed.), *The skin senses.* Ch. 6. Springfield, Ill.: Charles C. Thomas.

Wever, E. G., and Bray, C. W. 1930. The nature of acoustic response: The relation between sound frequency and frequency of impulses in the auditory nerve. *J. Exp. Psychol.,* 13, 373–387.

Woolsey, C. N. 1958. Organization of somatic sensory and motor areas of the cerebral cortex. In H. F. Harlow and C. N. Woolsey (Eds.), *Biological and biochemical basis of behavior.* Madison: University of Wisconsin Press. (By permission.)

Worden, F. G., and Marsh, J. T. 1963. Amplitude changes of auditory potentials evoked at cochlear nucleus during acoustic habituation. *Electroenceph. Clin. Neurophysiol.,* 16, 866–881.

Wyckoff, L. B. 1952. The role of observing responses in discrimination learning. *Psychol. Rev.,* 59, 431–441.

Wyrwicka, W., Sterman, M. B., and Clemente, C. O. 1962. Conditioning of induced electroencephalographic sleep patterns in the cat. *Science,* 137, 616–618.

INDEX

BEHAVIORAL
OBJECTIVES

CHAPTER ONE: NEUROBIOLOGY

The student should be able to:

1. *Distinguish* between the central and peripheral nervous system.
2. *List* general trends in evolutionary development of the nervous system.
3. *Compare* the similarities and differences between nerve cells and other body cells.
4. *List* the subdivisions of the central nervous system and *give* the functions of each subdivision described in the text. (Note that these structures are presented in text in a general posterior to anterior order. The student should learn to list them in that order so that he has a rough idea initially of the relative location of these structures.)
5. Be able to *identify* all structures in Figure 1-8, if the figure is presented without labels.
6. *Draw* a neuron (as in Figure 1-11) and label its principle components.
7. *Describe* how an action potential differs from an EPSP or IPSP.
8. *Describe* the electrical processes involved in synaptic transmission.
9. *Memorize* the different classes of drugs and their general effects on behavior.

The student should memorize the following definitions:

Action potential   the sudden variation in voltage that propagates down the axon of a nerve fiber when stimulated; the all-or-none spike discharge of a neuron

Arousal   the nonspecific component of motivational states; state of excitability, activity, reactivity consciousness, etc.

Autonomic nervous system   the division of the peripheral nervous system controlling the emotional aspects of behavior, hormonal regulation, smooth muscle, etc.

Axon   that portion of the nerve cell which conducts information away from the cell body

Brain   the enlarged collection of cells and fibers inside the skull

Dendrite   that portion of the nerve cell that conducts information toward the cell body

Depolarization   a positive-going change in voltage; a change in the resting membrane potential toward zero

Efferent   travelling away from the central nervous system; motor

Electroencephalogram (EEG)   a record of the electrical activity of the brain over time; a record of the voltage variations of less than about 70 hertz occurring in the brain

Excitation   the process by which neural or behavioral events are initiated or increased

Excitatory postsynaptic potential (EPSP)   the depolarization produced on the cell body or dendrites by an excitatory synaptic transmitter substance; the result of activation of an excitatory synaptic connection

Ganglion   a collection of nerve cell bodies which occurs outside the central nervous system

Hyperpolarization   a negative-going change in voltage; a change in the resting membrane potential away from zero; i.e., toward being more negative

Inhibition   the process by which neural or behavioral events are stopped or decreased

Inhibitory postsynaptic potential (IPSP)   the hyperpolarization produced on the cell body by an inhibitory synaptic transmitter substance; the result of activation of an inhibitory synaptic connection

Metabolism   refers to all chemical processes in the body related to the production and utilization of energy

Nerve   a collection of nerve fibers which occurs outside the central nervous system

Neuron   a single nerve cell with its associated fiber processes

Neurochemistry   the study of the chemical processes of the nervous system, particularly of neurons

Parasympathetic division   the subdivision of the autonomic nervous system responsible for vegetative-digestive functions; the energy conserving division of the autonomic nervous system

Psychogenic drugs   drugs that produce psychotic-like symptoms in subjects

Psychopharmacology   the study of drugs that influence experience and behavior

Psychotherapeutics   the use of drugs in the treatment of mental illness

Resting membrane potential   the potential difference (voltage) which exists across the membrane of cells; approximately −70 millivolts across the membrane of a nerve cell

Spinal cord   the collection of cells and fibers contained within the vertebral column

Sympathetic division   the subdivision of the autonomic nervous system that prepares the animal in case of emergencies; the system that tends to mobilize resources

Synapse   the functional connections between neurons

Synaptic vesicle   the small specialized structure found in the axon terminal

Threshold   the point at which a stimulus will fire an action potential; the minimum stimulus energy necessary for perception

Tract   a collection of nerve fibers which occurs inside the central nervous system

Transmitter   the chemical substance which crosses the synaptic connection between neurons to excite or inhibit the neuron on which it acts

The student should be able to *identify* the following terms:

Acetylcholine   the synaptic transmitter substance at the neuromuscular junction; one synaptic transmitter substance in the autonomic nervous system; a presumed synaptic transmitter substance in the brain

Acetylcholinesterase   the enzyme that hydrolizes (breaks down) acetylcholine

Alpha rhythm   8 to 13 cycle per second voltage variations in the cortical EEG

Basal ganglia   a collection of nuclei lying in the ventral portions of the cerebral hemispheres concerned primarily with motor functions

Biogenic amines   a class of transmitter substances including norepinephrine, dopamine, serotonin, and related substances

Brain stem   refers to all structures contained within the hindbrain and midbrain

Cerebellum   a large structure overlying the pons concerned primarily with sensory-motor coordination

Cerebral cortex   an outer layer or covering of the forebrain containing cell bodies and fibers; greatly enlarged in higher mammals

Corpus callosum   the large band of fibers interconnecting the two cerebral hemispheres

Dendritic spines   the small specialized structures found on dendrites which appear to form a synapse with an opposing axon terminal from another cell; the point at which excitatory synapses are formed in some cases

Dopamine   a suspected transmitter substance in the brain; one of the biogenic amines

Engram   the individual unit of memory

Golgi bodies   organelles found in nerve cells and other cells specialized to secrete substances

Hypophysis   pituitary gland

Hypothalamus   an important grouping of nuclei lying on the ventral surface of the midbrain concerned with hormonal regulation, eating, drinking, and other emotional-motivational aspects of behavior, sleep, etc.

Mitochondrain   an organelle which converts foodstuff and oxygen into metabolic energy

Norepinephrine   a suspected transmitter substance in the brain and peripheral nervous
   system; one of the biogenic amines
Nucleus   the central portion of a cell which contains DNA; a collection of nerve cell
   bodies which occurs inside the central nervous system
Organelle   small specialized structure within the cell responsible for metabolism, respiration
   or synthesis
Reticular formation   the centrally placed cellular network of the brain stem concerned
   with reflex excitability, the arousal response, alerting or attention, sleep and
   waking, pain, etc.
Serotonin   a suspected transmitter substance in the brain; one of the biogenic amines
Soma   cell body of a neuron
Thalamus   the large grouping of nuclei located just above the midbrain including sensory
   relay muclei and various association and nonspecific nuclei; the primary relay
   station for sensory information going to the cerebral cortex

CHAPTER TWO: SENSORY-MOTOR INTEGRATION

The student should be able to:

1. *List* and *describe* the sequence of events in the sensory coding process.
2. *Explain* the principle of "specific nerve energies."
3. *Name* the wavelength range of visible light.
4. *List* three physical characteristics of light.
5. *List* the subjective counterparts for the three physical characteristics of light.
6. *Name* and *define* the basic parts of the human visual system.
7. *Name* the two types of retinal receptor elements, their location in the retina,
   what type of vision they mediate, and what pigment each contains.
8. *Compare* and *contrast* the Young-Helmholtz three-receptor theory and the
   opponent theory of color vision.
9. *Identify* general structures of the ear and structures within the cochlea.
10. *Describe* how von Bekesy integrated the place theory and the frequency theory
   of hearing.
11. *List* six major types of somatic sensory sensation.
12. *Compare* and *contrast* the neural pathways which mediate somatic sensory experience.
13. *Name* two common features of sensory systems.
14. *Discuss* the organization of movement with particular reference to its control by
   motor cortex.

The student should *memorize* the following definitions:

Adaptation   the ability to change in response to the environmental requirements; an
   alteration in receptor sensitivity as a response to some alteration in the environment
Afferent   travelling toward the central nervous system; sensory
Basilar membrane   the receptor membrane of the cochlea containing the hair cells
Brightness   the subjective experience of light intensity or luminance
Cochlea   the receptor mechanism of the ear which contains the hair cells, basilar and
   tectorial membranes, etc.
Cochlear microphonic   the piezo-electric signal produced at the cochlea which is
   believed to be a generator potential for auditory receptor cells
Color   the subjective experience of light wavelength; hue
Columnar organization   the vertical functional organization of cells in some specific
   sensory areas of the cerebral cortex such as the discrete somatic sensory area

Cone   one of the two basic types of receptor cells in the retina

Efferent   travelling away from the central nervous system; motor

Fovea   the center of the retina onto which images are focused composed entirely of cones

Ganglion cell   the cell type in the retina that forms the optic nerve

Generator potential   the graded electrical response of a sensory receptor when activated by a stimulus

Hair cell   the receptor cell of the ear

Hertz   cycles per second

Homunculus   the form of the somatotopic representation on the somatic sensory cortex

Iodopsin   the light-sensitive chemical found in cones

Loudness   the subjective experience of sound intensity

Luminance   the physical intensity of light

Motor   of or pertaining to movement; fibers travelling away from the central nervous system

Perception   an interpretation of immediate experience in light of past experience, as distinguished from sensation

Photopic vision   vision utilizing only cone receptors

Pitch   the subjective experience of sound frequency

Receptotopic organization   the spatial representation of receptor surface on the surface of the cerebral cortex

Retina   the receptor apparatus of the eye

Retinotopic representation   the representation of the surface of the retina on the surface of the visual area of the cerebral cortex

Rhodopsin   the light-sensitive chemical found in rods

Rod   one of the two basic types of receptor cells in the retina

Saturation   the degree to which a particular light is composed of a single wavelength

Scotopic vision   vision utilizing only rod receptors

Sensation   the immediate experience of a stimulus, as distinguished from perception

Sensory   of or pertaining to sensation; fibers travelling toward the central nervous system

Somatic   of or pertaining to the body; refers to striated musculature; that portion of the peripheral nervous system controlling the striated muscles, i.e., voluntary behavior

Somatotopic representation   representation of the skin receptor surface on the somatic sensory area of the cerebral cortex

Tonotopic representation   frequency representation of tone in the auditory region of the cerebral cortex

Transduction   the process of changing forms of energy; the process of changing stimulus energy into neural impulses

Visual acuity   the ability to see detail; the sharpness or clarity of visual experience

CHAPTER THREE: SLEEP, DREAMING, AND ATTENTION

The student should be able to:

1. *Define* circadian rhythm and give examples.
2. *Discuss* factors which might control biological rhythms.
3. *Describe* the relationship between arousal level and ability to behave.
4. *Discuss* the relationship between behavioral arousal level and the EEG.
5. *Define* the various stages of sleep.
6. *List* five physiological correlates of the orienting reflex.

7. *Name* three stimulus categories which are confounded when a pure tone is presented.
8. *Describe* the problems which attentional variables may present an investigator.

The student should *memorize* the following definitions:

Alpha rhythm 8 to 13 cycle per second voltage variations in the cortical EEG

Arousal the nonspecific component of motivational states; state of excitability, activity, reactivity, consciousness, etc.

Attention stimulus selection; stimulus control of behavior

Circadian rhythm a biological cycle of about 24 hours duration; more generally, a cyclic variation in some biological function, such as activity level

Desynchronization a change in the cortical EEG from high amplitude, low frequency voltage variations, to low amplitude, high frequency voltage variations; also called cortical activation

Observing response a response which produces a stimulus for observation; a response indicating attention to some stimulus

Orienting reflex the series of physiological changes which occur when an organism attends to a novel stimulus

Pacemaker cells cells that exhibit some rhythmic or periodic activity; cells that control the rhythm of the heart

Paradoxical sleep see rapid eye movement sleep

Rapid eye movement sleep also called REM sleep; the stage of sleep characterized by rapid movements of the eyes and desynchronization of the cortical EEG; the stage of sleep during which dreaming usually occurs

Reticular formation the centrally placed cellular network of the brain stem concerned with reflex excitability, the arousal response, alerting or attention, sleep and waking, pain, etc.

Shadowing continuous monitoring of an auditory signal by verbal repetition

Sleep spindle an 8 to 13 cycle/sec voltage variation which exhibits rapid growth and subsequent decay in amplitude and which occurs during stage 2 sleep

Slow wave sleep the stages of sleep characterized by high amplitude low frequency voltage variations in the cortical EEG; deep sleep

Thalamus the large grouping of nuclei located just above the midbrain including sensory relay nuclei and various association and nonspecific nuclei; the primary relay station for sensory information going to the cerebral cortex

Transfer test a method of measuring attention in which two previously confounded stimulus attributes are tested separately to determine if the subject used one or the other in solving the initial discrimination problems

Vigilance task a method of measuring attention which requires that the subject continuously monitor some aspect of the environment, such as the bead on a radar screen, etc.

CHAPTER FOUR: MOTIVATION

The student should be able to:

1. *List* and *describe* three types of agonistic behavior.
2. *Identify* brain structures within the limbic system concerned with the various types of aggressive behavior.
3. *Name* and *define* two theories regarding what causes animals to eat.

4. *Name* the areas within the hypothalamus which mediate eating behavior and *describe* how they mediate it.
5. *Discuss* the peripheral and central theories of drinking.
6. *Compare* and *contrast* the ideas of Bernard and Cannon, Hull and Miller, and James and Lange regarding motivation theory.
7. *Describe* the nonspecific component of motivational states and its neurobiological substrates.
8. *Distinguish between* primary and secondary motivation.
9. *Define* cognitive dissonance and *relate* it to theories of less complex motivation.

The student should *memorize* the following definitions:

Aggression   the behavioral expression of anger; see agonistic behavior
Agonistic behavior   aggressive behavior; behavior characterized by flight, defense, or attack
Antidiuretic hormone   a chemical manufactured in the anterior hypothalamus which acts on the kidneys to conserve water
Aphagia   a syndrome characterized by a lack of eating and often consequent starvation, resulting from destruction of a lateral portion of the hypothalamus
Arousal   the nonspecific component of motivational states; state of excitability, activity, reactivity, consciousness, etc.
Attack   a form of agonistic behavior characterized by active initiation of fighting, as a predator after prey
Cafeteria experiment   an experiment in which animals are given a free choice of diets in order to determine if they are capable of regulating their own nutritional requirements
Cognitive dissonance   a theory of social motivation in which individuals are presumed to act in order to reduce the degree to which two or more aspects of information or opinion are contradictory
Defense   a form of agonistic behavior in which an animal fights only in order to protect his life, territory, family, etc.
Drive   a nonspecific state of the organism which increases motor activity and provides cues which direct behavior in ways which will reduce the level of drive; a hypothetical construct provided to account for motivated behavior; a source of motivation
Drive reduction   a theory of motivation which suggests that animals work to reduce their level of drive, that this reduction is rewarding, and that learning results from this form of reward.
Flight   a form of agonistic behavior characterized by active avoidance of some individual or object following an encounter.
Homeostasis   the theory that the body senses changes from an optimum point for some physiological process and then acts to restore the proper level
Hyperphagia   a syndrome characterized by overeating and consequent obesity caused by destruction of the ventromedial area of the hypothalamus
Hypothalamus   an important grouping of nuclei lying on the ventral surface of the brain close to the pituitary gland; concerned with hormonal regulation, eating, drinking, and other emotional-motivational aspects of behavior, sleep, etc.
Internal milieu   internal environment of the body
Motivation   see drive
Primary motivation   motivation "built in" to the organism without learning; often produced by tissue needs
Secondary motivation   learned motivation not dependent upon tissue needs; complex motivation such as curiosity, social needs, etc.
Sham rage   nondirected rage produced by removal of the forebrain rostral to the hypothalamus

CHAPTER FIVE: HEREDITY

The student should be able to:

1. *Defend* the position that heredity influences behavior. To do this properly, *describe* several types of evidence which suggest that heredity plays an important role in determining behavioral traits.
2. *Describe* the scientific advantages for using twin studies to identify the influence of heredity on behavior.
3. *Distinguish* between phenotype and genotype.
4. *Explain* the fact that it is interactions of heredity and environment that determine behavioral traits. Use phenylketonuria as an example.

The student should *memorize* the following definitions:

Allele   the alternate forms in which genes may exist at one locus on a chromosome

Chromosomes   the structures within the cell on which genes are located

Complete dominance   the mode of gene action in which the heterozygote has a phenotypic value identical to that of the homozygote

Concordant   the condition in which two identical twins are alike on some specified measure such as intelligence, schizophrenia, etc.

Correlation coefficient   a measure of the relationship between two sets of numbers

Deoxyribonucleic acid (DNA)   the genetic material contained within the cell nucleus

Discordant   the condition in which two identical twins are not alike on some specified measure such as intelligence, schizophrenia, etc.

Dominance   in genetics, the mode of gene action in which the phenotype is closer to that of the homozygous condition

Down's syndrome   mongolism

Gamete   a sex cell manufactured by the testis of the male or the ovary of the female

Gene   the basic element of heredity; the fundamental unit of hereditary substance

Genotype   the genetic composition of an individual; the genetic configuration necessary for the expression of a particular phenotype

Heritability   the proportion of phenotypic variability due to genetic differences among members of a population

Heterozygote   an individual possessing different allelic forms of a particular gene

Homozygote   an individual possessing identical allelic forms of a particular gene

Inbred strain   a population of animals resulting from the breeding together of closely related individuals

Klinefelter's syndrome   a condition of sexual and mental retardation characterized by the presence of an XXY chromosome configuration instead of the normal XY

Mongolism   a condition of mental retardation characterized by an extra chromosome, making the affected individual a 47 instead of a 46 chromosomal individual

Partial dominance   the mode of gene action in which the heterozygote has a phenotypic value close to but not identical to that of either homozygote

Phenotype   a trait which is expressed as a result of genetic endowment

Phenylketonuria   a disease characterized by mental retardation which results from a hereditary inability to metabolize dietary phenylalanine

Polygenic   a condition in which a number of genes each make a small contribution to the phenotypic expression of a particular trait; of or pertaining to many genes

Ribonucleic acid (RNA)   a copy of DNA which travels outside the cell nucleus to direct protein synthesis

Selective breeding   mating together of animals which display extreme levels of some phenotype

Sex linkage   the association of a particular phenotype with one of the sex chromosomes, X or Y

Trisomy   a condition in which there are three chromosomes instead of the normal pair

Turner's syndrome   a condition of space-form blindness and difficulty in numerical manipulation which results from having a single X chromosome instead of the normal XY configuration

MULTIPLE CHOICE
TEST

CHAPTER ONE: NEUROBIOLOGY

1. The spontaneous activity of the brain recorded with electrodes placed on the scalp is called the:
   a. polygraph
   b. electroencephalogram
   c. noise
   d. correlogram
   c. electro-oculogram

2. That portion of the peripheral nervous system which is most intimately concerned with the emotion aspects of behavior is the:
   a. central nervous system
   b. somatic nervous system
   c. peripheral nervous system
   d. autonomic nervous system
   e. muscle nervous system

3. Activation of the sympathetic division of the autonomic nervous system does not cuase:
   a. acceleration of the heart
   b. dilation of the pupils
   c. contraction of arteries
   d. inhibition of stomach contractions
   e. increased stomach secretions

4. The structure in the brain stem intimately concerned with the regulation of sleep and wakefulness is the:
   a. basal ganglion
   b. hypophysis
   c. reticular formation
   d. limbic system
   e. cerebellum

5. Which of the following responses can still be performed by a cat which has had all brain tissue above the midbrain removed:
   a. walk
   b. sleep
   c. vocalize
   d. eat
   e. all of the above

6. Which of the following structures is most intimately concerned with sensory-motor coordination:
   a. raphé nuclei
   b. cerebellum
   c. hypothalamus
   d. hypophysis
   e. thalamus

7. What is the area of the brain which controls the activity of the pituitary gland:
   a. thalamus
   b. cerebellum
   c. basal ganglia
   d. hypothalamus
   e. hippocampus

8. The cerebral cortex has increased its area appreciably through evolution by the development of:
   a. lobes
   b. cell bodies
   c. layers
   d. fissures
   e. associations

9. The organelle responsible for the conversion of foodstuffs into metabolic energy is called the:
   a. nissl body
   b. nucleus
   c. ribosome
   d. mitochondrion
   e. nucleuolus

10. Which of the following organelles is found in only neurons and other cells specialized to secrete substances:
    a. golgi bodies
    b. mitochondrion
    c. nucleolus
    d. ribosomes
    e. chromosomes

11. If an electrode is used to measure the voltage generated across the nerve cell membrane, a –70 millivolt potential will be observed and is called the:
   a. nerve cell potential
   b. action potential
   c. resting membrane potential
   d. axon potential
   e. graded potential

12. When an all-or-none action potential develops in the initial segment of a neuron, it travels down the:
   a. dendrite
   b. synaptic bouton
   c. cell body
   d. axon
   e. soma

13. The presynaptic ending of a synapse contains circular structures, believed to contain the chemical synaptic transmitter substance, called:
   a. synaptic vesicles
   b. dendritic spines
   b. postsynaptic vesicles
   d. nuclear vessels
   e. engrams

14. The type 1 synapse differs from the type 2 synapse because it involves:
   a. presynaptic endings
   b. dendritic spines
   c. transmitter substance
   d. a postsynaptic membrane
   e. action potentials

15. When an excitatory synaptic transmitter substance is released to cross the synaptic cleft, it causes in the postsynaptic cell body a(an):
   a. hyperpolarization
   b. repolarization
   c. depolarization
   d. presynaptic polarization
   e. prepolarization

16. Which of the following can be characterized as a "graded potential":
   a. inhibitory postsynaptic potential
   b. action potential
   c. resting membrane potential
   d. threshold potential
   e. all of the above

17. Which one of the biogenic amines has been used successfully in treating the disease, Parkinsonism:
   a. norepinephrine
   b. serotonin
   c. glycine
   d. dopamine
   e. acetylcholine

18. Which of the following drugs would not be considered a narcotic analgesic:
   a. amphetamine
   b. heroin
   c. morphine
   d. opium
   e. all of the above

19. Which of the following psychotherapeutic agents is classified as an antidepressant:
   a. imipramine
   b. chlorpromazine
   c. reserpine
   d. meprobomate
   e. chloriazepoxide

20. Strychnine act by blocking neural inhibition and are therefore classified as:
   a. depressants
   b. stimulants
   c. antidepressants
   d. narcotic analgesics
   e. psychogenic drugs

CHAPTER TWO: SENSORY-MOTOR INTEGRATION

1. Perhaps one of the first formal theories attempting to solve the problem of how nerve fibers code sensory stimuli was published in 1826 as the "Theory of Specific Nerve Energies" by:
   a. John Galton
   b. Erick Fromm
   c. Johannes Muller
   d. Young-Helmholtz
   e. Sigmund Freud

2. Which of the following cannot refer to a physical property of light:
   a. wavelength
   b. luminance
   c. purity
   d. duration
   e. color

3. An individual's perception of the "purity" of light is referred to as the light's:
   a. wavelength
   b. brightness
   c. saturation
   d. color
   e. luminance

4. The layers of receptors and nerve cells at the back of the eyeball is called the:
   a. lens
   b. cornea
   c. cochlea
   d. retina
   e. fovea

5. Rhodopsin, the photopigment in rods, when exposed to light breaks down into:
   a. retinene and photopsin
   b. retinene and opsin
   c. rhodopsin and photopsin
   d. iodopsin and opsin
   e. retinene and iodopsin

6. The spontaneous rate of synthesis of rhodopsin in solution follows very closely the time course of the following:
   a. cone dark adaptation
   b. the rate of synthesis of iodopsin
   c. rod dark adaptation
   d. synthesis of retinene
   e. the rate of synthesis of photopsin

7. The spatial representation of the visual world on the surface of the visual cortex is called:
   a. tonotopic organization
   b. columnar organization
   c. retinotopic organization
   d. dark adaptation
   e. form representation

8. The visual field which is focused onto the fovea will occupy approximately how much of the visual area of the cerebral cortex:
   a. 1%
   b. 2.5%
   c. 50%
   d. 90%
   e. 0%

9. The work of Hubel and Wiesel has provided evidence that single cells in the visual cortex of animals respond to:
   a. frequency
   b. color
   c. brightness
   d. form
   e. loudness

10. Pitch and frequency are:
    a. linearly related
    b. nonuniformly related
    c. unrelated
    d. logarithmically related
    e. opposites

11. The actual receptor mechanism of the auditory system is termed the:
    a. fovea
    b. ossicle
    c. tectorial membrane
    d. cochlea
    e. estachian tube

12. The vibrations of fluid in the cochlea cause which of the following to vibrate:
    a. tympanic membrane
    b. basilar membrane
    c. ossicles
    d. auditory meatus
    e. all of the above

13. The electrical response that follows the frequency and intensity of auditory stimuli and which can be recorded near the auditory nerve is called the:
    a. auditory nerve response
    b. evoked auditory potential
    c. cochlear microphonic
    d. auditory microphonic
    e. volley potential

14. Individual nerve fibers in the auditory nerve are capable of firing at the frequency of a tone up to about:
    a. 4000 hertz
    b. 15 hertz
    c. 100 hertz
    d. 1000 hertz
    e. 2000 hertz

15. Different groups of fibers firing out of phase with each other allow the auditory nerve response to follow sound frequencies up to about:
    a. 15 hertz
    b. 1000 hertz
    c. 4000 hertz
    d. 2000 hertz
    e. 100 hertz

16. The spinothalamic tract represents which of the following:
    a. the lemniscal system
    b. the discrete system
    c. the direct system
    d. the nonspecific system
    e. none of the above

17. The form of representation of the body surface on the somatic sensory cortex is called a(an):
    a. column
    b. homunculus
    c. topograph
    d. receptor surface
    e. organizational block

18. A particularly important functional principle of organization of all sensory systems appears to be:
    a. retinotopic organization
    b. columnar organization
    c. single neuron coding of frequency
    d. receptotopic organization of cortex
    e. tonotopic organization

19. The motor area of the human cerebral cortex represents:
    a. muscles but not movements
    b. movements but not muscles
    c. sounds but not muscles
    d. muscles and movements
    e. neither muscles nor movements

20. Removal of motor cortex in man will cause a loss of:
    a. fine and delicate movements
    b. all muscle tone
    c. loss of gross movements
    d. movements of the lower extremities
    e. loss of speech

CHAPTER THREE: SLEEP, DREAMING, AND ATTENTION

1. The alternation of sleeping and waking is a manifestation, in our lives and those of other animals, of the pervasive quality of:
    a. variation
    b. periodicity
    c. adaptation
    d. convolution
    e. discrimination

2. If illumination cues are eliminated from a rat's living cage, he will exhibit cyclic activity levels:
    a. identical to that with the light-dark cycle
    b. almost identical to that with the light-dark cycle
    c. completely dissimilar to that with a light-dark cycle
    d. activity will not be cyclic
    e. activity will be constant

3. The normal active period of a rat is during:
    a. morning
    b. afternoon
    c. light
    d. dark
    e. light and dark

4. The relationship between arousal level and the ability to perform in a well-integrated manner is best described by a(an):
    a. inverted-U shaped function
    b. U-shaped function
    c. linear function
    d. logarithmic function
    e. power function

5. The "alpha rhythm" occurs primarily during:
    a. stage 2 sleep
    b. REM sleep
    c. relaxed wakefulness
    d. excitement
    e. stage 4 sleep

6. The change from alpha rhythm activity to low voltage, fast activity on the cerebral cortex is often referred to as cortical:
    a. desynchronization
    b. depolarization
    c. synchronization
    d. respiration
    e. hyperpolarization

7. "Sleep spindles" occur during which of the following stages of sleep:
    a. stage 1 sleep
    b. stage 2 sleep
    c. stage 3 sleep
    d. stage 4 sleep
    e. REM sleep

8. Which of the following situations will dissociate the normal EEG pattern from behavioral indices (i.e., produce a sleeping EEG and a waking animal):
    a. injections of the drug amphetamine
    b. REM sleep state
    c. injections of the drug atropine
    d. peek emotional excitement
    e. relaxed wakefulness

9. Lesions (surgical removal) of the reticular formation in the brain stem have been found to produce:
   a. sleeping animals with waking EEG patterns
   b. no change in the sleep-wakefulness cycle
   c. waking animals but sleeping EEG patterns
   d. sleeping animals and sleeping EEG patterns
   e. permanently waking animals with waking EEG patterns

10. The areas of the reticular formation that appear most concerned with the induction of sleep are:
    a. more lateral areas
    b. more central areas
    c. more posterior areas
    d. more anterior areas
    e. more medial regions

11. Freud, in his extensive analysis of dreaming, emphasized the:
    a. symbolic content of dreams
    b. realistic content of dreams
    c. duration of dreaming
    d. forgetting of dreams
    e. sex differences of dreamers

12. The percentage of sleep-time spent in REM sleep in adult humans in about:
    a. 50%
    b. 20%
    c. 30%
    d. 90%
    e. 5%

13. Lesions of the following area tend to reduce or abolish REM sleep:
    a. raphé nuclei
    b. central reticular formation
    c. hypothalamus
    d. frontal cortex
    e. hippocampus

14. The following transmitter substance seems most closely associated with the induction of REM sleep:
    a. norepinephrine
    b. serotonin
    c. acetylcholine
    d. glycine
    e. gamm-amino butyric acid (GABA)

15. The serotonergic system associated closely with the induction or maintenance of slow wave sleep originates in the:
    a. cortex
    b. reticular formation
    c. raphé nuclei
    d. substantia nigra
    e. cerebellum

16. Which of the following is true of para-doxical (REM) sleep:
    a. the EEG shows slow waves
    b. decreased muscle tone
    c. increased muscle tone
    d. increased skin resistance
    e. none of the above

17. Which of the following organisms would you expect to have the least amount of REM sleep:
    a. monkey
    b. human
    c. human infant
    d. bird
    e. rat

18. An objective index of attention, which entails having the subject perform a discrete response in order to view a particular stimulus, is called a(an):
    a. orienting reflex
    b. flexion reflex
    c. observing response
    d. discrimination response
    e. shadowing response

19. Which of the following is one of the components of the orienting reflex:
    a. pupil dilation
    b. synchronization of the EEG
    c. vasodilation of the limbs
    d. initial acceleration of heart beat and respiration
    e. all of the above

20. Studies of evoked potentials during attention to a particular stimulus indicate that the amplitude of an evoked potential to an attended stimulus:
    a. increases in humans but not other animals
    b. decreases in humans but not other animals
    c. decreases in humans and other animals
    d. increases in all animals except humans
    e. decreases in animals but increases in humans

CHAPTER FOUR: MOTIVATION

1. Which of the following is not a commonly accepted form of agonistic behavior:
   a. flight
   b. defense
   c. fright
   d. attack
   e. all of the above

2. Among rodents, the following manipulation will produce an increase in fighting:
   a. increasing available food
   b. decreasing available food
   c. placing many females with one male
   d. placing a single male and female together
   e. increasing cage space for a limited group of animals

3. "Sham rage" can be eliminated by lesions of:
   a. hippocampus
   b. thalamus
   c. septum
   d. forebrain
   e. hypothalamus

4. The following brain regions have been importantly implicated in the control and maintenance of aggression:
   a. hippocampus
   b. amygdala
   c. hypothalamus
   d. a and b above
   e. a, b, and c above

5. The influence of the amygdala on agonistic behavior seems to operate through connections with:
   a. hypothalamus
   b. forebrain
   c. hippocampus
   d. thalamus
   e. it has no influence on agonistic behavior

6. Which of the following is an important determinant in feeding behavior:
   a. learning
   b. location of food
   c. taste of food
   d. nutritional value
   e. all of the above

7. The glucostatic theory of hunger maintains that an animal eats because of the following factor(s):
   a. state of dehydration
   b. blood sugar levels
   c. body temperature
   d. osmotic pressure
   e. salinity of the kidneys

8. Cannon suggested the influential but incorrect peripheral theory of thirst in which thirst was presumed to be caused by:
   a. stomach distension
   b. dryness of the mouth
   c. changes in blood sugar
   d. changes in osmotic pressure brain cells
   e. alterations in kidney salinity

9. Hyperphagia in rats is caused by:
   a. lesions of the lateral hypothalamus
   b. stimulation of medial hypothalamus
   c. lesions of medial thalamus
   d. lesions of medial hypothalamus
   e. stimulation of lateral thalamus

10. Andersson found that injections of the following into the anterior hypothalamus produced drinking in rats:
    a. glucose
    b. hypertonic saline
    c. asparatate
    d. norepinephrine
    e. acetylcholine

11. The following suspected neurotransmitter substance, when injected into a site where carbocol induces drinking, will often induce eating:
    a. glucose
    b. glycine
    c. norepinephrine
    d. dopamine
    e. acetylcholine

12. Drive reduction is presumed, in drive theories, to be:
    a. aversive   e. activating
    b. nauseating
    c. rewarding
    d. neutral

13. It is generally believed that "drive" itself is:
    a. nonspecific
    b. reinforcing
    c. specific
    d. primary
    e. secondary

14. Campbell and Sheffield demonstrated that the amount of activity emitted by rats during starvation was directly dependent upon which quality of the environment in which they were placed:
    a. richness
    b. color
    c. size
    d. density
    e. all of the above

15. The famous "inverted U-shaped" function is a graphic description of the relationship between behavioral performance efficiency and:
    a. learning
    b. arousal
    c. motivation
    d. hunger
    e. reward

16. The following region(s) of the brain is important in the control and elaboration of behavioral arousal level:
    a. reticular formation
    b. hypothalamus
    c. frontal cortex
    d. hippocampus
    e. all of the above

17. Rats will learn to press a bar for the folfowing as a reward:
    a. manipulation of an object
    b. electrical stimulation of lateral hypothalamus
    c. turning on a light in their cage
    d. turning a running wheel
    e. all of the above

18. Butler and Harlow found that monkeys would work very hard for the following reward:
    a. food
    b. visual exploration
    c. water
    d. drive reduction
    e. wet mash

19. Festinger's approach to human motivation has been termed:
    a. cognitive distance
    b. social discordance
    c. dissonant motivation
    d. cognitive dissonance
    e. achievement motivation

20. Cognitive dissonace bears similarities to:
    a. satiation
    b. drive reduction
    c. homeostasis
    d. food-seeking behavior
    e. stimulation of lateral hypothalamus

CHAPTER FIVE: HEREDITY

1. The first systematic attempt to carry out the family study method was undertaken by:
    a. Martin Kallikak
    b. Francis Ebbinghaus
    c. John Watson
    d. Erick Fromm
    e. Francis Galton

2. The difference in standing height between fraternal twins when compared with that of identical twins is:
    a. the same
    b. larger
    c. smaller
    d. less variable
    e. none of the above

3. When various components of intelligence are examined, which of the following is not found to be greatly influenced by heredity:
    a. verbal reasoning
    b. clerical speed
    c. abstract reasoning
    d. language use
    e. clerical accuracy

4. Which of the following neuroses has not been suggested to have a substantial hereditary basis:
    a. anxiety
    b. depression
    c. obsession
    d. hysteria
    e. schizoid withdrawal

5. Studies of twins reared apart from birth suggest that schizophrenia is influenced by:
   a. the I.Q. of the twins
   b. the adopted mother's personality
   c. the family educational background
   d. the adopted siblings' personalities
   e. heredity

6. Gregor Mendel's central discovery was that the hereditary substance is composed of particular elements now called:
   a. genes
   b. heterozygotes
   c. phenotypes
   d. genotypes
   e. polymers

7. The case in which a heterozygote has a phenotypic value closer to that of one of the homozygous parents, but not identical is called:
   a. genetic action
   b. partial dominance
   c. parental dominance
   d. recessive compulsive
   e. complete dominance

8. Example of behavioral and physiological characteristics affected by a single gene include:
   a. red-green color blindness
   b. phenylketonuria
   c. numerical ability
   d. a and b above
   e. b and c above

9. A male triple heterozygote can produce how many different kinds of sperm genetic configurations:
   a. 1
   b. 2
   c. 4
   d. 8
   e. 64

10. An important principle to be deduced from the many possibilities for genetic reorganization in offspring is that variability in living things is:
    a. solely environmental
    b. accidental
    c. purely genetic
    d. not accidental
    e. maladaptive

11. Within a single highly inbred strain of mice in which there is not genetic variability, the heretability of some trait, such as a loco-motor activity, is theoretically near:
    a. 0
    b. 0.5
    c. 1.0
    d. 1.5
    e. 10

12. In mice, inbreeding produces strains that are genetically:
    a. less variable
    b. more variable
    c. color blind
    d. more active
    e. random

13. Genetic information is coded by a sequence of substances along the DNA molecule called:
    a. enzymes
    b. RNA
    c. bases
    d. catalysts
    e. proteins

14. Phenylketonuria which results in severe mental deficiencies is caused by the body's lack of:
    a. phenolainine
    b. phenolpyruvic acid
    c. phenalalinine hydroxylase
    d. phenolacetic acid
    e. all of the above

15. How many pairs of chromosomes are found in the normal human cell:
    a. 21
    b. 22
    c. 23
    d. 47
    e. 48

16. The condition of having three chromosomes instead of a pair is called:
    a. homozygous
    b. trisomy
    c. anomalous rectification
    d. polygenic
    e. triple heterozygous

17. Which of the following chromosome configuration represents a normal male:
    a. XX
    b. X
    c. XY
    d. Y
    e. YY

18. Lack of a single chromosome pair is usually:
    a. harmless
    b. useful
    c. adaptive
    d. overcompensated
    e. fatal

19. Klinefelter's syndrome, which includes retardation of sexual development and mental retardation results from the following chromosome configuration:
    a. XXY
    b. XX
    c. XY
    d. XYY
    e. none of the above

20. A condition called Turner's syndrome is frequenctly found in females who have the genetic configuration:
    a. Y
    b. XY
    c. XX
    d. XXX
    e. X

MUTIPLE CHOICE TEST ANSWER KEY

CHAPTER ONE: NEUROBIOLOGY

1. b	2. d	3. e	4. c	5. e	6. b	7. d	8. d
9. d	10. a	11. c	12. d	13. a	14. b	15. c	16. a
17. d	18. a	19. a	20. b				

CHAPTER TWO: SENSORY-MOTOR INTEGRATION

1. c	2. e	3. c	4. d	5. b	6. c	7. c	8. c
9. d	10. d	11. d	12. b	13. c	14. d	15. c	16. d
17. b	18. d	19. d	20. a				

CHAPTER THREE: SLEEP, DREAMING, AND ATTENTION

1. b	2. b	3. d	4. a	5. c	6. a	7. b	8. c
9. d	10. c	11. a	12. b	13. b	14. a	15. c	16. b
17. d	18. c	19. a	20. a				

CHAPTER FOUR: MOTIVATION

1. d	2. b	3. e	4. e	5. a	6. e	7. b	8. b
9. d	10. b	11. c	12. c	13. a	14. a	15. b	16. e
17. e	18. b	19. d	20. b				

CHAPTER FIVE: HEREDITY

1. e	2. b	3. c	4. d	5. e	6. a	7. b	8. d
9. d	10. d	11. a	12. a	13. c	14. c	15. c	16. b
17. c	18. e	19. a	20. e				